Radical
Common School

'*Radical Education and the Common School* is a truly thoughtful book. It combines power-ful social and educational criticism with a sensitivity to powerful possibility. Reading it will demonstrate to critically democratic educators why we should be fully engaged with thick versions of democracy in education.' Michael W. Apple, *University of Wisconsin, Madison, US*

'Every now and then there comes a book on education to make the blood course through your veins and steel your resolve that 'It doesn't have to be like it is'; you know after reading it that something else better is possible. Paulo Freire's *Pedagogy of the Oppressed* and John Holt's *How Children Fail* spring to mind. Well here's another to stand alongside their work. Written with passion and incisiveness in equal measure, it will lift the spirits and re-energise all who are engaged in education not simply as a means of earning a living but as a way of changing the world for the better.' Tim Brighouse, *formerly London Schools Commissioner*

'This is a necessary book – particularly now! It is human and hopeful, but at the same time realistic and challenging. It builds its argument on cases, on practice and on experience to offer a different future for education – a democratic common school that serves the needs of students, communities and society. It should be compulsory reading for all would-be ministers of education.' Stephen Ball, *Institute of Education, University of London, UK*

'This is an important, timely and passionate book which should be read by anyone concerned with the future of education and democracy. In their clear-sighted vision of the common school as a laboratory for building a sustainable, inclusive and demo-cratic world, Fielding and Moss remind us not only that we can imagine alternative and better futures, but that there are steps we can take to build them.' Keri Facer, *Manchester Metropolitan University, UK*

What is education, what is it for and what are its fundamental values? How do we understand knowledge and learning? What is our image of the child and the school? How does the ever more pressing need to develop a more just, creative and sustain-able democratic society affect our responses to these questions?

Addressing these fundamental issues, *Radical Education and the Common School: a democratic alternative* contests the current mainstream dominated by markets and competition, instrumentality and standardisation, managerialism and technical practice. The book argues instead for a new public education, showing it is possible to think and practise differently. There are alternatives!

The authors argue for a radical education with democracy as a fundamental value, care as a central ethic, a person-centred education that is education in the broadest sense and an image of a child rich in potential. Radical education should be practised in the 'common school', a school for all children in its local catchment area, age-integrated, human scale, focused on depth of learning and based on team work. A school understood as a public space for all citizens, a collective workshop of many purposes and possibilities, and a person-centred learning community, working closely with other schools and with local authorities. The book concludes by examining how we might bring such transformation about.

Written by two of the leading experts in the fields of early childhood and secondary education, the book covers a wide vista of education for children and young people. Vivid examples from a range of stages of education are used to explore the full meaning of radical democratic education and the common school and how they can work in practice. It connects rich thinking and experiences from the past and present to offer direction and hope for the future. It will be of interest and inspiration to all who care about education – teachers and students, academics and policy makers, parents and politicians.

Michael Fielding is Professor of Education and **Peter Moss** is Professor of Early Childhood Provision, Institute of Education, University of London, UK.

Foundations and Futures of Education

Series Editors:

Peter Aggleton *School of Education and Social Work, University of Sussex, UK*
Sally Power *Cardiff University, UK*
Michael Reiss *Institute of Education, University of London, UK*

Foundations and Futures of Education focuses on key emerging issues in education as well as continuing debates within the field. The series is interdisciplinary, and includes historical, philosophical, sociological, psychological and comparative perspectives on three major themes: the purposes and nature of education; increasing interdisciplinarity within the subject; and the theory–practice divide.

Previous titles include:

Language, Learning, Context
Wolff-Michael Roth

Learning, Context and the Role of Technology
Rosemary Luckin

Education and the Family
Passing success across the generations
Leon Feinstein, Kathryn Duckworth and Ricardo Sabates

Education, Philosophy and the Ethical Environment
Graham Haydon

Educational Activity and the Psychology of Learning
Judith Ireson

Schooling, Society and Curriculum
Alex Moore

Gender, Schooling and Global Social Justice
Elaine Unterhalter

Education – An 'Impossible Profession'?
Tamara Bibby

Being a University
Ronald Barnett

Schools and Schooling in the Digital Age
Neil Selwyn

School Trouble
Deborah Youdell

Forthcoming titles include:

Irregular Schooling
Roger Slee

The Struggle for the History of Education
Gary McCulloch

Radical Education and the Common School

A democratic alternative

Michael Fielding and Peter Moss

 Routledge
Taylor & Francis Group

LONDON AND NEW YORK

First published 2011
by Routledge
2 Park Square, Milton Park, Abingdon, Oxon, OX14 4RN

Simultaneously published in the USA and Canada
by Routledge
270 Madison Avenue, New York, NY 10016

Routledge is an imprint of the Taylor & Francis Group, an informa business

Typeset in Garamond MT by Swales & Willis Ltd, Exeter, Devon
Printed and bound in Great Britain by TJ International Ltd, Padstow, Cornwall

British Library Cataloguing in Publication Data
A catalogue record for this book is available from the British Library

Library of Congress Cataloging-in-Publication Data
Fielding, Michael, 1945–
    Radical education and the common school / by Michael Fielding and Peter Moss.
    p. cm.
    Includes bibliographical references and index.
    1. Educational innovations. 2. Education—Aims and objectives.
    3. Educational change. 4. Education—Philosophy. 5. Radicalism. 6. Alternative education.
    7. Education—Experimental methods. 8. Educational innovations—Europe—
    Case studies. 9. Educational innovations—Great Britain—Case studies.
    I. Moss, Peter, 1945– II. Title.
    LB1027.F45 2011
    370.11′5—dc22
    2010022533

ISBN13: 978–0–415–49828–9 (hbk)
ISBN13: 978–0–415–49829–6 (pbk)
ISBN13: 978–0–203–83740–5 (ebk)

To the memory of Alex Bloom and Loris Malaguzzi who understood why democracy matters and what we might do to live and learn together more joyfully and more justly.

Contents

List of boxes and tables

Boxes

Tables

Acknowledgements

We would like to thank James Porter, Richard Hatcher and Patrick Yarker for their engagement with various stages of the writing of different parts of this book. Their challenges and their support are much appreciated.

1 The state we're in

> There is no single vital problem, but many vital problems, and it is this complex inter-solidarity of problems, antagonisms, crises, uncontrolled processes, and the general crisis of the planet that constitutes the number one vital problem.
>
> (Morin, 1999, p. 74)

This book is an exploration of social alternatives in the field of education, and argues for a new public education that we term 'radical education and the common school'. This exploration is made urgent by the parlous state that we, as societies and as a species, are in: Edgar Morin's 'number one vital problem'. It is inspired by a rich legacy of educational thinkers and doers and it is motivated by three desires: to overthrow the dictatorship of no alternatives, to practise an emancipatory social science and to pursue real utopias. The language we use to express these desires is borrowed from two social thinkers to whom we have frequently turned for their ideas about possibilities of social transformation: the American Marxist sociologist, Erik Olin Wright and the Brazilian social theorist, legal scholar and politician, Roberto Mangabeira Unger.

Unger's concern that we live today under the dictatorship of no alternatives – reminiscent of Margaret Thatcher's triumphant rallying cry 'There is no alternative' – reminds us of a powerful tactic of supporters of dominant discourses down the ages, and which today (or at least until recently) has been the clarion call of neoliberals and market fundamentalists, who have sought to turn a choice into a necessity. Thatcher and her ilk revelled in this dictatorship. Unger rebels, rejecting a poverty of political expectation that means 'the humanization of the inevitable has become the limit of transformative ambition' (2004, p. xviii).

Wright, too, believes in the possibility of alternatives. He coins the term 'emancipatory social science' to describe 'an account of a journey from the present to a possible future' containing three parts: the

> critique of society [that] tells us *why* we want to leave the world in which we live; the theory of alternatives [that] tells us *where* we want to go; and the theory of transformation [that] tells us *how* to get from here to there.
>
> (Wright, 2009b, p. 17; emphasis added)

Emancipatory social science leads Wright to an interest in 'real utopias', a term he uses to refer to 'utopian ideals that are grounded in the real potentials for redesigning social institutions'. While believing in the need for imagination and vision, to help us appreciate what might be possible, he also argues the need to eschew 'vague utopian fantasies', instead proposing utopian ideals that 'are grounded in the real potentials of humanity, utopian destinations that have accessible waystations, utopian designs of institutions that can inform our practical tasks of navigating a world of imperfect conditions for social change' (Wright, 2009a, p. 4).

In short, we need to work the tension between dreams and practice. Wright has sought to do so in his own work on 'real utopias', which has focused on a 'radical democratic egalitarian' alternative to capitalism. But he has also led a Real Utopias Project that has explored radical alternatives to existing social practices in a number of basic societal institutions including property rights, secondary associations, markets, the welfare state and gender relations in the family (Cohen and Rogers, 1995; Roemer, 1996; Bowles and Gintis, 1999; Fung and Wright, 2003; Ackerman *et al.*, 2005 and Gornick and Meyers, 2009).

What this book offers is a radical alternative to another basic societal institution, namely education, and an important educational environment, the school. It offers an alternative to what we view as the current dominant but failed and dysfunctional discourse about education and the school, of which more shortly, taking to heart Unger's comment that the dictatorship of no alternative cannot be overthrown without ideas. This offer comes from authors who share a particular perspective, both political and national, what might be termed left-wing English, though we hope that much of what we say resonates beyond England, indeed beyond the United Kingdom, and we draw widely for inspiration on people and places beyond the confines of our country.

The book also offers a contribution to Wright's emancipatory social science, focusing on the first two stages of that journey from the present to a possible future, critique and alternatives. Wright further applies three criteria to any consideration of alternatives: desirability, viability and achievability. We consider these criteria in more detail in subsequent chapters, but for the moment note that our focus is, again, on the first two: desirability, setting out an alternative that is strong on abstract but important principles; and viability, 'a scientifically grounded conception of viable alternative institutions' (Wright, 2009b, p. 16). In so doing, we set out what we hope is a real utopia, a fundamentally redesigned but pragmatically possible alternative for education and schooling.

There are other facets to the work of Wright and Unger that we find attractive. Their critiques of current economic and social conditions seem ever more necessary and urgent as these conditions come to be seen increasingly as inimical to flourishing, whether individual, societal or environmental. Their hopes for a better world are anchored in a strong belief in human beings and their capacity to act democratically, collaboratively and creatively. Their writing on alternatives and transformation is highly pragmatic, concerned with analysing how and why transformatory change might come about, rejecting both trivial revisions and revolutionary ruptures in favour of an incremental, cumulative and reactive process governed by a clear sense of direction – 'where to?' being the critical question – while at the same time eschewing the dangers of 'blueprint' utopianism. Wright, indeed, insists that the project of radical social change should be thought of less as providing a detailed blueprint or road map, with a clear itinerary marking the route unambiguously to a known destination and more as 'a voyage of exploration':

> We leave the familiar world equipped with navigational devices that tell us the direction in which we are moving and how far from our point of departure we have travelled, but without a map laying out the entire route from origin to end-point. This has perils, of course: we may encounter unforeseen obstacles which force us to move in a direction we had not planned . . . In the end, we may discover that there are absolute limits to how far we can go; but we can at least know if we are moving in the right direction.
>
> (Wright, 2006, p. 105)

We return in the final chapter to further discussion about the ways and means of transformation. Though the theory of transformation is not the subject for this book, we hope to leave the reader aware that such a theory is as important today as ever and that there exist some useful building blocks for creating a theory for the transformation of education. But we warn the reader in advance that, following Wright, we will not offer a detailed road map specifying the route and journey time to destination 'radical education'. We think such certainty neither desirable nor feasible. Unlike some educational pundits who have no doubts about direction or destination, the way ahead to us seems full of uncertainties: changing environments, unforeseen obstacles and unplanned deviations. It will take us to new viewpoints, leading us to review where we are heading towards and demanding route changes.

This talk of transformation, however, risks putting the cart before the horse. We start, in this chapter, therefore by paying particular attention to critique and why the current discourse of education and schooling is not fit for purpose, given the state we are in. In Chapters 2 and 3, we address alternatives. We propose desirable principles for redesigning education, a radical education that both looks backwards to draw on a rich educational legacy and looks forwards to offer an education that promises hope for the future; and for a school well-suited to practise a radical education, a common school. We also explore the viability of these alternatives, adopting Wright's understanding of viability as involving both 'systemic *theoretical models* of how particular social structures and institutions would work, and *empirical studies of cases*, both historical and contemporary, where at least some aspects of [our] proposal have been tried' (Wright, 2007, p. 27; emphasis added).

But before plunging into the sometimes gloomy topic of critique, we want to start on a hopeful note by offering two cases of viability: educational projects that have sought and, for a time at least, offered the prospect of real utopias in practice, and which provide some inkling of what we mean by radical education.

Two tales of hope

A community takes responsibility for its children's education

The city began its educational project more than 40 years ago. Today it runs a network of 34 municipal schools, for around 2,500 children, an expression of this community taking responsibility for the education of its younger citizens. Right from its beginning in the early 1960s, the project has been understood as, first and foremost, political and ethical, built on critical questions and explicit values. Critical questions have required choices to be made, and these choices have been made collectively and infused by values; once made, they have 'been reference points for us, guiding our experience, our journey' (Rinaldi, 2006, p. 71).

A central value has been democracy. The mayor at the time the city's project began talks about it as a reaction to fascism which 'had taught them that people who conformed and obeyed were dangerous, and that in building a new society it was imperative . . . to nurture and maintain a vision of children who can think and act for themselves' (Dahlberg, 2000, p. 177). Democratic participation – of children, parents, educators, other school staff and other citizens – is 'a value, an identifying feature of the entire experience, a way of viewing those involved in the educational process and the role of the school' (Cagliari *et al.*, 2004, p. 29). Other key values, important qualities that are precious to the education project, include dialogue and solidarity, uncertainty and subjectivity, plurality and border crossing.

The city's first question and choice was the most fundamental: what is our under-standing, what is our image of the child? And the city's answer has been that of the 'rich' child – 'rich in potential, strong, powerful, competent and, most of all, con-nected to adults and other children' (Malaguzzi, 1993, p. 10) – and the child as citizen and subject of rights.

The second question and choice has been: what is our theory of learning? From their questioning has emerged a distinctive approach. Learning, for instance, is not seen as a form of linear progression; it is not like a staircase, where you have to take the first step before you move onto and reach the other, en route to a known end point – it is not the learning of transmission and predetermined outcome. Rather learning is understood as a process of co-construction, building meaning in relationship with others, as this former director of municipal schools describes:

> Learning does not take place by means of transmission or reproduction. It is a process of construction, in which each individual constructs for himself the reasons, the 'whys', the meanings of things, others, nature, events, reality and life. The learning process is certainly individual, but because the reasons, explanations, interpretations and meanings of others are indispensable for our knowledge building, it is also a process of relations – a process of social construction. We thus consider knowledge to be a process of construction by the individual in relation with others, a true act of co-construction. The timing and styles of learning are individual, and cannot be standardised with those of others, but we need others in order to realise ourselves.
>
> (Rinaldi, 2006, p. 125)

The pathways taken by such learning and its outcomes are uncertain: learning 'does not proceed in a linear way, determined and deterministic, by progressive and predictable stages, but rather is constructed through contemporaneous advances, standstills, and "retreats" that take many directions' (Rinaldi, 2005, p. 19). Another leading educator in the municipal schools emphasises their ease with uncertainty of direction, their resistance to shackling learning and their belief in the potential of the rich child:

> It is important to society that schools and we as teachers are clearly aware how much space we leave children for original thinking, without rushing to restrict it with predetermined schemes that define what is *correct* according to a school culture. How much do we support children to have ideas different from those of other people and how do we accustom them to arguing and discussing their ideas with their classmates? I am quite convinced that greater attention to processes, rather than only the final product, would help us to feel greater respect for the independent thinking and strategies of children and teenagers.
>
> (Vecchi, 2010, p. 138; original emphasis)

Ideas about learning reflect ideas about knowledge. Knowledge, to quote the first director of the municipal schools, is like a 'tangle of spaghetti', a metaphor similar to Gilles Deleuze's idea of rhizomatic knowledge:

> something which shoots in all directions with no beginning and no end, but always *in between*, and with openings towards other directions and places. It is a *multiplicity* functioning by means of connections and heterogeneity, a multiplicity which is not given but constructed. Thought, then, is a matter of experimentation and problematization – *a line of flight* and an exploration of *becoming*.
>
> (Rinaldi, 2006, p. 8; original emphasis)

The process of learning as co-construction, in relationship with others and without the necessity of known outcomes, involves all concerned creating and re-creating theories:

> For adults and children alike, understanding means being able to develop an interpretive 'theory', a narration that gives meaning to events and objects of the world. Our theories are provisional, offering a satisfactory explanation that can be continuously reworked; but they represent something more than simply an idea or a group of ideas. They must please us and convince us, be useful, and satisfy our intellectual, affective, and aesthetic needs (the aesthetics of knowledge). In representing the world, our theories represent us.
>
> (Rinaldi, 2006, p. 64)

Theories are created and shared, questioned and re-formed. This requires listening to thought – the ideas and theories, questions and answers of children and adults alike; treating thought seriously and with respect; and struggling to make meaning from what is said, without preconceived ideas of what is correct or appropriate. Listening, therefore, is one of the foundations of the educational project,

> careful, respectful, tender 'listening' with solidarity to children's strategies and ways of thinking. Careful however! These are children who feel free to express

their opinions and who trust in the fact that they will be listened to carefully and respectfully. It is no coincidence that Jerome Bruner recalls that what struck him most on first entering [our] schools was a teacher who was listening to a child's theories on how shadows are formed. He emphasises how this listening was interested and serious, because the child was putting together a theory the credibility of which was not important. What was important was the process that led to the construction of the theory.

(Vecchi, 2010, p. 29)

The city's educators speak, therefore, of a 'pedagogy of relationships and listening'. Another pedagogical concept of great importance is the 'hundred languages of children', an idea that emerged early on in this municipal project, during debates about the privileged position given in traditional education to just two languages, speech and writing, which 'supported the power, not only of certain knowledges, but also of certain classes' (Rinaldi, 2006, p. 193). The 'hundred languages', a theory full of democracy, refers 'to the different ways children (human beings) represent, communicate and express their thinking in different media and symbolic systems; languages therefore are the many fonts or geneses of knowledge' (Vecchi, 2010, p. 9). These numerous linguistic possibilities range from mathematical and scientific languages to the poetic languages, 'forms of expression strongly characterised by expressive or aesthetic aspects such as music, song, dance or photography' (ibid.). The choice of a 'hundred' does not denote a precise count, but is intended to be 'very provocative, to claim for all these languages not only the same dignity, but the right to expression and to communicate with each other' (Rinaldi, 2006, p. 193).

A pedagogy of relationships is not only about interconnection and interdependency between people, but also between the 'hundred languages'. This means breaking down the divisions and opening up the compartments that too often exist in education with 'proposals for learning that do not hurry to fence the world in more or less rigid categories of thought; but, on the contrary, seek connections, alliances and solidarities between different categories and languages or subjects' (Vecchi, 2010, p. 32). Learning processes occur and are enriched when 'several languages [or disciplines] interact together' (ibid., p. 18).

The city has developed these ideas over nearly half a century, and put them to work in its schools, in a process of sustained and participatory experimentation. This ability to implement ideas in practice and to sustain the inventiveness and richness of the pedagogical thinking and work has not been a matter of luck. Apart from continuing political commitment from the city council and sustained public support, there have been strong organisation and effective tools – all based on explicit values; they never forget that 'behind every solution and every organisation, this means behind every school, there is a choice of values and ethics'. In short, the technical and managerial proceed from the political and ethical. In this way, the schools have moved from one to two teachers per group, to promote dialogue and multiple perspectives. Schools have *ateliers* (workshops) and *atelieristas* (educators with a background in visual arts) to develop the role of the visual languages in learning; working with these languages, ateliers and atelieristas help connect the cognitive, expressive, rational and imaginative, and bring an 'aesthetic dimension' to learning processes. Project work has a central role in learning. It is an ethos and a practice inscribed with the values of democracy and uncertainty, and enabling the co-construction of knowledge without a predetermined end point:

> It is sensitive to the rhythms of communication and incorporates the significance and timing of children's investigation and research. The duration of a project can thus be short, medium, or long, continuous or discontinuous, with pauses, suspensions, and restarts. The statement of a hypothesis on how the project might proceed is valid only to the extent that it is seen precisely as a hypothesis and not as a 'must', as one of a thousand hypotheses on the direction that might be taken. Above all, making hypotheses is a way to increase the expectations, excitement, and the possibilities for being and interacting, for welcoming the unexpected as a fundamental resource. . . . [Project work] is a way of thinking, a strategy for creating relations and bringing in the element of chance, by which we mean 'the space of the others'; i.e. that undefined space of the self that is completed by the thoughts of others within the relational process.
>
> (Rinaldi, 2006, pp. 132–33)

The city fosters collaborative relationships between its schools and between the city and its schools. A key role is played by the team of *pedagogistas*, experienced educators who act as pedagogical coordinators for the city's educational project, each working with a small number of municipal schools to help educators – teachers and atelieristas – deepen their understanding of learning processes and pedagogical work. Last, but not least, *pedagogical documentation* is a multi-purpose and participatory tool of great importance for many tasks: planning, researching, professional development and evaluation.

Put simply, pedagogical documentation makes learning processes and educational practices visible by being documented in various ways (by means of notes, photographs, videos, recordings, children's artistic or other creations, etc.) so that they can be shared, discussed, reflected upon, interpreted and, if necessary, evaluated. It can and does involve everyone – children, teachers, auxiliary staff, families, administrators and other citizens – and gives 'the possibility to discuss and dialogue "everything with everyone" and to base these discussions on real, concrete things' (Hoyuelos, 2004, p. 7). It makes education and the school transparent by enabling 'the active and visible exchange of ideas between a school and its surroundings including the families, community members, and political leaders'; and it transforms a school 'to become a meeting place of co-construction . . . [and] a place of democracy [by inviting] multiple ideas, debate, and negotiation among different points of view of an experience' (Turner and Wilson, 2010, p. 10). Pedagogical documentation is another expression of the project's commitment to democracy, an example of democratic practice at the heart of the school in which all participants must take responsibility for education, not ceding it to outside experts applying supposedly objective indicators.

One answer to the question, 'does this educational project work?' is to say: 'participate with the citizens of the city in documentation and take responsibility for answering your own question and making your own judgement of value'. By looking at and trying to understand what children actually do, at their learning processes and theories, not assessing whether children meet certain predefined norms, educators and others in the city find that children in their schools are capable of original, creative and unpredicted thought and learning: children and educators alike are open to surprise, wonder and amazement. There is recognition that there are different 'languages of evaluation' and that the choice of language has deep implications.

The second answer is to point to the tens of thousands of people from outside the city who visit its schools or look at their work presented in an exhibition that has been travelling the world for more than 20 years – and are impressed, excited and inspired by what they see. For this is a local experience that has now created a global network of enthusiasts, convinced that something important and special is going on in this project and wanting to develop their own educational projects in relationship with the city and its schools. Among these thousands of enthusiasts are some of the leading educationalists of the day. Howard Gardner has been a long-term admirer:

> most important, is the capacious and inspiring conception of children – as active, engaged, exploring young spirits, capable of remaining with questions and themes for many weeks, able to work alongside peers and adults, welcoming the opportunity to express themselves in many languages . . . it is what first brought me [there] in the early 1980s and inspired me on many memorable trips since.
>
> (Gardner, 2004, p. 17)

Jerome Bruner, another frequent visitor, describes 'a city of courtesy, curiosity and imagination', and of not being prepared for what he saw on his first visit: 'it was not only the fact that the [schools] were better than anything I had ever seen before . . . [What struck me] was seeing how imagination was cultivated there, reinforcing at the same time the children's sense of the possible' (Bruner, 2004, p. 27). Gunilla Dahlberg is part of a strong and long-standing Swedish relationship with the city, and speaks of an evolving understanding of the significance of the educational project:

> Many of us in Sweden then [in the 1980s, when Swedes first came into contact with the city] thought it was about children making art and not about pedagogy in a broader sense. This was because of the beauty and the sophistication of the art [in the city's travelling exhibition]. Extensive reading and two decades of study visits to [the city] helped us to see a bigger picture. We started to understand their practice as similar to ours in Sweden, but simply better . . . [But] today our understanding has moved on again. We have come to understand that [the city] has indeed constructed a new and different pedagogical space. A relational space where making connections is a primary concern. In this space there is room for celebrating the complexity of thought processes by exploring new relations with art, design, architecture, science, philosophy.
>
> (Dahlberg, 2004, p. 22)

This is both a very local and a very cosmopolitan experience, firmly rooted in a particular political and historical context but attaching great importance to border crossing and driven by an endless curiosity. They are visited from, and in turn visit, all over the world. They relate to a network of schools and educators in many countries that draw inspiration from the city – an example of a global community of learners. They are open to many influences, reading widely, though recognising that reading is an interpretive process – Piaget, Morin, Dewey or Vygotsky become 'our Piaget', 'our Morin', 'our Dewey' or 'our Vygotsky'. And they avidly explore disciplines, theories and contemporary issues, straying well beyond the borders of education, to make connections, discover new perspectives and deepen understandings of the context within which their education is situated.

The people of this city have had the courage to take responsibility for the education of young citizens and to think for themselves. They have dared to make the choice of understanding the child as a rich child, a child of infinite capabilities, a child born with a hundred languages. They have risked and indeed welcomed uncertainty and complexity. They have built a new pedagogical project foregrounding relationships and encounters, dialogue and negotiation, reflection and critical thinking, border crossing and multiple perspectives.

A democratic school for human flourishing

The school began its work in 1945, in a context where democracy itself had been under global threat. Whilst it is not, perhaps, surprising that the work of the school was animated by a vibrant awareness of the fragility of democratic ways of life, what was remarkable was the quiet and resolute insistence of the head teacher, Alex Bloom, that democracy was to be its animating, overt dynamic. He unambiguously insisted that 'a piecemeal approach could not work. A consciously democratic community could not be formed gradually by the removal of one taboo after another' (Bloom, 1948, p. 120). Despite some internal difficulties and some initial hostility, the school grew to become not only one of the most radical examples of a democratic secondary school within the state system of secondary schooling, but also one of the most successful. Relatively early on in its ten-year history, a glowing inspection report talked of '[t]he pioneering missionary work which has been carried out over the past two and half years, always in a spirit of confident adventure'. Such work, it affirmed, 'has attained not only the goal which the school set itself from the beginning, but also something much more – it has given a vision of what the new form of Secondary School can be' (Ministry of Education, 1948, p. 11).

One of the key consequences of taking democracy really seriously was that it formed the bedrock of all that went on in the school, for democracy was understood and practised not primarily as a mode of decision-making; it was a way of living and learning together.

> It is a vital part of our belief that the *modus vivendi* claims paramount importance. We are convinced not only that the overall school pattern – the democratic way of living – precedes all planning, but that it proclaims the main purpose of

education in a democracy. Our aim is that our children shall learn to live creatively, not for themselves alone, but also for their community.

(Bloom, 1949, p. 170)

This learning by being and doing is to be distinguished from learning *about* these matters. Anticipating the work of Lawrence Kohlberg 20 years later in the US (discussed further in Chapters 2 and 3), Alex Bloom argued that

> Lessons about cooperation or tolerance or injustice will not form right attitudes nor change wrong ones. By living experiences within the community the child learns; the fuller and deeper the comprehension of the experience the more they 'cut into' the fibre of his being and become an integral part of his self. This way of living established, the 'work' can, with understanding guidance from the staff, be left to achieve itself.
>
> (ibid., p. 170)

His view was that education was 'fundamentally a matter of relationships', that '[h]e is educated who is able to recognise relationships between things and to experience just relations between persons' (Bloom, 1952, p. 136), and that the art of living can only be learned through the kinds of contexts just described. It was imperative, he believed, to replace the debilitating influence of fear as the prime incentive to educational 'progress'. 'Fear of authority (. . . imposed for disciplinary purposes), fear of failure, (. . . by means of marks, prizes and competition, for obtaining results); and the fear of punishment (for all these purposes)' must be replaced by 'friendship, security and the recognition of each child's worth' (ibid., pp. 136–37).

The school thus 'began without regimentation, without corporal punishment, without competition' (Bloom, 1948, p. 120); and in order to overcome staff concerns about its novelty and its presumed impracticability, substantial time was devoted to discussing and getting a feeling for what was known as 'The School Pattern' and the principles underlying it. In contrast to current predilections for avoiding matters of principle and the philosophical foundations of what we aspire to achieve in our daily work, this is precisely where the head teacher started and through 'peaceful penetration, courage and patience' there evolved 'within two and a half years, a homogeneous, living force' (ibid.).

What then were the key elements of the 'daily design for living' (Bloom, 1953, p. 177), which 'The School Pattern' expressed? The only surviving copy of what was an intentionally-evolving document opens by suggesting that:

> At school the child has two loyalties which we aim at making two accepted duties . . . one to himself, the other to his community. We must give him the freedom to develop himself as fully and as finely as he can for his own sake and for the sake of his community. The art of compromise is thus, an essential lesson in learning to live dynamically, but at peace, in and with a community.
>
> (Bloom, n.d.)

Human flourishing is relational and dynamic, and best nurtured through the daily realisation of the mutually conditioning twin principles of freedom and equality, which together constitute the living reality of a just, inclusive, caring community. What is particularly interesting is the equal stress placed by the school on the child's uniqueness and her obligation to contribute to the community; and on the community's responsibility to create spaces for freedom and to earn the allegiance of the child.

1   the child must feel that . . . he *does* count, that he is wanted, that he has a contribution to make to the common good;
2   the child must feel that the school community is worthwhile.

(Bloom, n.d; original emphasis)

In helping young people to grow in this way, 'objective rewards and punishments are false stimuli, for, unless the right thing is done for the right reason one lives unethically . . . Similarly, objective competition is wrong; it is not only unethical but it tends to destroy a communal spirit'. In eradicating it, 'because there are neither carrots nor goads, there will be no donkeys, for when children are treated as we would have them be, they tend to reach out accordingly' (Bloom, 1949, p. 171).

The key role of staff was to model these aspirations in a kind and tolerant way and 'through wise guidance and unobtrusive supervision' help the child to 'comprehend the freedom given him'. 'The School Pattern' concludes by suggesting that '[p]erhaps the crux of things, now, lies in the realisation of the individuality of each child with all that this implies of individual treatment, individual approach, individual work'. Or, as Bloom puts it in one of his best known pieces: 'Perhaps what is needed most of all by teachers is a larger faith in the natural fineness of the child and in his inner potential' (Bloom, 1949, p. 171).

If the school's image of the child was one in which 'natural fineness' and curiosity were best addressed within the context of a vibrant democratic community expressive of a relational, inclusive view of individuality, what were the commensurate views of learning made real in the daily practice? In earlier years, Bloom tried a range of approaches to collaborative, student-centred learning. These included projects, 'centres of interest' and social studies which were approached individually, in small groups and as class or Form studies. However, after wide experience of all these approaches, the school came to the view that 'the most effective learning is achieved and the keenest interest maintained' through what they called 'School Study' (Bloom, 1953, p. 175). In order to retain the commitment to engaging with the interests of students, broad topics, such as 'Man's Dependence on Man', were collectively agreed by staff. Each Form then took one of the agreed facets of the School Study as its own theme and divided it into group topics. Students worked in self-chosen groups 'making their notes, building charts, paying their visits, while the teacher proceeded with them as co-adventurer, stimulating them and acting as their ever present help' (ibid.).

The collegial individuality at the heart of Form studies was then further developed and nested within the larger communal engagement of the whole school, attended by about 260 children. 'Once a fortnight the whole school met in the Hall to receive reports from the children in each Form on the progress being made in the study, a member of staff taking the chair' (Bloom, 1953, p. 175); and once a year, there was a School Conference planned and arranged by the staff. Here, each Form teacher gave the school a résumé of their work connected with the School Study. There then followed a film illustrative of the theme of the School Study before students broke into mixed age discussion groups whose representatives subsequently reported the tenor of their discussions to the whole school.

Here we have the vibrancy of individual interest and energy stimulated and developed through the increasing breadth and depth of collaborative research, and in such a way that communities of enquiry feed off each other in a nested, cumulative way that is informative, stimulating and celebratory. In the head teacher's own words, from their approach to School Study the following values emerged and in an order he regarded as significant and deliberate:

> Curiosity and Thought are aroused;
> By learning how to satisfy this curiosity children learn how to learn
> (through books, visits, interviews, chats, and so on);
> The living experience of group working is vital to the promotion of
> just human relations;
> Understanding rather than knowledge collecting is achieved;
> The skills of communication are sharpened in purposeful situations.
>
> (Bloom, 1953, p. 176)

School Study took up much of the work of the school in the mornings. In the afternoons, Elective Activities continued the commitment to communally situated choice. Here, we have daily arrangements in which 'children make up their own afternoon timetable' (Bloom, 1953). Students themselves not only made choices from staff offerings, but also suggested offerings themselves. What is as pertinent and even more compelling is the head teacher's evaluation of Elective Activities in action:

> Need one elaborate the value and joy of these afternoons? Groups which are cross-sections of the school, meeting for their self-chosen activities, purposefully employed. Through the abundance of their creative experiences the children find an emotional release in an atmosphere that is *sympaticos*. And always with them rests the satisfaction that they, *they* have made the choice.
>
> (Bloom, 1953, p. 176; original emphasis)

In the school there was not only an emphasis on communally-situated choice and an emergent approach to a broadly conceived notion of learning. There was also a companion emphasis both on continuity of relationships with a class teacher and on multifaceted communal engagement with other students and staff. Underpinning all this was an immensely strong belief in what we later refer to as 'the insistent affirmation of possibility' and its resultant hostility to any kind of ability grouping or means of labelling children. In addition, there was strong commitment to learning outside the physical confines of the school, including, at the time highly unusual, extensive use of the wider city as a learning resource and regular residential experience in the form of school camps on the coast. Lastly, anticipating and exceeding even the most radical forms of student voice in contemporary schooling, students' own evaluations of their curricular experience in both its broad and narrow senses were sought and acted on through Weekly Reviews in which each child commented on any aspect of their learning and staff teaching they felt appropriate.

Democracy was not confined to how children and adults lived together and related to each other: organisation mattered. The school had a remarkably sophisticated formal democratic structure consisting of the Staff Panel, the Pupil Panel, and, at the school level, the Joint Panel and the School Council/School Meeting. The Staff Panel met every Monday lunchtime and included all staff, about ten people. The Pupil Panel comprised the Head Boy and Head Girl, their two Deputies and the Secretary, all of whom were elected by students. It also included elected Form Representatives. This Panel met every Friday morning in school time and considered all school matters. There were reports from Form Representatives and business sent by staff. It also appointed a range of Pupil Committees which took responsibility for running various aspects of school life, for example:

- Dance – midday dancing in the Hall;
- Meals – organising break-time canteen and helping with midday meals;
- Sports – playground games, sports equipment, outside matches (Non competitive! They did play matches with other schools but, even when they 'won' always requested they be recorded as 'friendlies' and not count in the league);
- Tidy – appearance of the school;
- Social – concerts, parties, visitors.

Each Committee was linked to a member of staff who undertook a liaison role. Form Meetings took place every Monday morning, in part to hear reports of the previous Friday's Pupil Panel meeting.

The Joint Panel met on the last Friday of the month. It included members of both Staff and Pupil Panels and chairs of all Pupil Committees. Reports were given by a member of staff for the Staff Panel, by the Head Girl or Head Boy for the Pupil Panel and by chairs of the various Pupil Committees. On the Monday following the Joint Panel Meeting, there was a School Council/School Meeting presided over alternately by a member of staff and by a member of the Pupil Panel, agreed at the previous Full School Meeting.

One of the most innovative aspects of the democratic structures and practices of the school was this School Council and its attendant School Meeting. This was a school council and not what are often now called 'school councils', but which are in fact student councils. It involved every teacher and student in the school gathering together in the hall to reflect on their work and lives together. Purposes and aspirations, the touchstones of meaning-making, framed the opening and closing of the event; reflection, dialogue, disagreement and celebration enabled contributions from all ages and identities in ways which challenged traditional hierarchies within the context of an insistent, demanding mutuality. A range of voices were heard, not only through the narratives of learning, but also through the leveller of laughter and the eagerness of exploration. And all through this ran the excitement of the unpredictable and the reassurance of shared responsibility.

Summing up his reflections on the working of the School Council/School Meeting, its supporting committees and activities, and the range of engagements in formal and informal learning exemplified in the school's day-to-day life, the head teacher concluded:

> It will be seen that we, as *teachers*, have very little power. Nor do we need it. We are, by the nature of our work, in authority. Our School Council prevents us from being authoritarian. A large part of the school organization is in the hands of the children themselves, and the value of the experiences afforded by the School Council in responsible, democratic and constructive living is great. To the children the school becomes *our* school with a consequent enrichment of community feeling.
>
> (Bloom, 1953, p. 175; original emphasis)

Hope and despair

The educational project with which we began this chapter is Reggio Emilia, a city of 150,000 inhabitants in Northern Italy, and its 'municipal schools' are for children from a few months old to six years. In the complex context of Italian pre-school education, these municipal schools are not the only services for young children in the city, with the state and private (mainly religious) organisations providing many schools for three- to six-year-olds. Although the city lacks sufficient resources to provide for all of its children, it has built up an extensive and widespread network, for children under and over three years, all within an integrated 0–6 (*zerosei*) education system – and its educational project remains energetic and innovative more than four decades after the first centre opened, and more than 15 years after the premature death of Loris Malaguzzi, the first head of the city's schools and a leading figure in twentieth century education. Reggio Emilia stands today as a continuing and flourishing example of what Unger calls 'islands of productive and educational experimentalism where collective learning and permanent innovation already rule' (Unger, 2004, p. lvi).

The school described in our second case example was St George-in-the-East, a secondary modern school (intended for children defined dismissively as 'non academic') in Stepney, one of the toughest areas of the East End of London. It flourished under Alex Bloom's leadership from 1945–1955 and became hugely well-known, both internationally and amongst progressive educators in England. However, whilst the school welcomed visitors from all over the world and the local community was hugely supportive, the education authorities in London were more wary.

In September 1955, Bloom died suddenly at the age of 60. His death was prominently reported in such disparate national newspapers as *The Times*, the *Evening News* and also the *Daily Mirror*, which ran a double-page centre spread with vivid pictures of distraught adults and children mourning his passing. Roy Nash, at that time education correspondent of another national daily paper, the *News Chronicle*, was moved to remark that:

It was an incredible thing to happen, absolutely unique in State education history. In my time I've reported funerals of prominent people, but I've never seen such genuine grief as on that day in the East End. It showed the humanity of true education.

(Berg, 1971, p. 37)

Honoured, too, by the anarchist weekly newspaper *Freedom* and the only secondary school within the state sector to be visited and supported by A. S. Neill (Croall, 1983, p. 334), Bloom is now virtually unknown.

These two examples are different in many respects. Reggio Emilia is a whole city in a prosperous part of Italy. Its educational project consists of a network of schools supported by the city, for children below compulsory school age. That project continues today, after more than 40 years and having weathered the loss of its first inspirational leader, Malaguzzi. St George-in-the-East was a secondary school, for children from 11 to 14 years. It served a desperately poor and neglected part of London, though one with its own vibrant political and cultural heritage – the Battle of Cable Street on 4 October 1936 was the first mass opposition to the rise of fascism in England. Whilst this brave educational project did not long outlast the death of its remarkable head teacher, its legacy resonates through the radical traditions of public education on which this book draws and to which it offers its own small contribution.

But they have much in common, which is why we start with them. First and foremost because they set the scene for the book, which proposes the need for a new public educational system based on what we term radical education and the common school. The examples illustrate some of the features of a radical education, including democracy as a fundamental value of education. They are examples of a community's and a school's imaginative engagement with an agreed set of radical democratic educational principles. They are instances, too, of a willingness to experiment, fuelled by a shared reaction to a recent history of totalitarian regimes that imposed conformity and obedience – the dictatorship of no alternative; both welcome plurality and the unexpected. Both also place great importance on a pedagogy of relationships and listening, in which knowledge is the outcome of an educational process of co-construction, and on fostering cooperation and solidarity, between people and (in the case of Reggio) between schools. With these collaborative and democratic values and with their emphasis on groups and networks, neither chose to organise education around the unit of the individual learner. Finally, we can point to the attention paid by both to value-based organisation and to the small scale of the schools.

As such they offer two local experiences that are very much at odds with today's educational mainstream, which we see as dominated by markets and competition, instrumentality and standardisation, managerialism and technical practice, and increasingly irrelevant to the perilous state in which we, humankind, find ourselves. The school has always been at risk of being a place of regulation and normalisation, tasked with producing subjects fit for the purposes of the nation state and the capitalist economy; in today's case, that means the autonomous, flexible, calculating, self-regulating and high consumption subject required of advanced liberalism and globalised hypermarket capitalism. Reggio Emilia and St George's remind us that the school can be something other, making an active and critical contribution to a demo-cratic and responsible society, whose citizens combine singularity with solidarity, and who commit to something considered of enduring value.

Reggio Emilia and St George-in-the-East run like threads through this book. We refer to them frequently, right up to the end, partly because we know them well, partly because they are well-documented, and partly because they are rich and relevant expe-riences of what we understand as radical education and how it operates in a holistic way that integrates all aspects of its work and aspirations. But they are not the only experiences, not by any means, and we present further local experiences throughout this book, experiences that serve as further reminders that alternatives are not just possible in theory, but in practice too. Indeed, if we began to systematically document and take stock of such experiences, past and present, at home and abroad, we might well find that there exist far more countercurrents than we thought and stand a little less in awe of the mainstream. Which last point leads us to conclude that education today needs fewer large-scale quantitative studies comparing performance on pre-determined outcomes, and more critical case studies of possibility, opportunities to enrich our imagination and vocabulary and to explore the potential of what Roberto Unger terms 'democratic experimentalism'. It also gives us some hope for the pos-sibility of change, that possibility being another theme of our book: how might it be possible to extend radical education and the common school?

Our introductory examples bring together two fields of education: early childhood and secondary. We plan to maintain and develop the relationship throughout the book, and include primary education too, aware that these parts of the education system too rarely appear together, let alone dialogue – a failure to connect found as much among academics as practitioners and policy makers. We want to contribute to building a relationship of equality, dialogue and mutuality across the education system, what the OECD (2001) has called a 'strong and equal partnership'. We are convinced that much learning can follow if 'meeting places' can be created, places of encounter for all parts of the education system where co-constructive learning can take place through a pedagogy of relationships and listening. Too often, though, the education system consists of one level seeking to impose on the one below, in a colonial and undemocratic process that some in the early childhood education field call 'schoolification'.

These two examples also illustrate the importance of working with experiences from other times and other places. This does not mean a nostalgic desire to return to the past or a simplistic belief in imported solutions. It means that there are many traditions in education (as in other fields) that we can benefit from engaging with, and this means making connections, both with other times and other places, by crossing borders, temporal and spatial. This can offer access to the accumulated wisdom of people who have puzzled away at important questions over many years; this can help us to be self-critical, by making the familiar strange and suggesting questions and per-spectives that may be new to us or which we may have simply forgotten about; it can offer us a different language and provoke our imaginations; it serves to remind us that there are alternatives and to reflect about the conditions under which these alterna-tives may best flourish. Why, for example, the reader may already be pondering, has

Reggio Emilia flourished for more than four decades, while St George-in-the-East survived barely more than one? In sum, engaging with different traditions, looking back in time and looking transnationally, provides another 'meeting place' where we can again co-construct new understandings – a process of learning.

Last but not least, and mindful of Henry Giroux's call for educators to 'combine a discourse of critique and resistance with a discourse of possibility and hope' (Giroux, 2008, p. 5), we start with these two cases because they give cause for hope, cause to believe in the world again. They remind us of what education and schools can be capable of, they remind us of their potential for excitement and inspiration, engagement and connectedness, amazement and wonder. This hope provides an antidote to the despair with much mainstream discourse about education and schooling that has given birth to this book.

If economics has gained a reputation as the 'dismal science', then education today has surely become the 'dismal subject'. In England today (but we suspect the same applies in many other parts of the world), hardly a day goes by without some depressing item in the media about education: parents scrambling to get their children in, by hook or by crook, to some schools, while turning their backs on others, with accusations of lying, fraud and theft; ever more testing and examinations for children, with raging disputes about the meaning of the results (more exam passes than ever, standards rising – Ah! but exams aren't what they used to be, so it doesn't count, in fact we are going to the dogs); teachers and schools reeling from one set of prescriptions to another, subjected to 'high stakes' testing, and constantly under the harsh gaze of government and inspectors; seemingly endless negative reports about children and their behaviour in and out of school – the school as battlefield for discontented youth; the school failing to deliver employers with what they want; the school turned to as a cure-all for society's mistakes and discontents, as yet another 'subject' is added to the brimming curriculum; and yet another plan to further privatise, marketise and re-structure the education system, in the hope that business know-how, the 'invisible hand' or some new form of school management will produce better performance, freeing us all from responsibility. The language used to talk about education in the mainstream is similarly dreary and off-putting, projecting the image of a human treadmill: 'goals', 'outcomes', 'performance', 'standards', 'indicators', 'delivery', 'measurement', 'high stakes tests', 'assessment', 'league tables', 'efficiency', 'competition', 'parent power', 'incentives', 'sanctions', 'inspection', etc.

What emerges from this impoverished and impoverishing public discourse is an image of the child as an empty vessel, to whom information, prescribed by the curriculum, must be 'delivered'; the teacher as technician, whose task is to unwrap and present packages of prescribed information; the parent as autonomous consumer, concerned only with securing the best buy for their child; and the school as a business, competing against other school-businesses for the custom of these parent-consumers, and whose 'mission' is to use technician-teachers to apply prescribed 'human technologies'[1] to achieve predefined outcomes. Children, teachers and schools are all evaluated by their conformity to ever more standardised norms, with standardised achievement the main currency of education. Education and the school have become a machine for ever more effective governing – of children, of teachers and of parents – in the interests of producing a flexible, self-managing workforce for an increasingly competitive and increasingly consuming global economy. They have become enclosures for deploying technical practices, underpinned by an extremely instrumental rationality, in a project reduced to identifying the most effective means to achieve predetermined ends – 'what works' is the slogan.

Education so reduced to a technical practice has come to epitomise the contention of Carlo Ginzberg, the Italian historian, that we live today in a culture where we are constantly offered solutions before we have asked the critical questions (Dahlberg *et al.*, 2007). So the public discourse of education rarely gives voice to such critical questions: What is education for, what is its purpose, both here and now and looking to the future? What should be its fundamental values and ethics? What do we mean by knowledge and learning? What is our concept of education? What is our image of the child, the teacher, the school? Who is responsible for education and what does it mean to be responsible?

The triumph of technology over thought and the failure to create an informed, relevant and critical public educational discourse about purposes, values, ethics, concepts, understandings and responsibilities, led one of us to observe at the end of the first term of the English 'New Labour' government that:

> What we cannot do is continue as we are but more persistently and more intensely. . . . We have to break free from our current modes of thinking and exhibit . . . 'a preparedness to think radically outside the frame'. Unless we do so we will fail profoundly and persistently to educate ourselves, our contemporaries, and our children's children. At this juncture our most important tasks are intellectual. We are operating in the wrong frame of reference and as a consequence our lives will continue to become more busy, more exhausting, less humanly productive or satisfying and increasingly devoid of meaning. Alternative frameworks exist that are likely to serve our human needs more profoundly and more engagingly: it would be foolish to ignore them.
>
> (Fielding, 2001a, p. 13)

In the absence of these alternatives, we are left with a simplistic, mechanistic and out-dated narrative, which invites incredulity: education for a competitive market society and a growth-based and consumption-led economy. The narrative is not outdated just in the sense that it has – as we shall argue later – been overtaken by events and by increasing disbelief in a future that is simply more of the same, a future of markets and growth-based economics. It is outdated in a more profound sense, offering a Victorian narrative for a twenty-first-century world.

The Victorian era seems to spring readily to mind when reflecting on education today. The philosopher John White argues that we have entered the twenty-first century with an educational system based on the values and practices of the nineteenth century (White, 2007). The recent *Cambridge Primary Review*, an independent investigation into the condition and future of primary education in England, concluded that in many ways – including the primacy of the 3Rs, the range of subjects and the class-teacher system – 'today's primary schools would not look unfamiliar to the Victorians' (Cambridge Primary Review, 2009, p. 10). This view is echoed by an English secondary head teacher who writes of attempts by some schools 'at rescuing young people from the complex and frequently alienating experience that many urban schools and academies have become in their relentless adherence to nineteenth century forms of organisation and control' (Davies, 2009, p. 10). Internationally, an OECD report adopts the same theme, criticising the 'organisation, curriculum and decision-making in schools [that] continue to resemble 19th century patterns: curricula imbibed with the certainties of the past, formal testing of discrete skills and knowledge items and the "balkanisation" of teachers into separate classrooms and disciplines' (OECD, 2006, pp. 221–22). It is not so much that Mr Gradgrind still rules in the classroom, but that education still espouses the individual subject as its basis, not the connectedness across borders that marks out the thematic and project approach of Reggio Emilia and St George's.

The failure of public thought and deliberation that has led to the survival of this outdated educational narrative reveals a society in which political discourse has been hollowed out, 'drained of great ideas in favour of economic goals' (Morin, 1999, p. 112). It is a process in which the social and the political have been collapsing into the economic, so that 'all aspects of social behaviour are reconceptualised along economic lines' (Rose, 1999, p. 141), with markets as 'the primary instrument for achieving the public good' (Sandel, 2009b, p. 2). Apple argues that the upshot has been 'a dangerous shift in our very idea of democracy – always a contested subject – from "thick" collective forms to "thin" consumer-driven and overly individualistic forms' (Apple, 2005, p. 11).

The metaphors vary – draining, collapse, thinning – but all evince the same idea: a serious weakening of democracy and the rise and rise of economism. Education epitomises this process, as Stephen Ball has vividly shown in his study of the privatisation of English education. He concludes that:

> education is increasingly, indeed perhaps almost exclusively, spoken of within policy in terms of economic value and its contribution to international market competitiveness . . . Within policy this economism is articulated and enacted very generally in the joining up of schooling to the project of competitiveness and to the 'demands' of globalisation and very specifically through the 'curriculum' of enterprise and entrepreneurship.
>
> (Ball, 2007, pp. 185–86)

But 'economism' – the reduction of everything to economic values and ends (or, at least, a certain understanding of economic values and ends), 'the propensity to avoid moral considerations, to restrict ourselves to issues of profit and loss' (Judt, 2009, p. 86) – is part of a wider phenomenon: the dominance of technical practice and its expert practitioners in pursuit of taken-for-granted and uncontested ends. Morin talks of 'democratic regressive processes', which include 'technobureaucratic development [that] brings about the domination of experts in all fields that, until then, had been answerable to political discussions and decisions' (Morin, 1999, p. 91); the pretext that only such technocratic experts are competent to make major political decisions, atrophies the competence of citizens, endangers diversity and degrades civic spirit (Morin, 2001, p. 91). Gert Biesta, in his powerful critique of the 'what works?' mentality, applies this generic process specifically to the field of education. He observes that 'a democratic society is precisely one in which the purpose of education is not given but is a constant topic for discussion and deliberation', then argues that 'the current political climate in many Western countries has made it increasingly difficult to have a democratic discussion about the purposes of education' (Biesta, 2007, p. 18).

A related example is the area of child well-being, a subject rising up the national and international policy agenda. The previous English government centred its 'children's agenda' – referred to as *Every Child Matters* – on five themes or outcomes, to be applied to all services for children, including schools: being healthy; staying safe; enjoying and achieving; making a positive contribution; and achieving economic well-being (for further information, see the English government's *Every Child Matters* website at http://www.dcsf.gov.uk/everychildmatters/). The choice of these is not, of course, self-evident – a further five or more outcomes could be readily produced. Nor is their meaning self-evident, each carries numerous possible and contestable meanings. But rather than holding open a space for continuing democratic discussion about meaning and purpose, government dashed on to doing, its whole machinery focused on 'delivery', inspection and assessment. Instead of a proposition for democratic deliberation in an open-ended politics of childhood, the 'five outcomes' were treated as a statement of fact, part of a managerial exercise, a corporate mission statement providing a rationale for a complex web of human technologies – 'national public service agreements', 'departmental strategic objectives', 'quality of life indicators' and 'quality of service measures' (http://publications.everychildmatters.gov. uk/eOrderingDownload/DCSF-00331-2008.pdf) – the effect of which is the closer governing of children and adults alike.[2]

As international organisations such as OECD and UNICEF enter the same field of children's well-being, the risk intensifies of education, a primarily political and ethical issue, being reduced to a technical issue of identifying universal, definitive outcomes, effective technologies for delivering these outcomes and means of objective assessment including 'indicators'. Debate about purpose and meaning will close, alternative perspectives and complexities will be simplified or sidelined, the technical will emerge triumphant. All that may come to matter is to find some way to drive one's country up this or that international league table, a technical task that surrenders deliberation and choices about critical questions to international technocrats.

We do not want to imply that there are no exceptions to this general picture. In our own country, England, but doubtless elsewhere too, there have been a number of important, high-profile independent interventions in recent years – for example, the *Cambridge Primary Review*, already mentioned, and the *Nuffield Review* (Nuffield Review, 2009), the largest independent review of education and training for 14–19 year olds in England and Wales for 50 years – which have insisted on a serious return to educational purposes within the context of a well-informed, wide-ranging public debate. But their treatment at the hands of government has been less than exemplary and, in its most extreme forms, pre-emptively and precipitatively dismissive. Rather than recognising the inevitability of plurality in education and seeking a *modus vivendi* between different perspectives, governing has become increasingly afflicted with a desire for rational consensus, an evidence-based right answer.

Questions of education and well-being cannot, of course, be confined to endless debate about meaning and purpose; decisions have to be made and actions taken. But there is a world of difference between the techno-bureaucratic desire for closure, leaving the way open to fixate on 'what works', and the political and ethical desire to leave meaning open as a 'constant topic for discussion and deliberation'. In a plural democracy, political and ethical practice should be held in tension with technical practice; a conflict of ideas and opinions should be expected and welcome; thought and action should inform each other; and education should be treated as a living, becoming and indeterminate project and not a closed, fixed and prescribed programme.

A combination of economism and techno-bureaucratism has enveloped education (and other sectors of public life). We are left with an enfeebled democracy practising a pseudo-politics and occupying a contracting public sphere; infused with a certain form of economic thinking and reduced to arguing differences of detail about technical and managerial matters; and subjected to an array of experts, consultants and entrepreneurs, who both build and assess the effectiveness of an increasing array of human technologies that are used to govern us ever more effectively. 'Policy making' has replaced 'politics'; the common good is left to the vagaries of the marketplace and management, not to collective deliberation and reflective practice; and constant action has substituted for argument and thought.

The politics of depoliticisation

> [Neoliberalism's restructuring of governance is] a political theory of performativity asserting that an effective public sphere will be one that makes public services answerable to the pressure of competition and the incentive of relative advantage of the marketplace . . . What this is eroding is any conception of the public good as collective good determined through democratic participation, contestation, and judgement in the public sphere. It seeks to replace politics (substantive rationality) with contract (technically rational solutions).
>
> (Ransom, 2003, p. 470)

We should be clear here. Our contention is that the political and ethical have been drained out of public discourse on education and schools: the discourse is reduced to discussion of the best technical solutions for achieving predetermined and self-evident ends, at the expense of debate about critical questions, purposes, values, understandings or concepts. But the draining of politics *is* political. Depoliticisation of education is part of what Biesta, quoted earlier, refers to as 'the current political climate in many Western countries'. An understanding of that climate helps not only to explain why education has become primarily a matter of technical debate – about techniques of management – but to make sense of an apparent contradiction in today's education: the strange mix of a rhetoric of choice and diversity with a practice of ever-tightening control and standardisation. We talk the talk of 'personalised learning' and 'individual choice'. But learning itself is increasingly prescribed; so while there may be some limited choice about process, as Lynn Fendler notes 'there can be no flexibility or variation in the outcome' (Fendler, 2001, p. 134), defined in terms of specified developmental goals. Marianne Bloch, too, identifies the strange mix of flexibility and standardisation:

> as globalizations of economies, outsourcing, and cultural and physical border crossings are enhanced, the young child and his parents must be standard, yet flexible and adaptive, competitive and collaborative . . . Teachers are asked to teach children to be members of a globalised world and at the same time to compete well for their own self, family, and nation.
>
> (Bloch, 2006, pp. 34–35)

The political forces creating the political climate for education and its depoliticisation, embodying flexibility and standardisation, are a partnership of neoliberalism and neoconservatism. Both 'isms' share certain values. Both value untrammelled markets and competition in the economic field, along with individual consumer choice and inequality as an inevitable and necessary driver of efficiency, effort and individualism. Both show profound suspicion of democratic politics: markets are inhibited by politics and 'governance by majority rule is seen as a potential threat to individual rights and constitutional liberties . . . Neoliberals therefore tend to favour governance by experts and elites' (Harvey, 2005, p. 66). Both are deeply suspicious of anything public, deemed inherently inefficient and hindering competition. Public assets should be privatised, public spaces are either eliminated or increasingly colonised by private interests (most visibly, the remorseless spread of advertising and sponsorship) and private business solutions are preferred to public provision of goods and services.

But neoconservatives part company somewhat with neoliberals when it comes to the social and cultural; the former worry that total laissez faire will cause irreparable damage in these areas, with bad consequences for the fabric of society and the order of things. They are 'deeply committed to establishing tighter mechanisms of control over knowledge, morals and materials through national or state curricula and national or state-mandated [and very reductive] testing' (Apple, 2004a, p. 175).

Harvey has pointed to 'the increasing authoritarianism evident in neoliberal states such as the US and Britain', equating this authoritarianism with a strain of neoconservatism which is:

> entirely consistent with the neoliberal agenda of elite governance, mistrust of democracy, and the maintenance of market freedoms. But it veers away from the principles of pure neoliberalism and has reshaped neoliberal practices in two fundamental respects: first, in its concern for order as an answer to the chaos of individual interests, and second, in its concern for an overweening morality as the necessary social glue to keep the body politic secure in the face of external and internal dangers.
>
> (Harvey, 2005, p. 82)

Michael Apple, an observer of educational developments in the US and UK, also describes neoliberalism and neoconservatism as forming 'a new alliance that is exerting leadership in educational policies and educational reform'. He adds a third partner to this alliance, a particular fraction of the middle class who have thriven in education and schooling being treated as technical and managerial subjects, to be governed by experts and managers. This partner is a group:

> from a particular fraction of the professional and managerial new middle classes ... [which] gains its own mobility within the state and within the economy based on the use of technical expertise. These are people with backgrounds in management and efficiency techniques who provide the technical and 'professional' support for accountability, measurement, 'product control', and assessment that is required by the proponents of neoliberal policies of marketisation and neoconservative policies of tighter central control in education.
>
> (Apple, 2005, p. 20)

We might add to this interest group a growing band of entrepreneurs who have profited from the increasing privatisation of education and schooling, supplying a complete range of services as education and schooling is commodified, and social and political relations are replaced by the contractual relations of the marketplace. Stephen Ball has described how public education in England has become 'big business', identifying some of the key actors in this process, the networks developing between these actors, and the blurring of public/private boundaries and identities:

> increasingly the private sector is inside policy and inside the state bringing its interests and its discourse to bear and earning money from consultancies which recommend a greater role for the private sector in the delivery of public services – a closed circle of the obviousness within policy.
>
> (Ball, 2007, p. 83)

This schema of neoliberalism and neoconservatism, with the avid backing of a fraction of the managerial and entrepreneurial middle class, reduces somewhat a more complex situation of multiple, sometimes conflicting beliefs and identities. Neoliberals are not always entirely wedded to laissez faire, some seeing the need for some regulation to achieve the good neoliberal citizen – in Margaret Thatcher's words '[e]conomics are the method; the object is to change the heart and soul' (Butt, 1981). For neoliberalism requires a very particular subject: flexible, competitive, entrepreneurial, choice-loving and autonomous, able to thrive in markets; and it requires considerable management to produce this subject – starting from the earliest age. Some neoconservatives are motivated by concerns other than order and security and see strong governing using new techniques, including harnessing the market to social ends, as a means for social progress.

Still, the consequences of this alliance of ideologies and interest groups, with the ensuing techno-managerialist dominance of education, are serious. Politics and ethics are drained, leaving economics: education as an economic commodity, education as a source of private profit, economic performance as education's primary goal. Any idea of education as a public responsibility and site of democratic and ethical practice is replaced by education as a production process, a site of technical practice and a private commodity governed by a means/end logic – summed up, again, in that supremely techno-managerial question 'what works?'

With the leaching of politics and ethics and their replacement by management, technology and production comes cliché-ridden jargon ('quality', 'excellence' and 'world-class'), vacuous at best, technologies of normalisation at worst, and gross simplification with the means/end logic 'transforming what were complex, interpersonal processes of teaching, learning and research into a set of standardised and measurable products' (Ball, 2007, p. 186). The technocratic and economic brings with it what Morin terms the 'logic of the artificial machine', mechanistic, fragmented, compartmentalised, reductionist, seeking quantification and ignoring context; and that logic produces the dreary public discourse we have complained of already, the language of the management seminar and technical manual rather than of civic debate and public deliberation.

But perhaps the worst consequence of all is wasted time and missed opportunities, when we have no time to waste and cannot afford to miss any opportunities. For we need to create an education and a school capable of responding to the dangers and possibilities of today and tomorrow – and an apolitical discourse dominated by thinking that takes a 'technocratic and econocratic form' (Morin, 1999, p. 70) simply will not do. We shall explore this contention in more detail throughout the rest of the book, but let us give some preliminary indications of our case here, looking at two examples of wasted time and missed opportunity.

Some missed opportunities

> I also want to trouble and challenge what is going on in the educational arena today, where pedagogical practices are being increasingly mainstreamed and normalised in relation to universal standards . . . [T]he more we seem to know about the complexity of learning, children's diverse strategies and multiple theories of knowledge, the more we seek to impose learning strategies and curriculum goals that reduce the complexities and diversities of learning and knowing. The more complex things become the more we seem to desire processes of reduction and thus control, but such reduction strategies might simultaneously shut out the inclusion and justice we want to achieve.
>
> (Lenz Taguchi, 2009, pp. 4, 8)

> Humanity's basic problem has four interlinked parts. First, we are already living well beyond our planet's capacity to regenerate itself . . . Secondly, not only is global inequality in income and wealth untenable . . . but trying to grow the world out of poverty by raising everybody's income further is untenable . . . Thirdly, our economic system is highly unstable . . . Fourth, for many people on earth, 'more' and 'better' have parted company. More wealth is not translated into greater wellbeing. Each of these problems is recognised by policy-makers, but only to some degree. What they don't recognise is the way they link together, their systemic nature and their inter-relationships . . . What is on offer is a return to 'business as usual' with a green tint.
>
> (Wallis, 2010, p. 28)

In his writing about social transformation and social change, Erik Olin Wright identifies four linked components: social reproduction, gaps and contradictions of reproduction, trajectories of unintended social change and transformative strategies. It is the second and third of these components that we want to highlight here (we look at transformative strategies later): gaps and contradictions in processes of social reproduction and trajectories of unexpected social change, both as rationales for change and as potential drivers of transformation – reasons why we need change and reasons why change is likely. For our following examples, of what we term missed opportunities, all point to gaps and contradictions in the current educational project, making it no longer (if it ever was) fit for purpose. They also indicate some important trajectories, which require both conscious change but also have unintended consequences which undermine presumptions and goals that sustain the current mainstream approach to education.

Education today is out of step with new understandings of knowledge and learning

What do we mean by knowledge? How do we understand learning? In recent articles, Gert Biesta and Deborah Osberg develop a critique of two key assumptions about knowledge and learning in modern schooling. The first is a representational view of knowledge, understanding knowledge to be an objective, stable and accurate representation of a pre-existing reality, a literal reproduction. The second is that because knowledge is representative of a real and relatively stable world, it can be transferred exactly, for example from one mind (the teacher) to another (the pupil). This assumption – 'that communication is unambiguous and unmediated and results in unproblematic transference with full conservation of intent' (Roy, 2004, p. 297) – inscribes the prevailing instrumentalist and techno-rational approach to education.

Then, drawing on complexity theory, Biesta and Osberg explore another understanding of knowledge, related to the 'notion of emergence', *'the creation of new properties . . . a process whereby properties that have never existed before and, more importantly, are inconceivable from what has come before, are created or somehow come into being* for the first time' (Biesta and Osberg, 2007, p. 33; original emphasis):

> We believe that a complexity inspired epistemology suggests a 'pedagogy of invention' (we borrow this phrase from Ulmer, 1985) for it brings into view the idea that knowledge does not bring us closer to what is *already* present but, rather, moves us into a *new* reality, which is incalculable from what came before. Because knowledge enables us to transcend what came before, this means it allows us to penetrate deeper *into that which does not seem possible from the perspective of the present*. Knowledge, in other words, is not conservative, but radically inventionalistic. This means that when we think about schooling, we should not think of it as primarily being about providing children with knowledge of a predetermined world.
>
> (Biesta and Osberg, 2007, pp. 46–47; original emphasis)

Complexity is also central to Edgar Morin's view of knowledge, as is context: he calls for thinking in context and thinking the complex, 'a kind of thinking that relinks that which is disjointed and compartmentalised, that respects diversity as it recognises unity, and that tries to discern interdependencies' (Morin, 1999, p. 130). He is particularly scathing of overspecialisation and the adverse consequences of disciplinary (subject) thinking that artificially separates an interdependent and complex world. For him, learning is about making connections and working with complexity and context, but it is also about interpretation and construction:

> All knowledge, as well as all perception, is an act of translation and reconstruction (see Morin, 1985), that is, interpretation. The reality of anything taken as whole can only manifest itself through theories, interpretations, and systems of thinking . . . The paradigm of disjunction/reduction, which controls most of our modes of thinking, separates the different aspects of reality from one another and isolates objects or phenomena from their environments. . . . That is why all knowledge of reality that is not animated and controlled by the paradigm of complexity is bound to be mutilated and, in this sense, to be lacking in realism.
>
> (Morin, 1999, p. 101)

The approach to education at St George-in-the-East was an early attempt to work with complexity and context, making connections and constructing knowledge. Pedagogical thought and practice in Reggio Emilia develops this approach. It has much in common with the idea of a pedagogy of invention and attaches great importance to complexity and context, interpretation and construction, research and experimentation. The educators in that city were, says Vea Vecchi, one of the earliest atelieristas in the municipal schools, among the first in Italy to discuss Morin's theories of complexity (but also, to illustrate the importance attached to border crossing, 'the theories of Ilia Prigogine on entropy and time flow, Francisco Varela's theories on learning, Gregory Bateson's on mind and ecology, Mandelbroot's on fractals and other experiences' (Vecchi, 2010, p. 134)). Their educational project, which we outlined at the start of this chapter, views knowledge as created through relationships, theory building, listening and making connections. Learning, Vea Vecchi contends, 'takes place through new connections between disparate elements', and so 'aesthetics can be considered an important activator for learning' (ibid., p. 9). Drawing on Morin's work, Vecchi is concerned with the way modern education and schools tend to fragment, compartmentalise and reduce what is complex, interdependent and transdisciplinary, be they disciplines, subjects or different aspects of our humanity:

> the development of thinking is limited by systems of teaching that tend to separate the different disciplines; . . . by working in this compartmentalised way we come to break reality up into little pieces and make a more general, more complete understanding of things more difficult; . . . this division poses obstacles to opportunities for grasping elements capable of establishing connections which constitute the support, the strong links, in comprehensive networks of knowledge.
>
> (Vecchi, 2010, p. 17)

When we are born, she says, 'we are a whole, and the whole of our senses strains to relate with the world around us in order to understand it'. Very quickly, however, we find ourselves

> 'cut into slices' . . . the state of separation in our culture which forces us to pursue knowledge on separate paths . . . We need to reflect seriously on how much individual and social damage is being caused by education and culture which prefer to separate than to work on connections.
>
> (Vecchi, 2004, p. 18)

Reggio Emilia is not alone in acknowledging and working with 'the complexity of learning, children's diverse strategies and multiple theories of knowledge'. There are other honourable exceptions all of which take seriously notions of curriculum integration and the co-construction of knowledge, e. g. Futurelab's *Enquiring Minds*, the RSA's *Opening Minds* and the Paul Hamlyn Foundation's *Learning Futures* and their radical, disgracefully forgotten predecessors such as Charity James's IDE (Interdisciplinary Enquiry) work at the Goldsmith's College Curriculum Laboratory in the 1970s, Jerome Bruner's *Man: A Course of Study* (MACOS) and Lawrence Stenhouse's *Humanities Curriculum Project* in the 1960s and 1970s, and Helen Parkhurst's earlier Dalton Plan in the first half of the twentieth century. But far more often, modern education and schooling, as Lenz Taguchi observes in the quotation that begins this section, seek 'to impose learning strategies and curriculum goals that reduce the complexities and diversities of learning and knowing' and the 'more complex things become the more we seem to desire processes of reduction and thus control'. Thought and knowledge are stifled by separating things out and from their contexts, ignoring many of the hundred languages of childhood, and insisting on there being one right answer, one acceptable outcome, in the belief in a certain, stable and objectively knowable world. How much, asks Vea Vecchi:

> does a school which works with decontextualised objects and situations lead to thinking in separate fragments and mistaking information for knowledge, which is only obtained by organising and placing parts in relation to each other? How much does ignoring the fact that emotions are an integral part of learning and educational processes distort the global process of knowledge building?
>
> (Vecchi, 2004, p. 19)

For Vecchi, like Biesta and Osberg and Morin, what is important in learning is the emergence through relations and connections of new interpretations, new perspectives, new thoughts and how to create space for this creativity and independent thinking.

These ideas are not new; as we keep coming back to, education has traditions which provide a rich legacy, and which we are foolish to ignore. To take just one notable example, John Dewey, the great American educationalist from an earlier generation, shared this position of the indeterminacy of education. Viewing education as value-based, the world as not knowable with certainty or objectively, and learning as a process of cooperative learning within educational communities, for Dewey the outcomes of this process could not be precisely predicted or predetermined.

We are dealing here with fundamental educational issues of epistemology and pedagogy. Such matters are, of course, contentious. Many readers may not find the reflections of Biesta, Osberg, Morin, Vecchi, or the many others who share their perspectives, convincing. They have chosen to situate themselves in particular paradigmatic positions, which many readers may not choose to share.

But the point is that there *are* different positions, producing different perspectives and understandings; there *are* choices to be made; and these differences and choices should be at the heart of a political and ethical discourse about education. As Vea Vecchi puts it: 'schools need to consciously take a position on *which knowledge* they intend to promote' (Vecchi, 2010, p. 28; original emphasis). They can pursue an idea of teaching that chooses 'to transmit circumscribed "truths" in various "disciplines"'; or they can choose 'to stand by children's sides together constructing contexts in which they can explore their own ideas and hypotheses individually or in groups and discuss them with friends or teachers' (ibid.). Or, they could choose something else, as there are more than two ways of thinking about knowledge and learning; we need to think more in terms of 'and, and, and' than 'either/or'.

But in the modern impoverished techno-managerial public discourse, schools or others concerned with education have little or no space for such matters. There is no encouragement to think duality let alone plurality, no future in exploring alternatives. Technicians are not supposed to question what they are doing or why they are doing it. They need to keep themselves busy ensuring the technology works and performance does not flag. Opportunities for rich learning are ignored, education atrophies and democracy withers.

Education today is irrelevant to the enormous dangers facing humankind

What is education for? What is its purpose? Put another way, if (as Giroux (2008) argues), education always presupposes a vision of the future, what is the vision? These seem the most fundamental of questions to be asked about education. Fundamental because they are the most critical political and ethical questions to be asked of education; and also because answers, however provisional and uncertain, form the basis for deciding more specific aims and, hence, deciding issues of practice such as pedagogical and curricular approaches.

Today, the public discourse assumes, to the extent it articulates its views about educational purpose, that education is about the accumulation of competencies and qualifications that will fit children for becoming flexible, self-regulating and risk-managing workers and citizens in a world made up of nation states competing in a global market economy driven by ever-increasing consumption and growth. We, individually and collectively, need ever higher standards of skill and education for future prosperity and well-being. The future, it is assumed, is a continuing trajectory of the present, more of the same. At the moment of writing, societies are watching with bated breath for signs of returning economic growth, the resumption of business as usual after the 2007/2008 financial crisis and ensuing recession – so the world can get back on track, returning to 'business as normal'.

But this assumption that the future is just more of the same is now incredible because that trajectory and the world it presumes clearly have no future. We are instead on a new trajectory, bringing unexpected and unintended social, economic and political changes. The point is starkly put in an important report from the Sustainable Development Commission, the UK government's independent advisory body on sustainable development.

> A world in which things simply go on as usual is already inconceivable. But what about a world in which nine billion people all aspire to the level of affluence achieved in the OECD nations? Such an economy would need to be 15 times the size of this one by 2050 and 40 times bigger by the end of the century. What does such an economy look like? What does it run on? Does it really offer a credible vision for a shared and lasting prosperity?
>
> (Jackson, 2009, p. 6)

Shortages of vital resources – water, food, fuel – are already apparent and, without profound changes, will (in the words of the then UK Government Chief Scientist, Professor John Beddington) create a 'perfect storm' by around 2030 that 'threaten[s] to unleash public unrest, cross-border conflicts and mass migration as people flee from the worst-affected regions' (Sample, 2009). Commenting on a UN report published later the same year, predicting that Asia faces an unprecedented food crisis and huge social unrest unless hundreds of billions of dollars are invested to ensure sufficient water for growing the huge increase of food needed, the Director-General of the World Bank-funded International Water Management Institute said:

> The agriculture of tomorrow will need a lot more water. Given that one litre of water is used to produce one calorie of food, the world will need up to 6,000 cubic kilometres of additional water every year to feed another 2.5 billion people 2,500 calories per day. This is almost twice what we use today and is not sustainable.
>
> (Vidal, 2009)

All this plus global warming, already showing clear signs of the catastrophic conse- quences to come once it exceeds (as seems very likely) two degrees centigrade and prolif- erating nuclear weapons. Little wonder that the Bulletin of Atomic Scientists decided in 2007 to move their 'doomsday clock' – conveying how close humanity is to catastrophic self-destruction – two minutes closer to midnight, re-setting it to 23.55 (http://www. thebulletin.org/content/doomsday-clock/overview). Or that Edgar Morin refers to the planet's 'Damoclean Phase', as it faces 'deadly global threats' (1999, p. 75). Or that historian of education Richard Aldrich comments on the qualitatively new situation we have brought upon ourselves as a species, the potential to self destruct:

> Current problems are frequently, and somewhat mistakenly, expressed in terms of saving the planet. The Earth has existed for some four and a half billion years

and may well survive for a couple of billion more. In contrast it is the human species, with a history that can be measured in terms of some 200,000 years, that is
in immediate danger. Our first concern should no longer be as it was for much of
the nineteenth and twentieth centuries the origin, but rather the death of species
– especially our own.

(Aldrich, 2010, p. 2)

The problems that put our species at risk are not only global in scope, so that no
individual country can escape their consequences. They are also man-made, the result
of recurrent human failings: the will to master nature and a relationship of exploitation with the planet; progress in science and technology unmatched by comparable
progress in ethics and politics (Gray, 2009); blindness to the complexity, interconnectedness and the unpredictability of life; and a pervasive irresponsibility expressed
in a carelessness about the consequences of our actions for other humans, other species and the planetary environment. We are indeed reaping the rewards of our arrogance, moral underdevelopment and thoughtlessness – and we might say the failings
of decades of education, up to the present day, to consider these as issues of the
highest priority.

While such behaviour and attitudes are hardly new, their consequences are increasingly global and catastrophic. A recent instance is the financial storm of the late 2000s,
brought about by a toxic mix of belief in the infallibility of self-regulating markets, of
hope that mathematical formulae could predict the workings of markets, of the global
integration of poorly-regulated and irresponsible financial markets, and of the phe-
nomenal greed and lack of wisdom of a financial community fixated with the technical
(including the exotic and impenetrable financial products that fed the near collapse of
the banking system) and the material, while lacking any ethical sense or historical perspective. Moreover, many of those most culpable were the elite produced by the current education system: as one of the more astute observers of the debacle observes, 'a
generation of brilliant young graduates with advanced numeracy has been persuaded,
by lavish incentives, to devote their intelligence to financial inventiveness, rather than
the more tedious and less lucrative alternatives of the laboratory or classroom' (Cable,
2009, p. 26). Even in 2008, when the banking crisis was breaking, one fifth of graduates from Oxford University, a pinnacle of the traditional UK education system, went
into the City (i.e. financial services) (Chakrabortty, 2009).

But perhaps, some might argue, the damage wreaked on the planet, the threat of
instant annihilation hanging over us, and the traumas of a near global financial melt-
down is a price worth paying (especially, if others mostly pay the price). Perhaps, the
education that has contributed is justified. Because, despite the downsides, surely
they have brought health, happiness and a sense of well-being to many? But this is
not the case.

Increases in material living standards *in poor countries* do 'result in substantial
improvements both in objective measures of wellbeing like life expectancy, and in
subjective ones like happiness'. But as countries 'join the ranks of the affluent developed countries, further rises in income count for less and less' (Wilkinson and Pickett,
2009, p. 8). In short, there is a law of diminishing returns: after a certain point, the

benefits of increased wealth simply peter out to be replaced by growing discontent. Indeed,

> it is a remarkable paradox that, at the pinnacle of human material and technical achievement, we find ourselves anxiety-ridden, prone to depression, worried about how others see us, unsure of our friendships, driven to consume and with little or no community life . . . we seek comfort in over-eating, obsessive shopping and spending, or become prey to excessive alcohol, psychoactive medicines and illegal drugs.
>
> (Wilkinson and Pickett, 2009, p. 3)

Elsewhere, the economist Richard Layard has similarly noted no striking improvement in well-being in richer countries, with no evidence that 'developed' societies are any happier today than they were 50 years ago. In short, 'ever-increasing consumption is not making us any happier' (New Economics Foundation, 2009, p. 23), and as Stewart Wallis observes in the quotation with which we start this section, 'for many people on earth, "more" and "better" have parted company'.

So, while education is always likely to have an economic purpose, what exactly that purpose is seems increasingly hard to determine. Even if we could ignore the unsustainability and deep discontents of growth-based, market capitalism, the mantra of education as societal and individual preparation for competition within a global knowledge economy does not seem to stack up. Based on the Beyond Current Horizons Programme, commissioned in 2007 by the English Department for Children, Schools and Families to inquire into possible future trajectories for socio-technical change, Keri Facer and Richard Sandford question this economic role for education:

> The vision of a universally beneficial knowledge economy with high levels of creative and rewarding employment seems to be unsustainable based on current trends . . . [which] make it increasingly unlikely that any country will be able to employ all of its citizens in high value, highly rewarded work . . . Such a landscape hollows out the middle tier of employment and creates an increasingly polarised labour market with significant challenges for compulsory education in terms of motivation and aspiration.
>
> (Facer and Sandford, 2010, p. 86)

The authors go on to discuss a number of choices that they see for education in such uncertain conditions, alternatives that question 'preparation for competition within a knowledge economy [remaining] a primary goal of education' (Facer and Sandford, 2010). But simply contributing to more of the same, better performance in an endless round of growth and consumption, seems even less sensible and plausible an aim if we factor in, as we must, the apparent failure and unsustainability of our current economic model. Education for such a purpose hardly seems to measure up to the state we, humankind, are in. Indeed, this precarious state leads Aldrich to argue that an 'education for progress', with material progress high on the agenda, is now well past its sell-by date, a delusional idea with dangerous consequences. Similarly, Morin's view of the interdependency and complexity of the world and its problems – in which the 'number one vital problem' facing us is the many problems and crises facing us – leads him to conclude that an education based around separate disciplines/subjects is 'not fit for purpose': it is, he contends, 'impossible to conceive of our earthly identity and of anthropolitics without a thinking capable of relinking disjointed notions and compartmentalised areas of knowledge' (Morin, 1999, pp. 129–30). We need to learn about the world in all its complexity and interconnectedness, to recognise and understand the huge problems facing us – but 'our compartmentalised, piecemeal, disjointed learning is deeply, drastically inadequate' (Morin, 2001, p. 29). Indeed, as Wallis points out, what policy makers, often among the best educated members of society, 'don't recognise is the way [problems] link together, their systemic nature and their inter-relationships' (Wallis, 2010, p. 28).

We need, this much seems clear, an education that is transdisciplinary and connective, that rejects the principle of reduction for the principle of complexity, and which has as its first and foremost purpose the goal of surviving – what Aldrich terms an 'education for survival'. Aldrich defines an education for survival as having two main aims: to make preparations for survival following any catastrophes; and '"living well" to prevent or reduce the incidence of major catastrophes that threaten human and other species and the Earth itself'. We can understand the goal of living well as care for the planet as one side of a coin, the other side being promoting personal wellbeing or flourishing. Human flourishing, Wright proposes,

> is a broad, multidimensional umbrella concept, covering a variety of aspects of human well-being . . . [including] the absence of deficits that undermine human functioning . . . [and] the various ways in which people are able to develop and exercise their talents and capacities, or, to use another expression, to realise their individual potentials.
>
> (Wright, 2009b, p. 9)

Such potentials can and do take many forms – intellectual, emotional, spiritual, artistic, physical and more – none of which is inherently more worthy than others; we have, to return to Malaguzzi's metaphor, the potential of a hundred languages.

The concept of flourishing, or as some might term it personal well-being, 'is pivotal to sound thinking about education' (White, 2005, p. 3). And taking the two sides of living well, the environmental and personal, into account we might perhaps develop Aldrich's concept and propose an 'education for survival and flourishing', understood as living well *and* within limits, a reminder that personal flourishing cannot be divorced from collective, even species flourishing. Those limits include at least two important and interrelated dimensions. The limits imposed by what the planet itself can bear – the limits of sustainability; and the limits imposed by social justice – the limits of distributional equity. For in a world of enormous inequality, within and especially between countries, where so many are so far removed from the material conditions of the minority, planetary sustainability calls for a 'new macro-economics for sustainability' that 'must abandon the presumption of growth in material consumption as the basis for economic stability' and 'ensure distributional equity' (Jackson,

2009, p. 10). Here would appear to be an important component of an 'education for survival and flourishing'.

We are not saying that survival or flourishing, however qualified and elaborated, are the only purposes of education. There is an economic purpose too, though as just indicated, what that is and how it would be consistent with the purposes of survival and flourishing needs far more thought and deliberation. And doubtless others, too. Moreover, such broad purposes not only need further and continuing debate about meaning (which can and should never be finally nailed down), but should also lead to a denser tangle of more specific aims, needed to achieve the overarching purposes. These aims help to define education and to determine its structures and processes, including the school, the workforce, the curriculum and evaluation. The aims for what we term radical education are discussed more fully in the next chapter, but include fostering the values of democracy, justice, solidarity and experimentation, and the ethics of care and encounter.

Although our purposes and our aims for education are not original, indeed they can trace their roots back to important traditions and experiences, such as those examples with which we began this chapter, they are at odds with much of mainstream education today. What we find both shocking and depressing about this dominant discourse on education – with its endless talk of choice and competition, standards and assessments, businesses and privatisation – is its lack of interest in and reflection about its implication in the economic and environmental crises confronting us; about the part that education can and should play in averting future disaster and creating a good life founded on sustainability, equity and respect for diversity and complexity; and about education's responsibility for the condition of democracy, both here and now and in the future. As the doomsday clock ticks, educational systems seem stuck in a time warp, suffering both historical amnesia and future myopia, displaying an unwillingness or inability to engage with either new thinking or the state we are in – and worse, the state we are heading towards.

Putting education in perspective

> The rise of the social service state, the century-long construction of a public sector whose goods and services illustrate and promote our collective identity and common purposes, the institution of welfare as a matter of right and its provision as a social duty: these were no mean accomplishments . . . Others have spent the last three decades methodically unravelling and destabilizing those same improvements: this should make us much angrier than we are.
>
> (Judt, 2009, p. 96)

We are great believers in education and schools; we hope that is apparent from what we write. However, our belief is not absolute but qualified. It depends what is meant by education and what is the image of the school; what we mean by education and school, what we believe in, will be the subject of subsequent chapters on radical education and the common school. Furthermore, following Foucault's warning that 'everything is dangerous' (Foucault, 1984, p. 343), we recognise that education and the school can be powerful means for governing, children and adults alike. They can contribute to Gilles Deleuze's 'societies of control' characterised by constant monitoring, heterogeneous and fast-changing standards, and never being finished, with 'lifelong learning' cited as an example of this emergent society (Deleuze, 1992). Attention must be paid to ways of making them less dangerous, and here the values and ethics we propose and discuss in the next chapter play an important part.

Last but not least, we think that education has an important contribution to make to survival, flourishing and democracy, and that these are important purposes of education. But we do not believe that education can by and of itself achieve these purposes. The wider society must have the political will to pursue them in all it does; it cannot subcontract the task to education, washing its hands of responsibility.

This is also the case when it comes to a range of more specific social and health problems, where there is a tendency today to see education as a cure-all, a technical solution to political and ethical problems. This is most apparent in contemporary attitudes to early childhood education, where enormous claims are made for the benefits of 'early intervention', with mouth-watering returns on investment promised (sometimes as much as $16 or $17 back for every $1 spent – the dollar signs indicating the American source of such financial calculations). This excerpt from an official report from a Canadian provincial government is typical of its kind:

> Every dollar spent in ensuring a healthy start in the early years will reduce the long-term costs associated with health care, addictions, crime, unemployment and welfare. As well, it will ensure Canadian children become better educated, well adjusted and more productive adults.
>
> (David Butler-Jones, Canada's Chief Public Health Officer, quoted in Pascal, 2009, p. 12)

Let us leave aside for the moment the philosophical and political questions surrounding the meaning of terms such as 'better educated', 'well adjusted' and 'more productive' (these claims for early childhood education typically assume the meanings of such goals to be self-evident and uncontentious, no obstacle therefore to the economic calculations that follow). Let us accept that early induction into formal educational settings – two or three years of nursery schooling – will produce some improvement in performance in compulsory schooling, at least in the first years, in effect preparing children for the educational regime to come. But when we look further into claims that early education will, of and by itself, produce huge, long-term changes in societies, such claims fail to hold up. The evidence, essentially local knowledge drawn from US studies undertaken in very particular temporal and social contexts, needs careful interpretation and is insufficient to sustain universal conclusions (Penn *et al.*, 2006); they are falsely premised on social sciences being able to emulate natural sciences by producing cumulative and predictive theory; and the causal model is naive, as if one particular and targeted intervention can unravel and solve a complex and deeply-entrenched set of problems and causes. Why, one asks, if the studies 'proving' these amazing effects are correct is the site of most studies, the US, still one of the worst performing of all 'rich' countries on social and health indicators despite having substantially higher per capita income than the best performers, the Nordic states (cf. UNICEF, 2007; Wilkinson and Pickett, 2009)? Don't these studies ignore Morin's call for contextualised and complex thinking?

The work by Richard Wilkinson and Kate Pickett on (to use the subtitle of their book) 'why more equal societies almost always do better', brings us back to reality and points to a clear conclusion: 'inequality seems to make countries socially dysfunctional across a wide range of outcomes' (Wilkinson and Pickett, 2009, p. 174). At the 'healthy end of the distribution' consistently come the Nordic states and Japan, countries with relatively low income inequality. At the opposite end, 'suffering high rates of most of the health and social problems, are usually the USA, Portugal and the UK' (ibid.). Further, more equal societies 'are more socially cohesive and have higher levels of trust which foster public-spiritedness' (ibid., p. 227), which may make them better able to respond to challenges such as global warming.

Successful societies like the Nordic countries, without the chronic levels of dysfunctionality of countries like the US, are the product of an interconnected bundle of values, policies and services. They are lower on inequality (not only income but also gender) certainly, but also higher on democracy (Skidmore and Bound, 2008), solidarity and taxation. They fare well on early childhood education and also on many other services and benefits (see, for example, the high standards of Nordic countries in the area of parental leave (Moss, 2009)). The need for this kind of broad approach, which recognises that successful societies have many and interconnected reasons for their success, and due scepticism for placing too high expectations on one 'magic' solution, like early intervention, is expressed by the American researcher Ed Zigler, in an article titled 'Forty years of believing in magic is enough':

> Are we sure there is no magic potion that will push poor children into the ranks of the middle class? Only if the potion contains health care, childcare, good housing, sufficient income for every family, child rearing environments free of drugs and violence, support for parents in all their roles, and equal education for all students in school. Without these necessities, only magic will make that happen.
> (Zigler, 2003, p. 12)

In the same vein, the Beyond Current Horizons Programme warns that no 'silver bullets' are in prospect for complex educational problems: 'despite the continuing demand for quick fixes, neuroscience, computing and bioscience are not expected to provide easy solutions to educational issues over the next two decades' (Facer and Sandford, 2010, p. 85).

Yet despite these warnings about trust in magic potions and silver bullets and the clear evidence of 'what works', we have created instead, under the baleful influence of neoliberalism, less democratic and more unequal societies in which health and social problems have thrived. As Tony Judt argues, 'the common theme and universal accomplishment of the neo-Keynesian governments of the postwar era was their remarkable success in curbing inequality', but 'inequality has once again become an issue in Western society . . . [as] the inequality index has steadily grown over the course of the past three decades' (Judt, 2009, p. 88). By 'unraveling and destabilizing' the accomplishments of the 'social service state', we have abandoned 'the labours of a century . . . to betray those who came before us as well as generations yet to come'. We should, indeed, as Judt suggests, be angrier than we are – at the damage done, the opportunities wasted and the failure to take timely action to reduce the huge dangers confronting us.

The point we are making is that education and schools, especially the radical education and common schools we will be discussing, are very important public institutions with a vital role to play in the creation and maintenance of societies that are functional, cohesive, public-spirited. We will develop our understanding of this role and its importance in later chapters. But they cannot do it alone, they cannot 'solve the problems of a society unwilling to bear its burdens where they should properly be shouldered' (Noddings, 2005, p. 42). They can go with the grain, but not too far against it – they cannot, by themselves, bring democracy to societies which have let democracy atrophy, they cannot bring survival to societies that ignore sustainability, they cannot bring social well-being and individual flourishing to societies mired in inequality and unwilling or incapable of major political and economic reorganisation. In short, education and schools are a necessary but not sufficient condition for a good society.

Perhaps the title of our book, therefore, should have been 'Radical education, the common school and the equal society'. For our political and ethical belief in equality is reinforced by the clear evidence that more equal societies are one of the most important preconditions for human and societal flourishing. For those not convinced, listen to what Richard Wilkinson and Kate Pickett have to say after a working lifetime studying the issue:

> The evidence shows that reducing inequality is the best way of improving the quality of the social environment, and so the real quality of life, for all of us [including the better-off] . . . It is clear that greater equality, as well as improving the wellbeing of the whole population, is also the key to national standards of achievement and how countries perform in lots of different fields. . . . If you want to know why one country does better or worse than another, the first thing to look at is the extent of inequality . . . And if, for instance, a country wants higher average levels of educational achievement among its school children, it must address the underlying inequality which creates a steeper social gradient in educational achievement.
>
> (Wilkinson and Pickett, 2009, pp. 29–30)

To make the point – that greater equality makes for societies that do better – the New Economics Foundation (NEF) has undertaken an interesting exercise. It has calculated the cumulative gain for the UK, with its high level of income inequality (similar to that in Australia and New Zealand, lower than the highly unequal US), if it moved to the far lower level of inequality found today in Denmark. Bearing in mind that 'unequal societies have worse outcomes across nearly every social domain' (New Economics Foundation, 2009, p. 28), and on the assumption that attaining lower Danish levels of income inequality would reduce a wide range of social problems to Danish levels, NEF's model comes up with a cumulative gain – a sort of equality bonus – of £3,752 billion from 2010 to 2050! We might wish to treat this mindboggling number not so much as an exact prediction and more as an indication of possibility: indicative that addressing inequality directly, by redistributing income through taxation and other measures, is a necessary condition for a successful society in which individuals and their education can fully flourish.

And, we should add, what is true within rich countries is true within the global community. The huge inequalities between countries are bad for people and bad for the environment – in the words of a recent World Health Organisation report, 'social iniquities are killing people on a grand scale' (2008, p. 248). The whole world needs more and better education, but that needs grounding on far greater equality within and between countries.

Where to?

This is, says Roberto Unger, whose ideas about change we explore further in later chapters, the key question for bringing about what he terms 'revolutionary' or 'radical reform'. We have some ideas of the direction we would like to see education and the school move in, and the contribution we would like this book to make. We want to see a richer, deeper public discourse about education, which moves 'beyond the tyrannies of improvement, efficiency and standardisation to recover a language of and for education articulated in terms of ethics, moral obligations and values' (Ball, 2007, p. 191). We offer, we hope, some of that language throughout the book. We want to see a new public education, what we term a radical education based on the common school. We explore and imagine what 'radical education' and the 'common school' might be in Chapters 2 and 3. We recognise that we do not offer a perfect solution, nor do we think such a solution exists.

The trickiest bit, the thorniest of issues, is how to get there, in part because of the size of the task; in part because we are loathe to get drawn into prescribing detailed directions – giving instructions hardly seems in keeping with our democratic commitment, let alone being likely to achieve the required effect; and in part because the process of getting there may well lead to a somewhat different destination as we find other possibilities along the way and learn more about our original and other possible destinations. In short, we do not see how to separate process from outcome, journey from destination. We shall reflect more on this question, of how to undertake democratic reform to create a new public education, in the final chapter.

But for now we admit again to not knowing fully about our destination or direction of travel; many things are not clear and remain puzzling to us, not for want of evidence but because much of what puzzles us is of a political and ethical nature that no evidence can help with. In short, we do not have all the answers, and sometimes can only pose the questions. What we do want to make clear is that there are a number of possible destinations, so escaping from what Unger vividly calls the 'dictatorship of no alternative', that way of thinking and talking that says there is one right answer, one correct solution, one way that works, in short a best and evidence-based policy and practice that precludes messy political and ethical arguments, and ignores complexity and context. No destination and direction is perfect and foolproof, and each requires some compromise and falls short of perfection; there is, for example, always a degree of tension between diversity and coherence, individual and collective choice, consumer preference and common good, open and closed outcomes – and the best we can do is try to find a provisional and defensible relationship while recognising that not everyone will be satisfied.

We cannot claim to answer many questions about our destination and direction of travel, either to our own complete satisfaction or that of others. But what we want to open up is debate about where we and others might want to head towards: what type of educational project we should have the courage to embark on given current circumstances and likely future scenarios; what purposes and values, understandings and concepts, structures and practices we want to work with, and how we think they might work out. Above all, can we change education from being a techno-managerial exercise in control and normalisation into a democratic political and ethical project of participation and creativity? Can we (re)introduce surprise, wonder and amazement into education? Can we make the dismal subject exciting and relevant again, for children, for adults and for society as a whole?

One last thought for this preliminary chapter, a small pre-emption. For those who say, as they read on, that what we are exploring is unrealistic, impractical, irrelevant, visionary, idealistic or any other of the terms used to denigrate or devalue the possibility of alternatives, we would offer three initial responses. First, the present educational discourse, and the neoliberalism that underpins it, has no future, at least in a world that values sustainability, democracy, justice and flourishing; all it can offer is a vicious circle of ever greater marketisation and ever more controlling technologies and outcomes – more of the same that has palpably failed. There is, we would contend, no alternative but to explore alternatives.

Second, the present failing techno-managerial system has had immense amounts of money, manpower, research and policy lavished on it; too many eggs have been put in one – and we would argue, the wrong – basket. In the interests of diversity and survival, the time has come for documenting, promoting and supporting democratic alternatives and experimentation. We need to move on from the search for rational consensus to a truly democratic culture that recognises and welcomes irreducible plurality of perspectives, values and practices and believes that human beings can flourish in many ways of life (Gray, 2009).

Third, times change and nothing is forever. Looking back, Susan George reminds us that '[i]n 1945 or 1950, if you had seriously proposed any of the ideas and policies in today's standard neoliberal toolkit, you would have been laughed off the stage at or sent off to the insane asylum' (George, 1999, p. 1). While in the same vein and looking forward, the New Economics Foundation suggests that 'if governments could spend the last 30 years promoting competitive individualism and a wild enthusiasm for market solutions to local problems, why not spend the next few decades promoting the benefits of cooperation and interdependence' (New Economics Foundation, 2009, p. 53).

History after all has not ended and there are, it turns out, alternatives. Encouraged by this hopeful news, we are unashamedly utopian. But taking up the arguments of Erik Olin Wright, with which we began the chapter, we believe we are working with real utopias, mixing imagination with what is pragmatically possible.

2   Democratic radical education

> If the schools of a democratic society do not exist for and work for the support and extension of democracy, then they are either socially useless or socially dangerous.
>
> (Mursell, 1955, p. 3)

In recent years, attempts to envisage future scenarios – 'foresight initiatives' – have spread into the education field. Facer and Sandford count in the UK alone and just in the last five years 'four major educational futures projects, while the Organisation for Economic Cooperation and Development's strategic future scenarios have, since the early 2000s, played an influential role in shaping international thinking about educational policy' (Facer and Sandford, 2010, p. 75). Such exercises are important and useful, especially when they critique economic or technological determinism, 'challenging our assumptions about the inevitability of a single future trajectory', recognising 'the co-construction of society and technology' and the role for human agency in this process, and acknowledging that 'thinking about the future always involves values and politics' (ibid., p. 77). Undertaken in this way, work on future scenarios has the potential to contribute to democratic debate about alternatives and the collective choices facing us.

But setting out a range of future scenarios or alternatives is not our purpose in this book. Our purpose is more overtly utopian. It is to describe and argue the case for one scenario and alternative: a particular approach to education, one of many alternative approaches, one that we term radical education and the common school. In this chapter, we deal with radical education. We will define it in terms of the values, ethics, concepts and images with which it is inscribed, placing high priority on, inter alia, the value of democracy, an ethics of care, education-in-its-broadest-sense and the image of the school as a public meeting place, a collaborative *atelier* or workshop and a person-centred learning community.

We will then proceed to propose a dual rationale for this approach. First, we will argue for radical education in terms of its relevance to the present and future, the state we are and will be in, particularly given the enormous and interrelated dangers facing humankind. But we will also seek justification for radical education by looking to the past, and exploring how our concept of radical education continues and builds on a rich vein of educational tradition, including the legacy of progressivism and its companion socialist and libertarian critiques. Finally, we will propose some signs we think indicative of a school practising radical education.

Towards a radical education

The term 'radical' has always been contentious, either because of what it is perceived to advocate or because it remains such an elusive notion operating at the margins of mainstream thinking, whether of left or right. Its appeal is often that it serves as a corrective to wayward interpretations of a particular ideology or practice and brings advocates back to the roots or fundamentals of their aspirations. In this sense, part of the appeal of radicalism has to do not just with the fresh or adventurous nature of its outlook, with its break from a tired or overfamiliar present, but also with its allegiance to important ideals that have gradually been forgotten or, more seriously, betrayed by way of laziness or neglect.

Whilst there is clearly a place for this kind of argument at particular historical moments within particular traditions, it is not one that can bear too much intellectual weight without substantial qualification and elaboration. Thus, when Robin Barrow suggests that a radical is someone 'who wants change that involves going to the root of the matter, as opposed to one who wants no change at all or one who wants superficial change' (Barrow, 1978, p. 1), he is understandably taken to task by others, like Nigel Wright, who ask, 'how *much* change is required for it not to be superficial, and just what *are* the roots of the matter?' (Wright, 1989, p. 15; original emphasis).

We favour more the second sense of radicalism, which is less associated with a return to roots or forgotten customs and traditions – though we do argue strongly in this book that traditions of thought and action have a role to play in a radical education. This is a reading of radicalism that seeks to transcend existing frameworks and to advocate a new line of thought and action, often enacted through prefigurative practices that anticipate and, it is hoped, help bring about a quite different way of being in the world (we elaborate this concept in Chapter 4). It is this second sense of radicalism for which we are arguing in this book: radicalism as transcendence, radicalism as a set of aspirations that stretch beyond the reach of innovation to imagine and enact a future that rests on very different assumptions and values to those which define the basis and the boundaries of the current system. With Brian Simon, we would argue for a radicalism that 'sees educational change as a key aspect (or component) of radical social change' (Simon, 1972, p. 9).

Values

Our discussion of values, and of ethics later, illustrates the falsity of the distinction, much beloved in managerial thinking, between process and outcome. What we are talking about here are values and ethics that should be the aims of a radical education, but which also constitute the way that education is practised. Democracy, we contend and argue further later, must be learnt by doing, so an education for democracy must be inscribed with democracy as a value. Or, to take another example, the inculcation of an ethic of care is most likely to come about in an institution that practises that ethic in its everyday life and relationships. So radical education is both a doer and producer of values and ethics, and is supported in both roles by the concepts and understandings or images it adopts.

Democracy at the heart

> Democracy and day nursery are two terms that are not immediately associated with each other. But where and when does democracy start? In pre-school? In day care? In school? Or only when people are old enough to vote? Knowledge and insights gained from the evaluation of the project 'Living democracy in day care centres' show that the basis for an everyday democratic culture can indeed already be formed in the day nursery.
>
> (Priebe, cited in George, 2009, p. 14)

The meaning of 'radical education' is not self-evident, indeed it is highly contentious. Today, many lay claim to it. For example, the reforms started in the United Kingdom under Margaret Thatcher, with their emphasis on marketisation, competition and parental choice can be termed radical. We, however, anchor our definition of radical in a particular value: for us, participatory democracy is at the heart of radical education.

When the term 'democracy' is used, for many people the first thing that comes to mind is the formal sphere of politics and the traditional practices that make up representative democratic government: the election of representatives to governing bodies operating at different levels, the working of these bodies (e.g. national parliaments, local councils, etc.), and the various rules and norms associated with such democratic forms of government (e.g. electoral procedures, an independent media, the rule of law, etc). As we have already indicated in Chapter 1, this dimension of formal representative democracy, with its established institutions and practices, is in a sickly state, struggling to respond to the contemporary challenges of a complex and threatened world and to retain the engagement of citizens (Bentley, 2005; Power Inquiry, 2006). Fewer people vote, elected representatives are held in low esteem, whole sections of the community feel estranged from mainstream politics while many others feel cynical or disinterested, and undemocratic political forces are on the rise. As Morin observes, we are in the midst

> of a draining and sclerosis of traditional politics, incapable of fathoming the new problems that appeal to it; in the midst of a politics that encompasses multi-faceted issues, handling them in compartmentalised, disjointed, and additive ways; and in the midst of a debased politics that lets itself be swallowed by experts, managers, technocrats, econocrats, and so on.
>
> (Morin, 1999, p. 112)

But this is only part of the story. For democracy is a multidimensional concept, with different forms and practices linked to each dimension. Skidmore and Bound, for example, in their work on democracy have created an 'Everyday Democracy Index' that covers six dimensions, ranging from 'electoral and procedural democracy' through 'activism and civic participation' and 'aspiration and deliberation' to democracy in the family, the workplace and public services. They argue that modern democracies must 'be rooted in a culture in which democratic values and practices shape not just the formal sphere of politics, but the informal spheres of everyday life: families, communities, workplaces, and schools and other public services' (Skidmore and Bound, 2008,

p. 9). Representative democracy has an important part to play. But modern democracies must also be 'Everyday Democracies', with participatory democracy present and practised in many settings and in many ways.

But democracy can also be understood in another and more pervasive sense: as a way of thinking, being and acting, of relating and living together. This is democracy, in the words of John Dewey, as 'a mode of associated living embedded in the culture and social relationships of everyday life' and as 'a way of life controlled by a working faith in the possibilities of human nature . . . [and] faith in the capacity of human beings for intelligent judgement and action if proper conditions are furnished' (Dewey, 1939). It is democracy, as Hannah Arendt sees it, as a form of subjectivity expressed as a quality of human interaction (Biesta, 2007).

Democracy here is a relational ethic that can and should pervade all aspects of everyday life: 'a way of being, of thinking of oneself in relation to others and the world. . . . a fundamental educational value and form of educational activity' (Rinaldi, 2006, p. 156). Ole Langsted, writing of an early example of listening to young children about their experiences of early childhood education, also makes the point clearly, when he argues that 'more important [than structures and procedures] is the cultural climate which shapes the ideas that the adults in a particular society hold about children. The wish to listen to and involve children originates in this cultural climate' (Langsted, 1994, pp. 41–42).

Beyond education, we can draw on broader traditions of democratic political theory that also regard democracy as not only being about formal governance but also about human flourishing and the conditions under which it can best be fostered. Within these traditions there is a recognition that whilst democracy is, of course, a political form, it is, in Macmurray's words 'not primarily a matter of political organisation'. Rather,

> [i]t is a quality of the personal life. The passion for freedom which makes men [sic] prefer death to servitude, the sense of human dignity and personal responsibility, the love of the fellowship of equals – these are the roots from which it springs.
>
> (Macmurray, 1943, p. 38)

A radical education built on the value of democracy and a multidimensional understanding of democracy expresses itself in a variety of ways: in the way educational politics and policy-making are conducted; in the governance of schools and decision-making large and small; in processes of learning and concepts of knowledge adopted; in ways of evaluation; and in everyday practices and relationships. We saw in the cases of Reggio Emilia and St George's, at the beginning of Chapter 1, a variety of examples of such democracy put into practice: a local politics of education rooted in an explicit commitment to democracy; learning as co-construction with an openness to unpredicted outcomes; the importance attached to listening and dialogue; participatory evaluation using pedagogical documentation; the Staff Panel, the Pupil Panel, the Joint Panel and the School Council/School Meeting. These cases are examples of schools become sites of 'everyday democracy' or what Michael Fielding (2007) terms 'educational sites of democratic living – i.e. democratic learning communities'

(Fielding, 2007a, p. 542). In such communities, Dewey believed, individuals 'learn to understand themselves as democratic individuals by becoming members of a community in which the problems of communal life are resolved through collective deliberation and a shared concern for the common good' (Carr and Hartnett, 1996, p. 63).

This idea of the school as a democratic community raises for us another notion: education as a site of democratic fellowship. In addition to reminding us not only of the importance, but also, and more importantly still, of the derivative justification of politics, there are two complementary radical points that writers like philosopher John Macmurray and the guild socialist political theorist G. D. H. Cole urge us to attend to through notions like democratic fellowship. These are, first, that fellowship is the point of politics. For Macmurray, politics 'has significance only through the human fellowship which it makes possible; and by this its validity and its success must be judged' (Macmurray, 1950, pp. 69–70). For Cole, '[b]eing democratic ... is not the same thing as believing in democracy. It starts from knowing your neighbour as a real person; unless it starts there, it does not start at all' (Cole, 1950, p. 100). Second, and too seldom acknowledged in the intensity of theoretical engagement, the companion argument is that democratic fellowship is not just the point of politics but the precondition of democracy's daily development and future flourishing: 'the extent and quality of such political freedom as we can achieve depends in the last resort upon the extent and quality of the fellowship which is available to sustain it' (Macmurray, 1950, p. 69).

In distinguishing the two aspects of democracy – as an organisational form, but also as a way of being in the world – we are deliberately opening up space to explore the relationships between different dimensions of democracy and the fundamental purposes that provide democracy's basic justification, including its capacity to enable us to become more fully human and lead good, creative lives together. By articulating the necessity of democratic fellowship, which is both a condition and an aspiration, not just of democratic politics but also of democracy as a way of life, we are affirming the need for an intellectual framework that places persons at the centre of any account of education and the nature of the good life. We explore this further later when discussing the concept of a person-centred or personalist education and our image of the school as a person-centred learning community.

Other values of a radical education

Alongside democracy, we would argue for four other cardinal values, which are interconnected and interdependent: justice, solidarity, plurality and experimentation. Justice spans both social justice and political justice, which are defined by Erik Olin Wright:

1 Social justice: *In a just society, all people would have broadly equal access to the necessary material and social means to live flourishing lives.* This is a fairly complex formulation, but the key idea is egalitarianism with respect to a fairly comprehensive understanding of the conditions which foster human flourishing.
2 Political justice: *In a politically just society, people should be equally empowered to contribute to the collective control of the conditions and decisions which affect their common*

fate. This is a principle of both political equality and collective democratic empowerment.

> Taken together these two claims call for a society that deepens the quality of democracy and enlarges its scope of action under conditions of radical social and material equality.
>
> (Wright, 2009b, p. 8)

Solidarity expresses a commitment to mutual support and collective action on matters of shared interest; it recognises individuality, but acknowledges that this is always constructed in relation with others and is enabled by common purpose and collective effort. Plurality acknowledges the irreducible multiplicity of values, perspectives, identities and ways of life, and the importance for creativity, democracy and experimentation of such diversity. Experimentation as a value expresses a willingness, a desire in fact, to invent, to think differently, to imagine and try out different ways of doing things; it is driven by the desire to go beyond what already exists, to venture into the not yet known, and not to be bound by the given, the familiar, the predetermined, the norm.

As Wright argued earlier, linking democracy and justice, and as we discuss later, in linking democracy and experimentation, all of these values are connected and interdependent.

Ethics and relationships

Two ethical ideas lie at the heart of our understanding of radical education: an ethics of care and an ethics of an encounter. Joan Tronto describes an ethics of care as involving particular acts of caring and a general habit of mind, that should inform all aspects of life, and which includes attentiveness, responsibility, competence and responsiveness. With Fisher, she defines caring as:

> a species activity that includes everything we do to maintain, continue and repair our 'world' so we can live in it as well as possible – a clear connection to the idea of 'living well' that we discussed earlier. That world includes our bodies, our selves and our environment, all of which we seek to interweave in a complex, life-sustaining web.
>
> (Fisher and Tronto, 1990, p. 40)

The concept, it should be noted, is broad enough to include our relationship with the environment as well as with people.

The ethics of an encounter, originating in the work of the Lithuanian-born French philosopher Emmanuel Levinas, attempts to counter a western tradition of 'grasping' the Other to make the Other into the Same, instead respecting the absolute alterity of the Other, the Other's absolute otherness or singularity: this is an Other whom I cannot represent and classify into a category, whom I cannot seek to understand by imposing my framework of thought. This means I have to abandon the security and certainty that comes from making the Other into the Same and try to forego the will to know. Dahlberg has outlined the enormous implications of this ethics for education:

> Putting everything one encounters into pre-made categories implies we make the Other into the Same, as everything which does not fit into these categories, which is unfamiliar and not taken-for-granted has to be overcome . . . To think another whom I cannot grasp is an important shift and it challenges the whole scene of pedagogy. It poses other questions to us pedagogues. Questions such as how the encounter with Otherness, with difference, can take place as responsibly as possible.
>
> (Dahlberg, 2003, p. 270)

Both ethics are situational and contextual, requiring an ethical sensibility and ethical judgements not the application of universal norms. Responsibility, too, is an important part of both ethics, essentially concerned as they are with relationships, including responsibility for others and for the environment.

Such ethics – emphasising responsible and 'non grasping' relationships – are also about how we relate to other humans, other species and the physical environment. They are supportive of certain types of relationship towards our natural world, and by implication towards prosperity, between each other and between the personal and the functional. A report to the European Commission on 'The world in 2025' (Gaudin, 2008) highlights the first relationship, reiterating the parlous position of humankind due to its irresponsible treatment to date of the environment, our natural world. We cannot, it argues, carry on as we have been without putting the future of our species at risk; for if we do, if the globalisation of a market economy and excessive consumption continues and spreads even further, 'it appears to lead to a global collapse' (Gaudin, 2008, p. 6), even perhaps another episode of mass extinction, this time including humankind. The report holds out the prospect of a second, more hopeful scenario, but one contingent on a profound change of relationship with our environment: instead of trying to control the planet, humanity manages to exert self-control, after the 'industrial age gave the illusion that mankind could master the world without mastering itself' (ibid., p. 88). Woman and man will have to shift from the attitude of the exploiter to the attitude of the gardener:

> more than a Producer, she/he is the guardian of life perpetuation, and also a poet modelling life as an artist . . . a guard of nature. She/he is not running away, leaving the weed invading the garden. She/he accepts the responsibility of modelling nature. She/he is on duty to care for nature, but also, this is the important point, she/he takes pleasure and accomplishment as an artist, because, ultimately, gardening is an art.
>
> (Gaudin, 2008, p. 75)

Hand in hand goes a different relationship to prosperity, turning away from equating prosperity with continual growth, and its attendant environmental depredations, to viewing prosperity as flourishing while leaving a vastly less material impact on the environment; as Jackson comments in his report for the Sustainable Development Commission, 'the possibility that humans can flourish and at the same time consume less is an intriguing one. It would be foolish to think that it is easy to achieve. But it should not be given up lightly' (Jackson, 2009, p. 7). It will mean weaning ourselves off novelty-based and status-driven consumption, the driver of materialistic individualism and a major contributor to our unsustainable growth-based economy:

> Structural change must lie at the heart of any strategy to address the social logic of consumerism. . . . [First] to dismantle the perverse incentives for unproductive status competition. [Second] to establish new structures that provide capabilities for people to flourish – and in particular to participate meaningfully and creatively in the life of society – in less materialistic ways.
>
> (Jackson, 2009, p. 11)

We will consider relationships with each other and between the personal and the functional later in this chapter, when we consider the legacy of the philosopher John Macmurray.

The concept of education

Education-in-its-broadest-sense

When we talk about radical education, what is our concept of education? We follow a long-established concept of education that understands education as fostering and supporting the general well-being and development of children and young people, and their ability to interact effectively with their environment and to live a good life. This is education as a process of upbringing and increasing participation in the wider society, with the goal that both individual and society flourish (Moss and Haydon, 2008). The concept might be termed 'education-in-its-broadest-sense' (EBS).

The notion of EBS is similar in many respects to the Continental concept and tradition of social pedagogy. Social pedagogy is a theory, practice and profession of working with people, originating in nineteenth-century Germany and with long and deep roots in many European countries. Its distinctive identity has frequently been lost in translation, pedagogy usually being translated into English as 'education/science of education'. One group of English researchers, who have worked over several years to understand the Continental tradition of social pedagogy and its application today in services for children and adults, describe it as implying:

> an approach to work with people in which learning, care, health, general well-being and development are viewed as totally inseparable, a holistic idea summed up in the pedagogical term 'upbringing'. The pedagogue as practitioner sees herself as a person in relationship with the child as a whole person, supporting the child's overall development.
>
> (Boddy *et al.*, 2005, p. 3)

Two German exponents develop this broad educational concept by suggesting four key principles underlying social pedagogy:

- Well-being: 'social pedagogy is essentially concerned with enhancing individual and collective well-being and human dignity.'
- Holistic learning: 'addressing "head, hearts and hands" in harmonious unity.'
- Relationships: relationships are viewed as central to well-being and learning, with 'social pedagogic practice as essentially relationship-centred' and 'seeing children as part of a group.'
- Empowerment: social pedagogy is 'very strongly based on promoting and enhancing children's rights . . . especially the right to meaningful participation in decisions affecting people's lives.'

(Eichsteller and Holthoff, forthcoming)

Not only does social pedagogy emphasise democracy, it also values justice and solidarity, seeing this and interdependence as complementary to the other goal of fostering personal development towards independence. Relevant to later discussions, education within the social pedagogic tradition is both community- and person-centred; the focus is on the individual, but the individual in relation with others and in society.

Social pedagogy, which we say more about in Chapter 3 when we discuss the profession of social pedagogue, can be contrasted with another concept of education, 'education-in-its-narrower-sense' (ENS), that equates education with schooling and certain kinds of formal learning focused wholly or mainly on cognitive capacities and, often, compartmentalised subjects. ENS is closer to the way in which education is often understood and publicly debated today. Both concepts of education are concerned with learning and this learning must be something the educator intends to bring about. But EBS, as we have indicated, takes a broad view of the scope of intentional learning, going beyond the cognitive or academic to encompass the social, aesthetic, ethical, cultural, emotional and physical domains. Such learning is understood to be inextricably linked to care, health and other conditions needed to live a good life and for a democratic community to flourish: learning contributes to these conditions and these conditions enable learning.

Radical education is also linked to particular ways of conceptualising learning and knowledge, ways that are illuminated for us by the practice of our two initial cases. Learning is not the transmission of pre-formed information, but a process of co-construction of meaning in relationship with others. It deploys a pedagogy of relationships, listening and invention, which emphasises connectedness and is open to the new and unexpected.

A personalist approach to education

Before leaving the concept of education, we want to develop one aspect that we touched on earlier, when noting that democratic fellowship and social pedagogy – or EBS – acknowledges an education that puts persons at the centre of any account of education: person-centred education, though one that finds no incompatibility with also being community-centred and about the relationship between the two, person and community. So our concept of education in a radical education includes a strongly personalist approach. But what do we mean by this?

First, it is important to say that 'personalism' stands in marked contrast to the now familiar notion of 'personalisation'. Personalism places the individual in an inescapably relational nexus, within which individuality emerges and learning occurs and from which community and all other human forms of engagement derive their vibrancy and legitimacy. Personalisation, by contrast, sees the individual in isolation, the autonomous learner restlessly seeking to become an ever-better entrepreneur of the self. From our perspective, despite its current popularity and enormous financial support from the former English government's Department for Children, Families and Schools, personalisation is intellectually bereft and in many other respects, cheerily reprehensible (Fielding, 2008a). Persistently prone to hyperbole, cultural insularity and self-induced historical amnesia, personalisation's current popularity is in large part due to its false hope of respite in a results-oriented scramble for success in school league tables. Despite its promising reminder of individual persons at the heart of the educational system, it is, in most cases and in ultimate intention, another articulation of market-led individualism.

Under the hegemony of neoliberalism, the notion of what it is to be and develop as a person has radically altered how we are invited to see ourselves and our relations with others. Personhood has become both atomised and collectivised and thus, despite its ideological protestations and first appearances, totalitarian in its propensities and inclinations. The animating drivers of neoliberalism are greed and self-interest legitimated and valorised through both the metaphors and the actualities of the market. Not only are we encouraged to see ourselves as atomistic, acquisitive and inveterately hard-wired into exponential consumption, we are required to do so through perpetual personal reinvention, the self as entrepreneur of the self, thus necessitating new products and patterns of consumption. Even during recent times of financial and economic crisis, when the dialectic of greed and mendacity reached its zenith, all were encouraged, despite dwindling means and growing reluctance, to resume consumption as a key remedial strategy. Here the collectivist, totalitarian propensities of neoliberalism become more apparent. Individuals have no intrinsic worth; their significance lies in their capacity to produce and consume ever more goods and services.

By contrast, personalism as a philosophical and political movement is antagonistic to both individualism and collectivism and argues for a deeply relational view of the self. Amongst its best-known twentieth century proponents were Emmanuel Mounier and Jacques Maritain in France and John Macmurray in the UK. Later thinkers with affinities to the movement include Emmanuel Levinas and Paul Ricoeur. In the spirit of that orientation what we wish to argue for, in developing further our concept of radical education, is an account of personhood that reverses much of what neoliberalism stands for, an account which is able to distinguish between instrumental and other-regarding forms of relation, value each differently according to context and purpose and, perhaps most importantly, offer a quite different view about the relative merits and proper relations between each of these forms. In pursuing this task, we begin by developing a personalist anthropology at the heart of which lies the mutually conditioning values of freedom and equality and the pervasive orientations of community and care.

Drawing on the work of John Macmurray, one of the most important philosophers of the twentieth-century English-speaking world, undeservedly neglected today, we presume an understanding of personhood that is relational rather than atomistic, heterocentric and other-regarding rather than instrumentally and prudentially-driven, and communally-situated rather than securely housed behind the gated privacies of acquisitive self-interest. The person is understood as irredeemably Other but also inescapably relational, persons bound to each other both by responsibilities and inter-dependencies and by the emergent energies and presumptions of Promethean possibility.

There are three key dimensions to Macmurray's thinking about persons that help us construct our own understandings of how best to enable each other to be and become more fully human. First, we need to recognise that human beings are deeply situated, communal beings whose personhood is steeped in mutuality. For Macmurray:

> human experience is, in principle, shared experience; human life, even in its most individual elements, is a common life; and human behaviour carries always, in its inherent structure, a reference to the personal Other. . . . [T]he unit of personal existence is not the individual, but two persons in relation; . . . we are Persons, not by individual right, but in virtue of our relation to one another. The personal is constituted by personal relatedness. The unit of the personal is not the 'I', but the 'You and I'.
>
> (Macmurray, 1961, p. 61)

In sum: 'We need one another to be ourselves. This complete and unlimited dependence of each of us upon the others is the central and crucial fact of personal existence . . . Here is the basic fact of our human condition' (Macmurray, 1961, p. 211). It is not just that '[h]uman personality is constituted by personal relations. It is only through our personal relations that we are human at all . . . The human individual – out of relation to all other human individuals – is a myth' (Macmurray, 1945, p. 8). It is also that the self is dynamic, shifting, constantly changing, constantly the expression of our lived and living relation with others: 'Our "personality" is not something that belongs to us as individuals; it is not *in* us but *between* us. Perhaps it is even true that we are different persons in different personal relationships' (Macmurray, 1945; original emphasis).

Second, Macmurray argued that there are two fundamentally different kinds of relation we have as persons, namely, 'functional relations' and 'personal relations'. 'Functional' or instrumental relations are typical of those encounters that help us to get things done in order to achieve our purposes: indeed, functional relations are defined by those purposes. Your relationship with those from whom you buy items or to whom you sell your services is defined by the purpose embedded in that encounter and when the transaction is completed your relationship ends. In functional relations, your engagement with others is partial and specific: partial in the sense that it does not draw on a whole range of attitudes, dispositions and capacities which you do in fact possess and use in other circumstances; specific in the sense that what is deemed appropriate or necessary in the exchange is circumscribed by its constitutive purposes, by the roles which shape the form and conduct of the encounter. For Macmurray, functional relations are typical of society; society is, in fact, an organisation of functions.

In contrast to functional relations of society, 'personal' relations of community are not aspectival, task-specific or role-defined; rather, they are expressive of who we are as persons. Whereas functional relations are defined by their purposes, personal or communal relations have no purposes beyond themselves: purposes are expressive of personal relations, not constitutive of them. Macmurray's preferred example to illustrate the differences between functional and personal relations is friendship. Friendship does not consist of common purposes. If you ask what the purpose of a friendship is, the asking of the question implies that it is not a friendship at all, but rather a relationship that, despite having the veneer of friendship, in fact has ulterior motives or instrumental reasons for its existence.

In a friendship, the common purposes arise from the care and delight in each other. If you care for someone you want to do something for them and with them, and the mutuality of those intentions gives rise to the practical ground of its shared reality. In a cooperative, functional relationship typical of society, if you change the purposes you dissolve the unity; in a communal relationship of friendship, far from the change of purposes dissolving the relationship, it both maintains and enriches the unity. Finally, it is important to stress that whilst society and community, the functional and the personal, are distinct they are nonetheless necessary to each other, though not of equal importance: 'We become persons in community, in virtue of our relations to others. Human life is inherently a common life. Our ability to form individual purposes is itself a function of this common life . . . Community is prior to society' (Macmurray, 1950, p. 56).

There are two further key points about Macmurray's philosophical account of community that need to be emphasised here and they concern community's constitutive philosophical principles, namely freedom and equality. Macmurray argues that there are two fundamental philosophical principles of community: these are the principle of freedom and the principle of equality. He suggests not only that freedom and equality are central to any adequate understanding of community or fellowship, but that these two principles have a mutually reinforcing relation with one another. His view is that:

> equality and freedom, as constitutive principles of fellowship, condition one another reciprocally. Equality is a condition of freedom in human relations. For if we do not treat one another as equals, we exclude freedom from the relationship. Freedom, too, conditions equality. For if there is constraint between us there is fear; and to counter the fear we must seek control over its object, and attempt to subordinate the other person to our own power. Any attempt to achieve freedom without equality, or to achieve equality without freedom, must, therefore be self-defeating.
>
> (Macmurray, 1950, p. 74)

Freedom for Macmurray is freedom to be ourselves, something we can only do in and through our relations with others, and only in certain kinds of relations. Friendship or community 'reveals the positive nature of freedom. It provides the only conditions which release the whole self into activity and so enable a man [sic] to be himself totally without constraint' (Macmurray, 1950, p. 73). Likewise, equality, understood in a personal rather than a functional sense, is enriching rather than diminishing: 'It is precisely the recognition of difference and variety amongst individuals that gives meaning to the assertion of equality' (Macmurray, 1938, p. 75).

For freedom and equality to become real presumes two things, the first being a positive motive between the persons involved. Community or fellowship is a relation in which we reciprocally enter with the whole of ourselves and rests upon our mutual affection and care for one another and stands in contrast to the prudential, aspectival relations of society. Second, the expression of freedom and equality in relationships of friendship or community is not only made possible by our care for each other, but also by the heterocentric nature of our mutuality.

> For each . . . it is the other who is important, not himself. The other is the centre of value . . . consequently he cares for himself only for the sake of the other. But this is mutual; the other cares for him disinterestedly in return.
>
> (Macmurray, 1961, p. 58)

One other aspect of Macmurray's account is important to bring out here and it relates to our earlier discussion on alterity in relation to an ethics of an encounter. Macmurray is at pains to point out that the unity of community for which he is arguing is '[n]o fusion of selves, neither is it a functional unity of differences . . . It is a unity of persons. Each remain a distinct individual; the other remains really other. Each realizes himself in and through the other' (Macmurray, 1961, p. 58). Community, the foundational basis of our development as persons, thus turns out to be adjectival, not substantival; it is not a group of people, nor is it the mere fact of a relationship; rather it is the shared mutuality of experience that is constitutive of it. Community is a way of being, not a thing. Community is a process in which human beings regard each other in a certain way (love, care and concern for the other) and in which they relate to each other and act together in mutuality as persons, not as role occupants. It is, furthermore, a mutuality informed by the values of freedom (freedom to be and become yourself) and equality (equal worth), which condition each other reciprocally and preserve the integrity of individuality through the heterocentric insistence of their care for and delight in each other.

The relational nature of persons and the key distinction between functional and personal modes of interaction comprise the first two dimensions of Macmurray's thinking about persons. The third, highly original and most important, dimension lies in his suggestion that the interdependence of the functional and the personal is both inevitable and desirable. The functional provides the concrete, instrumental means by which the personal expresses itself. If I care for you, that care achieves practical expressions as much through the rudimentary provision of daily necessities as it does through special acts of kindness. Community expresses itself or, in Macmurray's words, 'gets hands and feet' through the practical arrangements we enter into to express our shared humanity and the creativity of our differences.

Just as the personal needs the functional to realise itself in action, so too the functional needs some element of the personal to achieve its purposes. The key point here lies in Macmurray's further suggestions, not just of the interdependence of the functional and the personal, but the particular nature of that interdependence. For him, whilst the personal is through the functional – concern, care and delight become real in action through practical expression – crucially, the functional is for the sake of the personal. Thus, economic activity (the functional) is only legitimate insofar as it helps us to lead more fulfilled lives (the personal); politics and the fight for social justice (the functional) are the servants of communal flourishing (the personal). Within systems of compulsory public education, schooling (the functional) is for the sake of education (the personal); within schools themselves, administrative, management and other organisational arrangements (the functional) are for the sake of a vibrant and creative community (the personal).

Extending Macmurray's line of thinking, we argue that not only is the functional for the sake of the personal, and the personal achieved through the functional, but the influence of the personal on the functional is transformative of it: the functional should be expressive of the personal. Ends and means must be inextricably linked; the means should themselves be transformed by the ends by which they are inspired and towards which they are aiming. The functional ways in which we work together in schools to achieve personal, communal and educational ends should be transformed by the moral and interpersonal character of what we are trying to do.

The crisis we currently face in what we have termed the mainstream discourse of education has its roots in the fact that our dominant practical and intellectual frameworks reverse the very relation we are advocating. In what we term the 'high performance' model of schooling, the personal is used for the sake of the functional: students are included or excluded, valued or not, primarily on the basis of whether they contribute to the performance of the school. The pressure they and their teachers are put under to raise standards and improve performance marginalises the very educational aspirations that give schooling its justification and its purpose. Student complaints that schools do not care about them as persons, but only about them as bearers of results and measurable outcomes, are now ubiquitous. The same is true of teachers. In the radical education we are proposing, the relationship is reversed: in the school as 'person-centred learning community' and as 'democratic fellowship', students are viewed and treated as deeply-situated, communal beings whose personhood is steeped in mutuality; and the functional is used for the sake of the personal.

We explore and compare these different models of the school further in the next section.

Images

Last but not least, radical education is, for us, associated with certain images – or social constructions – of key actors and institutions. The child, as explicitly stated in Reggio Emilia and implicitly assumed in St George's, is the rich child:

> a child born with great potential that can be expressed in a hundred languages; an active learner, seeking the meaning of the world from birth, a co-creator of

knowledge, identity, culture and values; a child that can live, learn, listen and communicate, but always in relation with others; the whole child, the child with body, mind, emotions, creativity, history and social identity; an individual, whose individuality and autonomy depend on interdependence, and who needs and wants connections with other children and adults; a citizen with a place in society, a subject of rights whom the society must respect and support.

(Children in Europe, 2008, p. 6)

Our image of the teacher is similar, the 'rich' educator, with enormous potential, an active co-constructing learner, a reflective practitioner, multi-lingual (in the same sense as the child with a hundred languages), a critical thinker, a researcher and experimenter, and what has been termed a democratic professional. As such, the teacher may offer her 'reading of the world', but her role is to 'bring out the fact that there are other 'readings of the world' (Freire, 2004, p. 96), at times in opposition to her own. This concept of 'democratic professionalism' is based on 'participatory relationships and alliances. It foregrounds collaborative, cooperative action between professional colleagues and other stakeholders. It emphasises engaging and networking with the local community' (Oberhuemer, 2005).

And the image of the school in radical education? Our image is of the school as a public responsibility, a public institution and a public space; as a forum or place of encounter between citizens young and old, a space where all citizens for an important part of their lives come together; and as a collaborative workshop full of potential and possibilities, which is capable of many collective purposes and projects of common interest and benefit, including:

- Learning;
- Providing family support;
- Building community solidarity;
- Sustaining cultures and languages;
- Developing economy (including 'childcare');
- Promoting gender and other equalities;
- Practising democracy and active citizenship.

This list, we emphasise, is not comprehensive; it can, as we shall discuss in Chapter 3, be elaborated and developed by schools inscribed with values of democracy, justice, solidarity and experimentation.

We want to conclude this section by considering two further images or social constructions of the school in radical education: the school as 'person-centred learning community' and as a place of 'democratic fellowship', picking up on our previous discussion of a personalist approach to education. We contrast those images with three others: the school as 'impersonal organisation'; the school as 'affective community'; and the school as 'high performance organisation'. Developing Macmurray's insights and applying them to contemporary contexts of education and schooling, these five contrasting images – schematised in Table 2.1 – are produced from different orientations towards the functional/personal distinctions sketched earlier, which articulate

Table 2.1 Five images of the school: a typology

Schools as **Impersonal** Organisations	Schools as **Affective** Communities	Schools as **High Performance** Learning Organisations	Schools as **Person-Centred** Learning Communities	Schools as agents of **Democratic Fellowship**
The Functional marginalises the Personal	*The Personal marginalises the Functional*	*The Personal is used for the sake of the Functional*	*The Functional is used for the sake of the Personal*	*The Political expresses and supports the Personal*
Mechanistic Organisation	Affective Community	Learning Organisation	Learning Community	Democratic Fellowship
Efficient	Restorative	Effective	Existentially and instrumentally vibrant	Democratic living and learning

'impersonal', 'affective', 'high performance', 'person-centred' and 'democratic fellowship' modes of being and working together.

The first two, namely, the 'impersonal' and the 'affective', take diametrically opposite stances on the relation between the functional and the personal. In the image of the school as 'impersonal organisation', the functional marginalises the personal, which it sees as largely irrelevant and counterproductive of the core purpose of the school or business. It results in a predominantly mechanistic organisation that is primarily concerned with efficiency. It would typically be dominated by role relations and the prominence given to procedures.

In contrast, the 'school as affective community' valorises the personal at the expense of the functional. It is animated by an inclusive, restorative impulse rather than by the sifting, sorting and segregating predilections of efficiency. Its intense concern with the individual needs of young people results in little time or patience for the functional or organisational arrangements needed to translate the warmth and deeply held emotional commitments into practical realities that help young people learn in a variety of ways.

The other three images – the school as high performance organisation, the school as person-centred community and the school as agent of democratic fellowship – are particularly relevant to this chapter and our concept of radical education. They share a commitment to young people's achievement, but take very different stances towards how that achievement is conceived and how it is best realised within the context of a school. At first glance, the high-performance school and person-centred learning community seem very similar and it is that apparent similarity, or at least the sometimes extreme difficulty in telling the two apart, that suggests there may be important underlying issues to address.

However, on closer inspection, one school says 'Have a nice day' as part of a human relations mantra, whilst the other is genuinely welcoming and engaging of us. One uses extra time for tutorials to jack up test scores, whilst the other places personal encounter through dialogue at the very heart of its daily educational processes and intentions. In one the new sanctioning of creativity and personalisation is primarily the servant of the same narrow standards agenda, while in the other, creativity and engagement with young people as persons is the harbinger of a much richer, more demanding fulfilment of education for and in a democratic society.

These two schools are worlds apart; their felt realities are utterly at odds with each other. And yet, it is not always clear which frame is dominant, whose purposes are being served, whether we are the victims of those whose interests are quite other than those we would applaud, or whether we are part of something which is likely to turn out to be fulfilling and worthy of our support. In sum, it is not clear whether the personalisation claimed by both is a seductive re-articulation of corporate insinuation or a genuinely different orientation to what we do and how we might do it.

Much of the literature on performativity emphasises the extent to which it entails a denial of the personal, how through the 'emptying out' of social relationships any sense of caring for the young people with whom we work or for each other is marginalised or eradicated altogether. Certainly, the activities and worth of the school understood as a high-performance learning organisation are dominated by predefined outcomes, by measured attainment. Its form of unity is collective rather than personal or communal. The significance of both students and teachers is derivative and rests primarily in their contribution, usually via high stakes testing, to the public performance of the organisation and in this very real sense high-performance learning organisations are totalitarian.

Whilst much of this rings true, there is, however, something important that is missing here. Part of the power of contemporary performativity rests on its acceptance, not of a hollowed out ontology awaiting the fabrications of performance, but of its managerial reconstruction through the simulacra of care. The high-performing school is an organisation in which the personal is used for the sake of the functional: relationships are important; the voices of students are elicited and acknowledged; community is valued, but all primarily for instrumental purposes within the context of the marketplace. Social and, indeed, personal relationships are reduced to social capital; 'having relationships' moves subtly towards 'doing relationships', towards relationship management.

In contrast to the school as high-performance learning organisation, in its intentional, emergent mode the school as person-centred learning community is guided by its functional arrangements and interactions being firmly committed to wider human purposes. Certainly, the functional is genuinely felt to be for the sake of the personal. But, for a whole range of local and circumstantial reasons, the emphasis is on adapting traditional and more familiar arrangements to try to encourage and extend the school's basic commitment to the development of a learning community.

The organisational architecture of the school is heavily influenced by the acknowledged values and aspirations that express its distinctive character. Wide-ranging formal and informal arrangements amongst staff and between students and staff ensure many voices are heard and engaged. Pastoral and academic arrangements relate to each other synergistically with the needs of young people as persons providing the touchstone of aspiration and the arbiter of difficulty or conflict of interest. Continuing Professional Development is wide-ranging in both its processes and its substance. Often collegial, occasionally communal, it is enquiry-driven and learning-oriented e.g. hermeneutic or critical approaches to action research.

In its more fully developed, expressive mode the school understood as a person-centred learning community is one in which the functional is expressive of the personal, structures and daily practical arrangements having within them distinct traces of person-centred ways of being. Invariably, one sees the development of organisational forms that deliberately establish a sense of place, purpose and identity within which emergent, fluid forms of learning are encouraged. The revival of schools-within-schools, an implacable opposition to 'ability' grouping (see, for example, Hart *et al.*, 2004; Boaler, 2005, 2008), and more integrated, co-constructed approaches to curriculum together with wide-ranging use of the community exemplify commitment to more exploratory modes of being and development. Such schools deliberately develop more participatory, less hierarchical forms of engagement and decision-making. Distinctions between pastoral and academic become more problematic and ultimately less significant. Continuing Professional Development embraces more explicitly dialogic, even narrative forms of engagement such as action learning sets and self-managed learning groups (where small groups of participants not only set the agendas for their professional learning, but also identify key issues within the larger time frame of their own educational histories) and boundaries between status, role and function are increasingly transgressed through new forms of radical collegiality e.g. the students-as-researchers' movement in which staff and students work together on shared agendas of mutual interest (see *Radical Roles*, pp. 75–79 of this book).

Finally, if we extend the values and orientations of person-centred education to the domain of democratic praxis, it is clear they sit most comfortably within participatory rather than representative traditions of democracy. Arcing back to our earlier utilisation of the insights of John Macmurray, G. D. H. Cole and others on the nature and purpose of democracy as a way of life, we would thus wish to propose 'democratic fellowship' as the final articulation of our typology of school images. Here, the school as a person-centred learning community extends its commitment to education in its broadest sense in an explicitly democratic form. Not only is the functional expressive of the personal, the political is also utilised in the same way.

In reviving the notion of fellowship, we retain the essential link with democracy not just as a plural means of forming intentions, agreeing action and holding each other to account, but also as a deliberative, appreciative and creative form of personal and communal encounter; as a form of living and learning together; as a mutuality defined by the principles of freedom and equality within the context of kindness and care; as a shared commitment to a richly conceived, constantly developing search for and enactment of good lives lived in a just and diverse commonality.

The formal curriculum would explicitly encourage exploratory work, often on a thematic basis. Group work would be commonplace and the celebratory and interrogative occasions of shared enquiry, often between age groups, would feature strongly. Same-age and mixed-age mentoring and inter-generational learning (as in developments like 'Students-as-Learning Partners' where staff invite students to observe and co-develop their practice) would be approached within a shared commitment to the common good. Student and staff collaboration in 'Research Lessons' in which a small group of staff and students co-plan, observe and develop teaching approaches together exemplify approaches to professional learning that are individually and communally fulfilling. Finally, radical traditions of participatory rather than representative democracy exemplified in Alex Bloom's work at St George-in-the-East or the Just Community School movement in the US in the 1970s and 1980s (see Box 3.3 in Chapter 3) would push towards the development of School Meetings as the zenith of democratic fellowship.

We return in Chapter 3 to develop our ideas about the school best suited to provide a radical education, including issues of structure, organisation, workforce and practice. For the moment, we conclude by noting the hybrid and complex images of this 'common school'. Rather than the school as business or the school as high-performance organisation, we have a composite image that emphasises the school as public space, as a place of encounter for citizens, as a collective workshop and as a community.

Rationale for a radical education

The case for the kind of radical education we have outlined lies in the past, the present and the future. The sort of education we advocate is a response to our earlier discussion of missed opportunities: it seeks to take advantage of new understandings of learning and knowledge, and to confront the growing dangers facing humankind that prevent flourishing and even put our very survival at risk. If we are going to value and work with complexity and diversity, emergence and creativity; if we are to make connections and understand our inter-dependencies; if all of humankind is to survive and to flourish, and to do so on the basis of 'shared and lasting prosperity' and 'distributional equity', and these are all very big 'ifs' – then it seems important that education adopts certain values, ethics, concepts and images, such as the ones we have discussed. So, radical education, in our view, represents a necessary, but we repeat not sufficient, condition for survival and flourishing.

We take democracy as our starting point, not only as an important value in its own right, but because it holds an important key to how we, as societies and a species, may (if we are lucky) be able to defuse the dangers facing us and take a new direction that is better able to assure survival and flourishing. The case for democracy – our rationale for making democracy the basis of a radical education – can be clearly and concisely stated: 'Our society faces challenges where we need to act collaboratively more than ever. We need to deepen democracy through more deliberative and participative democratic mechanisms which spread democracy into the "everyday" of our lives' (Shah and Goss, 2007, p. 26). We need not only to think of democracy as multidimensional and multi-levelled, but to understand the interdependence of all dimensions and levels. Democratic education and the democratic school are an integral and necessary part of a democratic society and way of life for all of us: each depends on the other. Dewey put this well with a powerful metaphor: 'democracy needs to be reborn in each generation and education is its midwife'. He developed this at greater length, arguing that a democratic transformation of society requires a democratic transformation of education:

> Since, in a democracy, decision-making is no longer the preserve of an aristocratic elite, schools must become embryonic societies providing all pupils with

opportunities to develop the social attitudes, skills and dispositions that allow them to formulate and achieve their collective ends by confronting shared problems and common concerns. For Dewey, it is primarily by promoting the growth of social intelligence through cooperative problem-solving activities that schools can support and promote the evolution of a more democratic social order.

(Carr and Hartnett, 1996, p. 63)

What does current education and schooling have to offer in England? Too little. Take, for example, democracy, a value that we consider central to radical education. It is a fundamental value of the Swedish pre-school and school systems, spelt out as such at the start of the curricula for pre-schools and schools: 'Democracy forms the basis of the national school system . . . all school activity should be carried out in accordance with fundamental democratic values' (Swedish Ministry of Education, 1998, p. 3). Nor is this central role for democracy just in Sweden. The Nordic concept of a good childhood rests, Judith Wagner argues, on a number of 'bedrock ideals' including democracy:

> The Nordic notion of democracy as an essential feature of the good childhood requires that children experience democracy directly as an integral and consistent aspect of their daily lives at home, in school, and in their communities. Official policy documents and curriculum guidelines in the Nordic countries acknowledge a central expectation that preschools and schools will exemplify democratic principles and that children will be active participants in these democratic environments.

(Wagner, 2006, p. 292)

Nor is democracy as a central value of education confined to these countries. Another example, but by no means the only other, is, as we have seen, the municipal schools of Reggio Emilia. Moreover as Reggio Emilia and Sweden demonstrate, democracy as a value should be present from day 1; as the earlier quote from a project in the day nurseries in a German town puts it 'the basis for an everyday democratic culture can indeed already be formed in the day nursery'.

We are not arguing that every school in, say, Sweden is rigorously democratic in ethos and practice, but that democracy has a central and recognised place in the educational system: it is an explicit goal and aspiration. There is, of course, a strong democratic tradition in English education, to which we are connecting, and many teachers in England would regard democracy as a fundamental value. But democracy as a value has low visibility in the English education system, either in early childhood or compulsory schooling, making no explicit appearance in the early years curriculum and playing only a minor part subsequently as part of 'citizenship'. 'Citizenship' has been included in the English National Curriculum, as a non-statutory subject for the first two 'key stages', then as a statutory subject for older children, from year 7 (about 12-years-old) upwards. 'Democracy' appears here, but as a facet or 'key concept' of 'citizenship', making its first appearance only at key stage 2, for children from year 3 (8-years-old) upwards. Democracy is thus reduced to being a bit player in a 'subject', rather than a fundamental value running throughout the whole education system and process: democracy, we would argue, should precede citizenship.

The problem goes deeper than how and when democracy and citizenship appear in the curriculum. It lies in the whole approach, which is essentially individualistic and about fixing individual failings by bolting bits onto the education machine, in this case 'citizenship education':

> The first problem with the idea of citizenship education is that it is largely aimed at *individual* young people. The assumption is that they, *as individuals*, lack the proper knowledge and skills, the right values, and the correct dispositions to be the citizens they should be. This not only individualises the *problem* of young people's citizenship – and in doing so follows the neoliberal line of thinking in which individuals are blamed for their social malfunctioning. It also individualises citizenship itself, most notably through the suggestion that good citizenship will follow from individuals' acquisition of a proper set of knowledge, skills, values and dispositions.
>
> (Biesta and Lawy, 2006, pp. 71–72; original emphasis)

Worse, citizenship (and by implication democracy) are treated as predefined outcomes to be taught and delivered, 'a status that is only achieved after one has successfully traversed a specified trajectory'. Biesta and Lawy emphasise that citizenship, and by implication democracy, is not a subject to be taught but a practice to be learnt by doing:

> We suggest that citizenship is not so much a status, something which can be achieved and maintained, but that it should primarily be understood as something that people continuously do: citizenship as practice . . . This implies that a culture of participation should be a central and essential element of democratic citizenship.
>
> (Biesta and Lawy, 2006, p. 72)

The distinction – between teaching and doing – is central to our argument against the current educational mainstream and for a new public education. With its highly instrumental and technical orientation, and infused by neoliberal and neoconservative thinking, the mainstream treats democracy (and citizenship) as another and separate subject to be taught at an appropriate 'key stage', an addition to the already-lengthy subject shopping list of the curriculum, with measurable and predictable outcomes prescriptively-specified, expert-derived and uncontentious. This is far from the idea of democracy as a fundamental value to be practised – done – from the first day in nursery.

But the issue goes deeper than this. There is a fundamental distinction between a *marketised* system of education that treats schools as businesses and parents as consumers pursuing self-interest through individual choice and a *democratic* system of education that treats schools as public institutions and parents and children as citizens, capable of engaging in a democratic way of life and democratic forms of relationship, including participation in the making of collective choices. Carr and Hartnett have stated the distinction clearly:

> Any vision of education that takes democracy seriously cannot but be at odds with educational reforms which espouse the language and values of market forces and treat education as a commodity to be purchased and consumed . . . 'Freedom of choice' will be a major principle in determining educational policy, [but] the notion of 'choice' will not simply refer to the rights of individuals to pursue their narrow self-interests in a competitive marketplace. Instead it will be recognised that, in a democracy, individuals do not only express personal prefer-ences; they also make public and collective choices related to the common good of their society.
>
> (Carr and Hartnett, 1996, p. 192)

In a new public education, a radical education, democracy is a value and a practice, a way of living and relating, which pervades education and the school from day one and is learnt and contested, by children and adults alike, through its embeddedness in everyday life; it is a definition of the education and the school, how education is done, how the school operates, how young and old relate to each other – not just one of many predefined subjects and goals. We shall return to and explore further this theme in the next chapter when we go further into our understanding of democracy.

When it comes to justice and solidarity, the educational mainstream also offers little. Market systems emphasising individual choice are again not intended to pro-mote and support these values that we consider defining of radical education. Quite the contrary. A recent UNESCO report contains an overview of evidence on the consequences of increasing individual parental choice and intra-school competi-tion in school systems. What has emerged from 20 years or more of policy activ-ity? Overall, UNESCO is commendably wary of generalisations: 'Experiences and outcomes have varied . . . context is important' (UNESCO, 2008, p. 159). The results, however, provide no clear-cut endorsement for marketisation: 'The idea that increased parental choice leads to improved learning outcomes has intuitive appeal but is not well supported by evidence' (ibid., p. 160). For example, anal-ysis by OECD of results from the PISA (Programme for International Student Assessment) study of 15-year-olds in over 50 countries concludes that 'whether students are in competitive schools or not does not matter for their performance when socio-economic factors are accounted for' (OECD, 2007, p. 236); while in the US, 'advantages to academic outcomes stemming from voucher programmes are at most notably modest, and also certainly do not rise to the level anticipated by the early optimistic assumptions' (Lubienski, 2008).

But most germane to our discussion are the conclusions on equality. Here, UNESCO pointedly observes, '[t]he fact that competition by its nature creates losers as well as winners is sometimes forgotten' (UNESCO, 2008, p. 161). Indeed, 'school choice can exacerbate inequalities in many ways'. In particular, for a variety of reasons, disadvantaged children end up often concentrated in the worst-performing schools, while more advantaged families are best able to work the system:

Research in the United States shows that parents with wider social networks and more access to information are more likely to take advantage of choice policies and that they are better able to ensure that their children enter the higher quality schools they select.

(UNESCO, 2008, p. 162)

In other words, the children of middle-class parents are more likely to thrive in a system of choice and competition, able to deploy greater resources of knowledge, skills and contacts than less advantaged groups (see also Ball *et al.*, 1994; Whitty *et al.*, 1998; Lauder and Hughes, 1999; Ball, 2003; Apple, 2004b). As Stephen Ball observes, 'internationally, school choice policies are taken advantage of and primarily work in the interests of middle-class families' (Ball, 2003, p. 37).

Three specific examples can serve to illustrate this international phenomenon, of how marketised education systems foster inequality and, at the same time, undermine solidarity by encouraging parents to act as individual consumers competing for a scarce resource: the perceived 'high performance' school. The move to more parental choice in Swedish schools, with the promotion of independent but state-funded schools, has been studied by Skolverket, the Swedish National Agency for Education. The study finds that 'independent schools are chosen by parents with higher education and . . . that the likelihood of parents making a choice of school increases dramatically if they live in a city and are highly educated' (Skolverket, 2006, p. 31).

The same phenomenon has been reported in a study of Swedish pre-schools, centres taking children from 12 months to 6 years, and which all children in Sweden are entitled to attend. Government policy in recent years has been to increase private (though publicly-funded) pre-schools, to increase competition and parent choice. A study in Uppsala, the fourth largest city in Sweden, revealed the familiar story of marketisation: more advantaged parents are more likely to choose private pre-schools leading to increased segregation, which the researchers conclude is a consequence of 'a system which has abandoned the goal to provide equal opportunities, and instead has transferred the responsibility for these issues onto the unevenly distributed resources of the parents'. But the segregation of the market system goes beyond individual children and parents to affect the wider society. For the system creates conditions 'that make it virtually impossible for the pre-school organisation to achieve one of its central goals: to be a meeting place for children from different backgrounds' (Prieto *et al.*, 2002, p. 60).

Nearer home, our third example is a recent study that has found that so-called 'faith schools' in England increase social segregation, with no evidence of any compensatory increase in pupil attainment in their local areas (Allen and Vignoles, 2009); indeed, after 20 years of efforts by successive English governments to increase diversity of school types and hence competition, 'there is scant evidence that this approach has led to educational improvement' (Glatter, 2010, p. 1). Marketisation, once again, does not prove successful in its own 'school performance' terms, whilst doing nothing to reduce inequality or to foster solidarity. If anything, it works in the opposite direction: it is a case of everyone for themselves and their own interests.

An ethic of care also sits awkwardly in relation to education and the school in their mainstream manifestations. In England at least, but across many other countries too, policy and practice have treated 'care' as something distinct from 'education'. In early childhood, for instance, despite a policy rhetoric of 'care' and 'education' being inseparable, conceptually and structurally, the English system continues to be split between 'childcare' and 'early education', including separate workers – 'childcare workers' and 'teachers', the former as 'care workers' having lower qualifications, lower pay and lower status – and different relations between private and public: 'childcare' is viewed by government as an essentially private responsibility (albeit with some public subsidy to lower-income parents) while 'early education' is a public good, fully publicly-funded.

The position continues into school. 'Childcare' is separated off, as something that happens 'out of school' or 'wrapped around school', not as an integral part of education, and it is again undertaken by a lower-level 'care' workforce. Even in the classroom, the increasingly hierarchical school workforce – the product of what is termed in England 'school workforce remodelling' – reflects a fragmented approach to children, with the teacher leading on learning, while a much expanded team of less-qualified staff support learning and do supposedly less demanding care activities. Rather than a holistic approach to children, children are divided up with different fragments given to different occupational groups, graded according to qualifications and employment conditions.

Moving to secondary schools, in their evaluation of an English 'schoolswithin-school' (a model discussed in more detail in Chapter 3), the Sussex University research team point to the same separation of care as the norm, contrasting it with a minority – person-centred – tradition where education and care are closely linked:

> In the pastoral tradition, curriculum and care for the whole person are formally separated: curriculum is largely unalterable given that [it] is enabled and supported by structures and cultures that adapt young people to what is formally required of them. In what we might call the person-centred tradition, curriculum and care for the whole person are seen as inextricably linked and part of a wider educational undertaking that views learning as a much more collaborative, negotiated process that is not separable from your emerging identity as a person and your membership of a community.
>
> (Fielding *et al.*, 2006, p. 12)

The problem seems to reside in a Taylorist approach that has attempted to increase effectiveness and efficiency of production (including education) by breaking things (including people) into discreet bits, then applying different technologies and technicians to each bit – the factory model of division and specialisation writ large. Thus 'care' has been treated as a discreet activity and function, primarily undertaken by female relatives in the home and now, as 'care' is put increasingly onto the market and commodified to enable those relatives to take jobs, by low-status women workers – 'care workers'. Now that there is growing recognition of interdependency and connectedness – which applies to people as much as the environment – those societies most exposed to the Taylorist approach struggle over how to respond. What does it mean for a system based on division and specialisation to acknowledge care and education are connected or inseparable and what are the implications?

But other countries have less of a problem. In Sweden, according to the pre-school curriculum 'concern for the individual child's well-being, security, development and learning should characterise the work of the pre-school . . . [adopting] a pedagogical approach, where care, nurturing and learning form a coherent whole' (Swedish Ministry of Education, 1998, pp. 8, 14). Or, to take another example, in New Zealand, by the 1990s:

> 'early childhood education' had become the official term [for all early childhood services], as people took for granted that early education involved care as well – education is, again, understood as a broad, holistic concept, concerned with all aspects of well-being and development. 'Early childhood education' continues to be used as the generic term covering the diverse range of types of services in New Zealand.
>
> (Meade and Podmore, 2010, p. 32)

These are examples of countries that have adopted the concept of education-in-its-broadest-sense, which has a holistic approach as its default position, assuming education and care to be totally and inextricably interwoven; adherents find it hard to understand how the fragmentation approach – divide and rule – could ever have been adopted. How, they ask, could anyone ever have thought of learning, care and other facets of what it means to be human as separate?

Understanding care as an ethic provides an important means for putting Humpty together again, since it envisages care not as a separate activity or function, but as a way of relating that can and should pervade and shape every relationship – including that of teacher and child. Nel Noddings, writing from the US about the 'challenge to care in schools', recognises the ethical nature of care – 'no discussion of caring today could be adequate without some attention to the ethic of care' (Noddings, 2005, p. 21). She also recognises the centrality of care to education. The school, she argues, is a multi-purpose institution:

> It cannot concentrate only on academic goals any more than a family can restrict its responsibilities to, say, feeding and housing children. The single-purpose view is not only morally mistaken, it is practically and technically wrong as well, because schools cannot accomplish their academic goals without attending to the fundamental needs of students for continuity and care.
>
> (Noddings, 2005, p. 63)

Noddings, indeed, goes further. She argues that education itself should be organised around themes of care – 'care for self, care for intimate others, care for associates and distant others, for nonhuman life, for the human-made environment of objects and instruments, and for ideas' (Noddings, 2005, p. 47) – rather than traditional disciplines. Its main aim should be to produce people who are not only competent, but caring, loving and lovable.

If the relationship of care to modern education and schooling in England is, at best, uncertain and ambivalent, the relationship of an ethics of an encounter, with its deep concern for respecting diversity, is non-existent. Dahlberg is right to argue that '[t]o think another whom I cannot grasp is an important shift and it challenges the whole scene of pedagogy . . . [since it poses] questions such as how the encounter with Otherness, with difference, can take place as responsibly as possible' (Dahlberg, 2003, p. 270). But mainstream education has not begun to recognise these critical questions, let alone sought any answers. Instead, the trend towards categorisation, standardisation and normalisation, which seeks to place the Other into predefined positions, marches on relentlessly, reflecting the continuing will to master and govern, making the Other into the Same. We ask if Child X has attained standards a, b and c – not (as they do in Reggio Emilia) what has Child X learned and how, and what have we documented about Child X's learning that has surprised and amazed us.

We could go on, but hope the point has been made. For 25 or more wasted years education and schooling in England, and beyond, have been drawn into the gravitational pull of markets and techno-managerialism and been permeated by hyper-economism and instrumentality. The invisible hand with some help from experts and human technologies would, we were told, get education sorted out. Yet while all this has been going on, while huge amounts of time, money and mental effort have been lavished on getting the new system up and running, it has become increasingly clear that this type of education and the form of schooling it gives rise to have little to offer humankind, either for flourishing or for surviving the dangers already upon us and which, if not tackled, will be seriously harmful to our well-being, even perhaps fatally so.

And now the ideological foundations of the mainstream, the legacy of a generation of neoliberalism and neoconservatism, have cracked and are caving in. As Michael Sandel puts it, 'the era of market triumphalism has come to an end' (Sandel, 2009b, p. 2) and 'a politics of the common good' is called for, which 'invites us to think less of ourselves as consumers, and more as citizens' (ibid., p. 5). We need now to rethink 'the moral limits of the market' and the task of 'democratic governance', and we have to decide which we think more important:

> Democratic governance is radically devalued if reduced to the role of handmaiden to the market economy. Democracy is about more than fixing and tweaking and nudging incentives to make markets work better . . . [it] is about much more than maximising GDP, or satisfying consumer preferences. It's also about seeking distributive justice; promoting the health of democratic institutions; and cultivating the solidarity, and sense of community that democracy requires. Market-mimicking governance – at its best – can satisfy us as consumers. But it can do nothing to make us democratic citizens.
>
> (Sandel, 2009b, p. 4)

Current education and schooling have hardly begun to engage with the changes that are needed to exploit the opportunities or address the dangers confronting us. Indeed by their continuing entanglement in the current but bankrupt system preaching rising consumption, increasing growth, spreading commodification and intensified competition, they are part of the problem rather than the solution, part of the state we are in, not the state we might want to be in. As modern education has become 'increasingly an individual affair of learning competencies in view of private ends' (Simons, 2009, p. 1), with children and parents repositioned as individual consumers of educational products seeking competitive advantage in the marketplace rather than citizens with a shared interest in education as a public good and participant in democratic decision-making – so has education forfeited hope and become the 'dismal subject'.

We think the situation is very serious and should invoke a great sense of both anger and impatience for transformation. We repeat: mainstream education policy has wasted time and ignored opportunities that can be ill-afforded if we, humankind, and our societies are to survive and flourish and if democracy is to be reborn. Survival and flourishing is beyond any single intervention, but more likely, we contend, if a radical education centred on democracy is part of a concerted and sustained response to the dangers facing us and the possibilities arising from working with, rather than controlling out, diversity and complexity. However, as daily events keep reminding us, such a response is by no means certain and may prove beyond us as a species, both individually and collectively.

The diagnosis and prognosis is grim, but not beyond recall and not without hope. And that is the note on which we want to end this section. We introduced the book with two examples that offer cause for hope; there are many more, past and present and from many places, and we touch on some others later. Indeed, whilst recognising the influence and reach of the mainstream or dominant education discourse, we must avoid treating it as either universal or irresistible; there are many exceptions to the rule. Moreover even in the current system, dominated as it is by a dismal discourse, there are hopeful possibilities, features that could be worked with to contribute to a new direction for education and schools. In the case of England alone, we are thinking of such initiatives as Children's Centres and Extended Schools, which form part of *Every Child Matters*, the overarching policy of the New Labour government (1997–2010) covering all children and children's services, and which could possibly (though not necessarily) be the first steps towards recognition of education-in-its-broadest-sense.

In the next chapter, we will explain Children's Centres and Extended Schools in more detail and look at how their potential to contribute to a radical education and a common school might be realised. For the moment, we would note and welcome their potential, but suggest they are also examples of an all too common form of policy-making: attempting to produce technical solutions without first finding critical questions – restructuring without rethinking. They are 'programmes', with a means/end instrumentality and a desire for closure expressed in the techno-managerial language of delivery and targets. What they need to become are open-ended projects in which a community or communities take responsibility for the education of their children through processes of democracy, experimentation and research.

Drawing strength from the past

One of the distinct tragedies of today's school reform efforts is that the people involved have almost no knowledge of the long and valued tradition of like-minded efforts. Unfortunately, educators and citizens alike seem to have no collective memory of the many successful attempts at building more democratic schools. The history of progressive school reform documents the fact that thousands of teachers, administrators, community activists, and others spent their entire professional lives trying to build more educationally and socially responsive institutions. We have much to gain by reconnecting with their successes and with how they approached and overcame difficulties. All progressively inclined educators stand on the shoulders of these people.

(Apple and Beane, 2007, pp. 153–54)

There are other reasons for hope, other reasons for believing in the possibility of a democratic alternative, an education centred on the values, ethics, concepts and images we have espoused and termed radical education. Those reasons lie in the past, in the thinking and practice, the commitment and struggles, of our predecessors who have imagined and sought to embody an education with many of the features of radical education. The past in neoliberal times is either best forgotten or else held up as a dreadful warning, having nothing to teach us as we plunge on clinging to the juggernaut of market-driven change. Historical amnesia is the contemporary educational condition, as we are urged to focus our attentions on an education that will conform to market principles and deliver subjects for the market, individualistic consumers and flexible workers.

But we turn our backs on the past at great peril: 'society remembers less and less faster and faster. The sign of the times is thought that has succumbed to fashion; it scorns the past as antiquated while touting the present as the best' (Jacoby, 1977, p. 1). The past is traditions we can build on. The past is a treasure trove of experience and wisdom. The past is another environment to visit, which helps to make the contemporary familiar strange and hence, generate critical thought and questions. The past is peopled by exceptional individuals, like Loris Malaguzzi and Alex Bloom; is full of important experiments, like St George-in-the East, sources of inspirational energy; and the past is crossed by potent social movements, like the international New Education movement which spread across and beyond Europe in the late nineteenth century, inspiring and linking educational innovators such as John Dewey, Maria Montessori, Célestin Freinet and Janus Korczak. Times may change, but past thought and practice, these individuals and experiments and movements, still speak to us since they address concerns and hopes that are with us yet today.

In this section we can only scratch the surface of the past, pointing to a mere handful of important precedents to indicate the potential of past times for adding to both the rationale for and the practice of radical education as a new public education. The past confirms, for us, the importance of the values and other features that define our understanding of radical education, and provides us with valuable evidence that we can work with to develop and implement that understanding. We also touch on some past debates and criticisms, since the past is neither to be forgotten nor treated as sacrosanct. Indeed, the past politics of education is part of the rich legacy left for us, if we choose to use it.

Our starting point in this exercise of going back to the future is the now much disparaged notion of progressive education. Our search for alternative futures then takes us via left critiques of progressivism to the possibilities of radical education, both outside and, more contentiously, within the public system of education.

Progressivism: a legacy for radical education

If we are to understand the possibilities of transcending neoliberal and neoconservative approaches to education, we have also to understand the progressive consensus whose demise gave way to the quite different approaches that are now the norm in England and a number of other countries across the world. Whilst it can be sensibly argued that progressivism is largely a product of the late nineteenth century that came to hold sway, according to which country we are considering, during the 40 years between 1930 and 1970, its roots go back much further to writers like Comenius[3] and Rousseau, and its legacy remains a significant presence today (Darling and Norbenbo, 2003, p. 289). Given the richness and longevity of its traditions and the range of countries across the world that have embraced its thinking there is, inevitably and properly, no one account that can claim to be uncontested. That being said, Darling and Norbeno offer a useful starting point. They suggest five recurring themes that characterise progressive approaches to schooling, themes that show strong correspondence with the defining features of what we have defined as 'radical education' – criticism of traditional education, the nature of knowledge, human nature, democracy and the development of the whole person.

Progressivism's critique of traditional education – which in some important respects corresponds with the neoconservative element in what we have termed the current mainstream educational discourse – contains a number of strands, in particular, an antagonism towards models which rest primarily on the transmission of information, usually in an authoritarian instructional manner, with no significant place for the active involvement of the student in her own learning. More often than not delivered via compartmentalised school subjects, such approaches were frequently seen to operate at the expense of the life of the imagination.

Second, in the progressive account, the nature of knowledge is not, as is the case in traditionalist arrangements, to do with the acceptance of established truths. Rather, knowledge is seen as a personal acquisition: it is about personal growth and transformation through achieved experience. A heavily epistemological account of schooling, which emphasises the centrality of forms of knowledge, often takes too little account of the necessity of understanding, of making a difference to the life of the learner. In order to do that, progressives have argued that one needs to take seriously a whole range of other factors like the nature of the young person's previous experience, how they make sense of that experience, the kinds of things that intrigue them or interest them and the sorts of things they wish to explore. Such approaches, it is argued, are not only likely to be more successful, they are also more respectful of the student as a person.

Third, mainstream progressivism regards the child as naturally curious with an inveterate desire for learning. Consequently, it sees the role of the schools as, in the words of the Plowden report, 'to build on and strengthen children's intrinsic interest in learning and lead them to learn for themselves rather than from fear of disapproval or desire for praise' (Central Advisory Council for Education, 1967, p. 161).

The particularly important fourth strand of advocacy, which both united North American and European traditions of progressivism and expressed their cultural differences, was the insistence on the necessary link between schooling and democracy, not so much as a set of procedural arrangements, but rather as a way of learning and living together. Here the emphasis is not just on the child as a learner, but also the child as an agent in their own and each other's lives. The school is thus seen as a major site, not only of curricular engagement, but also of communal and ultimately, deliberative, democratic living.

The fifth and final strand of progressivism identified by Darling and Norbenbo has to do with the education of the whole person, what we have termed education-in-its-broadest-sense. This has partly to do with a rejection of too strong an emphasis on the notion of education as a preparation for later life. Whilst education is, to some extent, a preparation for something that is yet to come it is, just as importantly, to do with life lived now. Not only are we increasingly uncertain about what that future holds, part of what it means to lead a fulfilled life has to do with our willingness and capacity to form our own views, to live lives of integrity, to be and become good persons. In the words of Bill Taylor, '[p]rogressivism in education is essentially about putting persons at the heart of the learning and teaching processes . . . The uniqueness of the person must remain central to the learning process'. The school must empower the individual 'by nurturing personal dignity, worth and integrity' (Taylor, 1994, pp. 9, 11).

Critiques of progressivism

Neoliberal critiques

There are a number of reasons why progressive approaches to education are no longer sustainable in a systematic way under neoliberalism. One is that progressivism presumes a significant degree of autonomy for teachers who are free to make judgements about what is likely to benefit the children for whose learning and development they have a major responsibility. Since the mid-1970s, there has been a steady erosion both of teacher and local government autonomy and of the influence of teachers and their organisations at the level of policy making. Teachers and local authorities and, equally importantly, universities and colleges of education, have increasingly become the agents rather than the partners of central government.

The second reason is that the ideology of neoliberalism is fundamentally at odds with the foundational values and perspectives of most of what progressivism stands for. Instrumental rather than expressive, managerial rather than democratic in its relationships, extrinsic rather than intrinsic in its drives and dispositions, neoliberalism is dedicated to the creation and extension of a consumer society in which all are required to constantly re-invent themselves in an unending pursuit of material and instrumental gain. The mechanisms and mindsets of the market have not only undermined and displaced the core beliefs of progressivism – and of much else of value, like the notion of public service and pursuit of the common good – they have done so in a way that many new regimes have successfully employed in the past. For they not only introduce a new set of understandings and expectations that name and promote their preferred reality, but they also colonise aspects of the displaced discourse that retains some wider resonance. This can cause confusion and blur important political differences.

At first glance, the new set of understandings and expectations typical of neoliberalism seem to have much in common with certain elements of progressivism outlined earlier, particularly those to do with personal growth and transformation. However, on closer examination, the similarities are more apparent than real. Whilst, on the one hand, the Janus-faced imperatives of neoliberal discourse simultaneously include the ideologies of 'individual choice', of the 'customer', of 'ownership', of 'empowerment' and of 'personalisation', on the other hand, they also include the less visible, but equally powerful, regulatory mechanisms that operate at individual and macro levels of our lives. As individuals, we incorporate the dispositions and mechanisms of self-surveillance and the internalised requirements of incessant change and self-improvement. At macro levels of governmental policy, with apologies to F. D. Roosevelt, 'The only thing we have to choose is choice itself'. At the heart of contemporary neoliberalism lie not only the necessities of choice, of choice as an individual obligation, but also strong centralist requirements that insidiously define the boundaries and, increasingly, the terrain and targets within which particular kinds of choice are required of us.

There is one further companion issue to bring out here. It has to do both with the fact and the rationale of linguistic colonisation, of ways in which some of the language of progressivism has been appropriated rather than rejected by its neoliberal successors. Thus, if we look at each of the five hallmarks of progressive education identified earlier, within the neoliberal lexicon we can see an alternative reading which has some surface features and characteristics that retain a spectral link with a progressive past, but which, in reality, is creating a quite different future. Here, the invisible hand of the market rewrites progressive discourse in the image of atomistic acquisition.

The critique of traditionalist approaches now manifests itself in the ever growing requirement that we listen to 'the student voice' not as a democratic practice with emancipatory potential, but rather as means of keeping teachers up to the mark, of ensuring the voice of the fledgling 'consumer', well-schooled in the mechanisms and expectations of market, is validated, nurtured and made conspicuously visible in all spheres of life, even those in which issues of status and power have traditionally excluded their presence, let alone legitimated their interrogative potential (Fielding, 2004a, 2004b).

Instead of progressivism's commitment to knowledge as a personal acquisition leading to individual growth and transformation in a holistic sense, neoliberalism resorts to the learning style inventory and the enthusiastic championing of a persistently elusive notion of personalisation (Fielding, 2008a). Calibrated choice confined to pre-ordained options; loud and optimistic talk about co-construction cramped by the presumptions of ability labeling and the Damoclean sword of high-stakes testing; these and other dishonesties and delusions gain what validity they can, not only from the blandishments of the marketplace and the seductions of celebrity culture, but also from the instrumental co-option of progressivism's insistence on creativity and authenticity.

Instead of progressivism's insistence on the power and pleasure of intrinsic motivation and a profound personal, social and political understanding of a curriculum informed by children's interests, neoliberalism insists on the need to learn-how-to-learn, not as a life-world dynamic, but rather as an instrumental device, a social and economic capability recurrently required of the responsible and flexible consumer-worker.

The necessary link with schooling and democracy so typical of the Deweyan versions of progressivism is still there in neoliberalism, but its accounts both of democracy and of citizenship are transformed. Participatory democracy as a way of living good lives together is replaced by electronically-driven, representational forms of engagement. The common good is reduced to an aggregate compilation of consumer-citizen preferences and the high-performing school achieves its market position in part because it takes seriously the daily requirement that staff pay constant attention to the views of its young consumers.

Lastly, the education of the whole person, so central to person-centred versions of progressivism, is also taken seriously by neoliberalism. However, in doing so it invariably hollows out its substance replacing it with something much more utilitarian: with, for example, the skills and capacities of emotional intelligence (EQ), i.e. with the wherewithal, not of satisfying and fulfilling relationships, but rather with the knowledge and skills that enable one to get on in the world, that enable one to 'do relationships' as a necessary accomplishment of a successful economic repertoire. We are brought back to the school constructed as 'high performance organisation', where the personal is used for the sake of the functional.

Transforming the system: socialist critiques of progressivism

Neoliberalism's simultaneous appropriation and vilification of progressivism follows familiar trajectories of hegemonic ascendancy. Nonetheless and notwithstanding the subtleties and sophistications of its accomplishment, its view of human society in general and education and schooling in particular remain deeply objectionable. In our view what is needed is a narrative of education that is radically different, an account of sustainability, care and human flourishing which transcends the treadmill of self-interest and perpetual consumption and not only remains true to the creative, inclusive spirit of progressive education, but also goes beyond its propensity to offer a merely ameliorative response to the social injustices and spiritual degradations of its host societies.

These aspirations for radical educational change are, of course, the kinds of arguments for which many forms of progressivism prepare the ground. Where progressive versions often stop short and where we would wish to press ahead connects with long-standing arguments, particularly within socialist and libertarian traditions of educational debate, about how one goes about challenging and changing the *status quo* in ways that operate both at the level of daily practice and at the level of social and political strategy. We now take a brief look at some of the key strands in these debates.

There are, of course, many complex modes of thinking and practice that characterise the often interrelated nature of progressive and socialist education projects. Socialists more often than not share many of the criticisms progressives make of both traditional and neoliberal forms of schooling. What frequently divides them are arguments about *how* the *status quo* against which they are reacting can be seriously challenged and ultimately changed. The worry that socialists have about the ameliorative, humanising tendencies of progressivism is that, in the words of Quintin Hoare, 'throughout its long history this tradition has failed to transcend its oppositional, escapist character, and has failed to do more than salvage a minority from being broken by the system' (Hoare, 1965, p. 47). Whilst understanding the importance of providing an environment in which children can grow as freely and creatively as possible, progressivism is seen to have failed to fight or even comprehend the system that is so destructive of human flourishing and is thus seen as complicit in its perpetuation.

Similar sorts of concerns were also expressed in the mid-1970s about what was then known as 'the new sociology of knowledge', some of whose proponents championed a kind of naive 'possibilitarianism' (Whitty, 1974). Its advocates were seen to suffer, not from escapist tendencies, but rather from a debilitating naivety, an over-ambitious sense of the transformative powers of a radical pedagogy that encouraged students to contest the nature of knowledge and thereby come to see the social and political world as open to the possibility and the necessity of profound change.

Many feminists argued on similarly excoriating lines. On this view what was seen as the naive utopianism of the overweening aspirations of 1960s and 1970s progressivism placed impossible demands on a largely female workforce who blamed themselves, not the ideology or constraining macro contexts, for its frequent failure. Thus, for Valerie Walkerdine, progressivism is a 'fantasy of liberation' in which female teachers become 'the servant of the omnipotent child' (Walkerdine, 1992, p. 21). Furthermore, and equally damaging in its consequences, is progressives' denial of power relations, which thus makes powerlessness invisible. For Walkerdine, it is 'therefore very important to reassert the centrality of oppression and its transformation into a pathology in terms of a political analysis of the present social order' (ibid., p. 21).

The cumulative weight of the socialist argument is that changing schools is important, but that it cannot be achieved by more humane or searching practices that just focus on schools themselves. Richard Hatcher puts the matter cogently when he insists that change of the kind which will enable us to break from the suffocation of traditionalism, the alienation of neoliberalism and the injustice of both will only come through linking teaching to wider social struggles (Hatcher, 2007). Thus, the gender and race campaigns and the change in classroom practices they legitimated and supported within schools were successful because of wider social movements of the 1970s and 1980s they connected to. What is also needed are alliances between schools and local communities and with all those who have common cause through their marginalisation or oppression within current society.

Rejecting the system: libertarian transcendence

Whilst some radical forms of progressivism and socialism argue that our energies should be put into subverting and eventually transforming the current systems of education, other radical approaches, often with roots in anarchist and libertarian traditions, argue that any state system of education is inevitably oppressive and we would be better off either setting up bounded alternative schools within it or abandoning the idea of schools altogether. The former – alternative schools – approach, nicely summed by Roger Dale in the slogan 'community can compensate for society' (Dale, 1979, p. 196) is less concerned with extending deep social change than creating schools which enact their own view of a better society on a daily basis and ignore what goes on elsewhere. The latter – deschooling – approach, i.e. abandoning schools altogether, excited considerable interest in the 1970s, most prominently through the work of Ivan Illich.

At the heart of the libertarian critique lies the view that 'any successful radical change in society partly depends upon changes in the character, structure and attitudes of the population; a new society cannot be born unless a new person can function within it' (Spring, 1975, p. 9). Here, the argument is not only that the inevitable authoritarianism of schools blunts the creativity and spontaneity of individuals; it is also that it simultaneously creates a deep social and political dependency on schooling itself. We must, therefore, create other forms of education without recourse to schools. Among the most vibrant of its twenty-first century successors are Roland Meighan and Clive Harber, who through the collective 'Education Now' have since the 1980s advocated radical alternatives to schooling, state or otherwise, and who are now at the heart of the home education movement in the UK.

Our own view is that both the socialist and libertarian traditions we have described previously have much to contribute in helping us to develop a radical approach to social and educational change that moves beyond neoliberalism to a way of life that acknowledges the necessity of social justice and the common good as animating aspirations, albeit in ways that are cognisant of the pluralities that identities and difference demand and the inclusive communal contexts that freedom requires. How then might we articulate a convincing way forward that acknowledges the incommensurabilities as well as the possibilities that progressivism, socialism and libertarianism offer us?

We acknowledge the need for a radical education to be part of a wider struggle and that education by itself is not enough; as we noted in Chapter 1, we must always put education in perspective. We share the libertarians' suspicion of the governing potential of the school. We understand the chicken-and-egg dilemma that both traditions highlight: how can you have a radical education before you have a radical society and a radical subject, but how can you have this society and subject without first having radical education? But neither persuades us to abandon the search for a radical education nor to despair of the school as a place to help realise human potentiality and a democratic way of life. Instead of a simple model, in which education is either cause or effect, we need to imagine an education and school that is 'in between', neither the active originator of radical change nor the passive beneficiary of others bringing about such change, but engaged in a complex process of becoming.

Our response, therefore, is to seek theories of transformation – theories such as Wright's 'real utopias' and Unger's 'radical reform' – that envisage such a process and to advocate the role of radical education in that process through 'democratic experimentalism' and 'prefigurative practice'. We see in these a potentially feasible and substantive way forward that acknowledges the left's call for strategic acumen and progressive and libertarian calls for the necessity of grounding aspirational talk of a better future in the here-and-now of actual human encounter. We return to explain and explore these theories of transformation in Chapter 4, as well as the possible contribution of democratic experimentalism and prefigurative practice to challenging the status quo.

Democratic practice in radical education and the common school

In our next chapter we consider the form of school in which we believe a radical education founded on democracy might best be practised: the common school. Meantime, we round off our account of radical education by suggesting some features or aspects of democratic practice we would wish to see informing the kind of common school for which we will be arguing. These might be thought of as some of the signs or indicators that the visitor might look for to know whether she or he was coming to a school that practised radical education. We offer 10 below, though not claiming a comprehensive inventory:

- A proclaimed democratic vitality;
- Radical structures and spaces;
- Radical roles;
- Radical relationships;
- Personal and communal narrative;
- Radical curriculum, critical pedagogy and enabling assessment;
- Insistent affirmation of possibility;
- Engaging the local;
- Accountability as shared responsibility; and, lastly
- Regional, national and global solidarities.

Proclaimed democratic vitality

First, and of fundamental importance, a school for radical education will wish to foreground its interdependent commitments to (a) education as the most important rationale for schooling, and (b) democracy as both the end and the means, the purpose and the practice, of education. What this actually means will of course be something that those working in the school will need and wish to exemplify and share with their internal and external communities. Certainly, the narratives and exchanges that develop will be energised by a view of democracy that underscores the commitment to profound change in how we live and work now as a bridge to more just and more creative futures. Witness, for example, Alex Bloom, the great, radical pioneer head teacher, and his stated intention to create on 1 October 1945 '[a] consciously democratic community . . . without regimentation, without corporal punishment, without competition' (Bloom, 1948, p. 121); or the former mayor of Reggio Emilia who spoke in Chapter 1 of the city's desire 'to nurture and maintain a vision of children who can think and act for themselves'.

The key point here is that education in and for deep or 'high-energy' democracy has to be not just the starting point but what Elsa Wasserman, in her reflections on the relative success of the Just Community School movement in the US, calls the 'central educational goal' (Wasserman, 1980, p. 268) of the radical common school for which we are arguing (see Brookline school in Chapter 3, Box 3.3 for an example of a Just Community School). There has to be a proclaimed, not just an intended, democratic vitality, albeit one that bears in mind the vicissitudes of context and circumstance. It is important we learn from the successes and failures of iconic past attempts – for example, from England alone, not just Alex Bloom at St George-in-the-East but many others including Teddy O'Neill at Prestolee (Burke, 2005), Michael Duane at Risinghill (Berg, 1968), Tim McMullen and John Watts at Countesthorpe (Watts, 1977), and, more recently, Mike Davies at Bishops Park (Davies, 2005) to advance more radical forms of schooling within the public education system in England and beyond.

Radical structures and spaces

Our next three indicators comprise complementary aspects of the interpersonal and structural integrity of democratic living. They demonstrate the unity of means and ends, not only in matters of organisational structure, but also in the relational dimensions of daily engagement, which underscore the importance of care, respect and creative encounter as the foundational dispositions of social justice.

Structurally, the radical democratic school will be mindful of what might be called 'positional restlessness', that is to say, a libertarian and egalitarian insistence on the openness of opportunity, on the need to unsettle patterns and dispositions of presumption, and the need to open up much wider and more generous vistas of possibility for all members of a school community. Such a school will pursue a range of organisational articulations of participatory democracy at the heart of which lies an insistence on a permanent and proper provisionality. At both adult and student levels, this will include a permanent unease with hierarchy and a strong desire to create transparent structures that encourage ways of working that transcend boundaries and invite new combinations and possibilities.

There will also be substantial emphasis on the spatiality of democracy, on interpersonal and architectural spaces that encourage a variety of different forms of formal and informal engagement with a multiplicity of persons. These will include 'subaltern spaces' or spaces in which minority, marginalised or emergent groups can develop the confidence, capacity and dispositions that enable them to explore and name what is important to them and also gain the confidence and desire to engage with larger, different groups of people within and beyond the school community.

Pre-eminent amongst these other groups may be the School Meeting within which the whole school community will reflect on its shared life, achievements and aspirations. Here, young people and adults make meaning of their work together, returning tenaciously and regularly to the imperatives of purpose, not merely to the mechanics of accomplishment. Mindful of the challenges of difference, of identities as shifting and multiple, and of the recent re-emergence of group thinking and the perils of populism, we argue for an agonistic politics of radical democracy and a 'transformed conception of community' that arises from it.

Radical roles

Just as the structures and spaces within a common school practising a radical democratic education open up new possibilities, so too do the roles of those who work within them. True to the spirit of Roberto Unger's advocacy of 'role defiance and role jumbling', which we explore in the final chapter of our book, the radical democratic school will encourage this kind of fluidity and exploration, not only amongst staff but also between staff and students. It includes, amongst other things, a delight and belief in radical collegiality (Fielding, 1999), and inter-generational reciprocity that reflects deep-seated faith in the encounter between adults and young people as a potential source of mutual learning, not just in an instrumental, technical sense, but eventually in a wider existential and more fully educational sense.

Thus, in the re-emergence of the student voice movement over the past 15 years, student and staff roles have developed in a variety of significant ways hinted at by the sixfold typology below. The examples we cite are drawn both from work we have ourselves been involved in with schools and from published research studies.

Box 2.1

1. Students as data source
Staff utilise information about student progress and well-being

Classroom	*Unit/team/department*	*School*
• Lesson planning takes account of student test scores	• Samples of student work shared across staff group	• Student attitude survey

---

In Box 2.1, there is a real teacher commitment to pay attention to student voices speaking through the practical realities of work done and targets agreed. It acknowledges that for teaching and learning to improve there is a need to take more explicit account of relevant data about individual students and group or class achievement. At unit/team/department level, this way of working might express itself through, say, samples of student work being shared across a staff group, either as a form of moderation or, less formally, as part of a celebration of the range of work going on. At the whole school level, an example would be the now much more common practice of conducting an annual survey of student opinion on matters the school deems important.

In Box 2.2, staff move beyond the accumulation of passive data and, in order to deepen the learning of young people and enrich staff professional decisions, they feel a need to hear what students have to say about their own experience in lessons or their active engagement in contributing to its development via, for example, assessment

---

Box 2.2

---

2. Students as active respondents
Staff invite student dialogue and discussion to deepen learning/
professional decisions

Classroom	*Unit/team/department*	*School*
• Engaging with + adapting explicit assessment criteria	• Team agenda based on students' views/ evaluations	• Students on staff appointment panels

---

for learning approaches. Students are discussants rather than recipients of current approaches and thereby contribute to the development of teaching and learning in their school.

At unit/team/department level, this active respondent role might express itself through, say, every fourth meeting having a significant agenda item based on student views/evaluations of the work they have been doing. At whole school level, an example would be the inclusion of students in the appointment process for new staff.

Box 2.3

---

3. Students as co-enquirers
Staff take lead role with high-profile, active student support

---

Classroom	*Unit/team/department*	*School*
• How can we develop more independence in learning?	• Student evaluation of, e.g. History unit of work	• Joint evaluation of current system of Reports

---

In Box 2.3, we see an increase in both student and teacher involvement and a greater degree of partnership than in the previous two modes. Whilst student and teacher roles are not equal, they are shifting strongly in an egalitarian direction. Students move from being discussants to being co-enquirers into matters of agreed significance and importance. While the focus and the boundaries of exploration are fixed by the teacher, the commitment and agreement of students is essential. At a classroom level, we recall witnessing a wonderful infant school teacher ask her children what they felt independence in learning would look like if they saw it in a classroom. The ensuing discussion was recorded by the teacher to create, in effect, an observation schedule for the subsequent video recording of their work together. Teacher and children then sat down and looked at their joint work through the lens of their prior discussion, delighted in what they thought laudable and resolved to further develop ways of working that they thought would develop their adventure and both their independence and interdependence as learners. In the teacher's view, not only was this an important catalytic event for the class, it also revealed to her aspects of children's learning and her teaching that she would have been unlikely to have understood so deeply had she not involved her class as co-enquirers in what was, in effect, an elegant piece of classroom-based action research.

At unit/team/department level, this kind of approach might express itself through student evaluation of a unit of work, as, for example, undertaken by a group in a Portsmouth girls' secondary school calling themselves the 'History Dudettes'. At whole school level, an example would be a joint staff–student evaluation of the school system of reporting to parents on their children's progress.

Box 2.4

4. Students as knowledge creators
Students take lead role with active staff support

Classroom	*Unit/team/department*	*School*
• What seating arrangements assist in learning?	• Is the playground buddying system working?	• What is the cause of low-level bullying in class?

The development shown in Box 2.4 deepens and extends the egalitarian thrust of the co-enquiry approach. Partnership and dialogue remain the dominant ways of working, but here it is the voice of the student that comes to the fore in a leadership or initiating, not just a responsive, role. It is students who identify the issues to be researched and students who subsequently undertake the enquiry with the support of staff.

At classroom level, this has sometimes expressed itself through student-led research into what kinds of seating arrangements actually assist the learning processes in different year groups. At unit/team/department level, a good example comes from a School (Student) Council who were concerned that their playground buddying system was not working in the ways they had hoped. At whole school level, students in an innovative secondary school used photo-elicitation as part of their enquiry into the causes of low-level bullying that went largely undetected by staff (Thomson and Gunter, 2007).

The Joint Enquiry model shown in Box 2.5 involves a genuinely shared, fully collaborative partnership between students and staff. Leadership, planning and conduct of research and the subsequent commitment to responsive action are embraced as both a mutual responsibility and energising adventure.

At classroom level, this might express itself through the co-construction of, for example, a Maths lesson. At unit/team/department level, this might take the form of a Research Lesson (Dudley, 2007) in which, say, three staff and three students co-plan a lesson, observe it, meet to discuss the observation data, plan version two in the light of it and repeat the process. And all of this endeavour is undertaken on behalf of the

---

Box 2.5

---

5. Students as joint authors
Students and staff decide on a joint course of action together

---

Classroom	*Unit/team/department*	*School*
• Co-construct e.g. a Maths lesson	• Develop a 'Research Lesson' on behalf of dept	• Joint student + staff Learning Walk

---

team/department and their students. At whole school level, this kind of approach might express itself in a jointly-led Learning Walk (NCSL, 2005). Here a focus or centre of interest is agreed and the school (and any other participating school) becomes the site of enquiry within which the focused Walk is undertaken.

Finally, as shown in Box 2.6, the explicit commitment to participatory democracy and democratic fellowship extends the shared and collaborative partnership between students and staff in ways which (a) emphasise a joint commitment to the common good, and (b) include occasions and opportunities for an equal sharing of power and responsibility. At its best, it is an instantiation and explicit acknowledgement of the power and promise of inter-generational learning.

Box 2.6

---

6. Inter-generational learning as participatory democracy
Shared commitment to/responsibility for the common good

Classroom	*Unit/team/department*	*School*
• Students + staff plan lesson for younger students	• Classes as critical friends in thematic conference	• Whole School Meeting to decide a key issue

---

At classroom level, it might involve school staff, students and museum staff planning a visit to a museum for younger students. At unit/team/department level, this might take the form of classes acting as critical friends to each other within the wider context of a thematic or interdisciplinary project within and/or between years. At whole school level, this might express itself through the development of School Meetings that are such an important iconic practice within the radical traditions of both private education (e.g. the work of A.S. Neill at Summerhill (Neill, 1968) and David Gribble at Sands School (Gribble, 1998)) and public education (e.g. Alex Bloom at St George-in-the-East and Howard Case at Epping House School (Case, 1966)). Here, the participatory traditions of democracy find their fullest expression with key matters within the school decided on an equal basis by all Meeting members (Fielding, 2011, forthcoming).

Although all these examples of inter-generational learning and participatory democracy, and the radical roles for children and adults that attend them, come from the field of compulsory, and especially secondary, education, we can see them replicated by innovative early childhood education projects, such as Reggio Emilia, and the way these young students are understood and related to as citizens, and multi-lingual co-constructors of knowledge, researchers and experimenters. The consideration of radical roles can, indeed, be seen as one attempt to answer Loris Malaguzzi's foundational question: what is your image of the child?

Radical relationships

Just as the roles are more fluid and more diverse, so, within radical education the relationships between students and between adults and young people are not only less bounded and more exploratory, but also more openly informed by the dispositions and dynamics of care.

One aspect of a radical democratic practice in relational matters is caught by the notion of 'restless encounter'. Here, in tandem with the development of radical roles, is the development of radically different relationships to those that normally hold sway in schools. Such relationships enable us to 're-see' each other as persons rather than as role occupants, and in so doing nurture not only a new understanding, sense of possibility and felt respect between adults and young people, but also a joy in each other's being and a greater sense of shared delight and responsibility.

Another consequence of this relational re-centring of the educational process is that it enables us to look again at taken-for-granted aspects of the teaching and learning process and come to value them more profoundly and, as a consequence, engage with them more overtly and more deliberately. Our own advocacy of what we have elsewhere called 'the dialectic of the personal' (Fielding, 2000) is one which traces the mutually-conditioning interplay between the technical skills and the dialogic dispositions of teaching and learning.

An ethics and enactment of care are also more often than not dialogic in both form and intention and thus profoundly affect developments like student voice to which we have just alluded. Arguably, a dialogic approach to student voice – a pedagogy of listening – implies a fivefold, multifaceted engagement between adults and young people: first, a genuine openness towards each other, a reciprocity that is interested and attentive, rather than a cursory and incurious consultation; second, what we have elsewhere called a 'permanent provisionality', an understanding that we are not talking about a one-off event with little or no feedback or future engagement, but rather a pattern of continuing dialogue in which understandings and meanings are always open to new perspectives and interpretations and 'where you lose absolutely the possibility of controlling the final result' (Rinaldi, 2006, p. 184); third, a willingness to be surprised, to welcome the unanticipated as a mark of the partnership's potential to honour and deal with difference in ways that resist the silencing, homogenising tendencies of position and power; fourth, a pervasive rather than a compartmentalised approach, in which all young people in the school have many opportunities during the day for the kinds of encounters we have mentioned above. In contexts like these, student voice is neither exotic nor elitist; rather it is the lived expression of a shared delight and shared responsibility between adults and young people for a particular way of learning and living together. Lastly, a dialogic approach to student voice is, as much as any other, concerned about getting things done, about tackling real issues of current concern. However, it is also about how we make meaning together, how we understand the significance of our current work and our future aspirations.

These five elements of a dialogic approach all connect with a number of assumptions about education that see care and knowledge of persons as centrally important. Their pervasive reciprocity also nudge us away from the individualistic preoccupations of personalisation and high-performance schooling towards a person-centred approach that sees individual flourishing as intimately joyfully and necessarily bound up with relations with others, not as an instrumental lubricant for a smoother running organisation; towards a more communal orientation that sees democratic fellowship as both the means and the end of a broadly conceived, tenaciously intended radical education.

Personal and communal narrative

The notion of narrative is central to radical education in the democratic common school for at least two reasons. First, it is important both personally and communally because it connects in a fundamental way with one of the core processes of education, namely with the making of meaning. Narrative learning is mindful of the fragility of human endeavour, the need for recognition and significance, not in any flashy or self-aggrandising sense, but rather in terms of the moral and educational legitimacy of one's endeavours. It is precisely because narrative is about making meaning that the needs it expresses and the aspirations it voices lie at the heart of anything that can properly be called an educational undertaking.

Education is first and finally about how we learn to lead good lives together, lives that enable us individually and collectively to survive and flourish. Without some means of recreating a constant link to those profound matters of purpose, education becomes impossible and we have to make do with the thin and dispiriting substitutes of competitive schooling. As one head teacher remarked to us recently '[p]ersonal histories are tremendously important – giving yourself permission to have conversations with yourself. Keeping a handle on the past and what is right'.

Within the radical democratic school, there will be multiple spaces and opportunities for individuals, both young people and adults, to make meaning of their work, both personally and as a community. Indeed, the two are connected. The anthropology of the self presumed by most radical traditions of education is communal rather than atomistic. The anthropology of the 'transformed' notion of community for which we argued earlier is one that honours difference and presumes the sanctity of the individual person. Moreover, these multiple spaces and opportunities will recognise and support narrative as meaning-making, using the full range of the hundred languages of childhood.

The second reason narrative is important has to do with the necessary connection with history, with the radical traditions of education within which the work of the democratic school is located. Not only does history have much to teach its contemporary inheritors in a cautionary sense, it also provides many examples of counter-hegemonic significance and power that remind us not only of what has been but also that, in Terry Wrigley's resonant phrase, '[a]nother school is possible' (Wrigley, 2007). As Russell Jacoby so acutely observes, 'society has lost its memory, and with it, its mind. The inability or refusal to think back takes its toll in the inability to think' (Jacoby, 1997, pp. 3–4). In the decade and a half since Jacoby's remarks, things have got worse rather than better. With the preparation and continuing professional development of teachers becoming more and more focused on technologies of self and refinements of a frighteningly appropriate and increasingly compliant 'delivery', so professional engagement with alternative perspectives and possibilities rooted in philosophical and historical exploration of matters of enduring profundity and significance has all but ceased.

Radical curriculum, critical pedagogy and enabling assessment

At the heart of radical education's approach to the formal and informal curriculum must lie four imperatives. The first is a focus on the purposes of education, organising the curriculum around that which is necessary for a sustainable, flourishing and democratic way of life. The second has to do with the necessity of equipping young people and adults with the desire and capacity to seriously and critically interrogate what is given and co-construct a knowledge that assists us in leading good and joyful lives together. The third argues that whilst knowledge must transcend the local, it must, nonetheless, start with the cultures, concerns and hopes of the communities that the school serves. Lastly, whilst perhaps not a requirement of a radical curriculum, a consequence of taking these first three desiderata seriously leads to a curriculum that emphasises connectedness that is holistic in approach and organised around interconnected and interdisciplinary themes or areas, rather than separate subjects; and that encourages integrated forms of enquiry with students and staff working in small communities of enquiry, for example undertaking the kind of project or topic work described in our two cases at the start of Chapter 1.

Interestingly, this approach, which reached its apogee in compulsory schooling in England in the 1970s, is now undergoing, if not a revival (since our contemporary amnesiac culture denies both the fact and the power of history) then an unwitting return to integrated and interdisciplinary curricula, with two recent reports on primary education in England (Cambridge Primary Review, 2009; Rose, 2009) favouring a move away from discrete subjects towards wider 'areas of knowledge' or 'domains'. This is also one of the areas where compulsory education has much to gain through a strong and equal partnership with early childhood education, where interconnected approaches are more likely to be found (see, for example, the widely acclaimed New Zealand early childhood curriculum, *Te Whāriki*, literally 'a woven mat', with its strong emphasis on relationships, reciprocity, community, culture and language (New Zealand Ministry of Education, 1996)).

A critical pedagogy of a radical curriculum will develop a reciprocity of engagement and involvement not only with the immediate community, but also reach out to other communities, other ways of being, at a local, regional, national and international level.

Encounter with and delight in difference within the context of democratic values is central to the kinds of radical curriculum and pedagogy typical of the democratic common school.

When radical approaches to the curriculum have worked well, they have invariably been enabled by forms of assessment at both national and local levels that have had the flexibility to respond to the particularities of context and significant professional involvement of teachers in the assessment, moderation and examination process (for example, the Mode 3 system of examining in secondary schools in England in the 1970s and 1980s). At classroom level, they have incorporated high levels of peer and teacher involvement through assessment-for-learning approaches and additional community and family involvement through public, portfolio-based presentations. Once again, the compulsory education sector might have much to learn from the experience of early childhood education, in particular the latter's use of pedagogical documentation as a participatory process of evaluation that keeps open the issue of outcome rather than confining evaluation to the standardised and predefined.

Insistent affirmation of possibility

One of the most important confluences of the libertarian and egalitarian impulses that inform our advocacy in Chapter 4 of prefigurative practice is the insistent, persistent affirmation of possibility. Energised both by rage against 'the abandonment of ordinary humanity to perpetual belittlement' (Unger, 2005, p. 46) and by profound belief in the powers of ordinary men and women to create new and better ways of being in the world, this generosity of presumption requires us to keep options open, to counter the confinement of customary or casual expectation. This belief in the 'powers of ordinary men and women' is a key feature of radical education.

In the last chapter of their classic book *Education and the Struggle for Democracy*, Wilfred Carr and Michael Hartnett affirm that

> despite its portrayal as an institution of democratic education, all the evidence suggests that the comprehensive school has reinforced rather than challenged those non-democratic aspects of the English education tradition – exclusiveness, separation, segregation – that have always frustrated democratic educational advance.
>
> (Carr and Hartnett, 1996, p. 194)

Within the radical tradition, addressing these matters of 'exclusiveness, separation, segregation' is of paramount importance. So, too, is the insistence on keeping options open, on resisting closure, on a generosity of presumption that assumes the best rather than the worst of young people.

Thus, as we saw in Chapter 1 at St George-in-the-East, as in many other schools within the radical democratic tradition, there was a substantial attempt to replace the debilitating influence of fear as the prime incentive to 'progress'. For head teacher Alex Bloom, '[f]ear of authority [. . . imposed for disciplinary purposes]; fear of failure [. . . by means of marks, prizes and competition, for obtaining results]; and the fear of punishment [for all these purposes]' must be replaced by 'friendship, security and the recognition of each child's worth' (Bloom, 1952, pp. 135–36). Of the impediments mentioned, Bloom had a particular distaste for competition, arguing not only that it was unethical, but that it tended to destroy a communal spirit (for a philosophical companion piece see Fielding, 1976a, b). Indeed, a communally-oriented school does not need the artificial stimulus of 'carrots and goads': in such a school the children will

> come to realize the self that is theirs and respect the self that is their neighbour's. And because there are neither carrots nor goads, there will be no donkeys, for when children are treated as we would have them be, they tend to reach out accordingly.
>
> (Bloom, 1949, p. 171)

Finally, as was seen to be of paramount importance by many of the radical pioneers like Brian Simon, at St George-in-the-East there was no streaming or setting. For Simon, as for many others subsequently, not only were the presumptions of this kind of labelling false, its administration was more often than not crudely wayward, and its consequences deeply damaging (see Hart *et al.*, 2004, Chapter 2). For these and other reasons, an insistent affirmation of possibility denies the legitimacy of ability grouping, promotes emulation rather than competition, and prefers intrinsic motivation and communal recognition to the paraphernalia of marks and prizes. Loris Malaguzzi's image of the rich child born with a hundred languages could serve as the banner head for the affirmation of possibility.

Engaging the local

There are a number of reasons why a confident and expansive reciprocity between the school and its local community is of fundamental importance to radical education. Some of these reasons are philosophical and have to do with a view of radical education that sees education as a lifelong process and the school as a site of community renewal and responsibility in which young and old explore what it means to lead good lives together. Some of the most impressive work in this regard comes from developments like the Living Archive project in Milton Keynes (www.livingarchive.org.uk), where different generations make meaning out of an emergent, shared history – in one particular case, the chance discovery of a set of letters from an ordinary soldier in the First World War, which was later dramatised and enacted at a local school's community theatre and also published as a book (Mundy, 1991).

Others reasons for underscoring the nexus of the local are more pragmatic. Here, the community and the school are seen as reciprocal resources for broadly and more narrowly conceived notions of learning. If this is to become a living reality, it requires school and community to problematise institutional boundaries and thereby encourage a mutual re-seeing of presumed identities. They need each other more fully and more insistently if they are to thrive, both in the hurly-burly of the here-and-now, and in the excitement of an organically shared and mutually shaped future.

Alex Bloom was at the forefront of developments to involve parents in a whole range of ways and the school was often both host to and the driving force behind local cultural and communal events. He also earned the love of the community in less formal ways, for example, by providing warmth and shelter at the school long before it formally opened for lessons in the morning; by ensuring good-quality meals were served for all at lunchtime; by his deep knowledge of the families and the struggles they faced; and by his care and compassion for individuals – there are numerous accounts of students without adequate footwear being bought shoes by Bloom himself.

Similarly, the municipal schools in Reggio Emilia have a close, reciprocal engagement with their local community, both immediately around the school but also with the wider city, with which both children and adults strongly identify. This close relationship is typified by an invitation to one of Reggio's schools, for three- to six-year-olds, to design and create a theatre curtain for a historical city theatre. Vea Vecchi, the atelieristas involved, remembers that:

> it was 1998 and the project was a courageous one, both for Antonio Canova who was director of the Reggio Theatres and suggested the project with Mayor Antonella Spiaggiari's enthusiastic approval, and for us who accepted because it was by no means a simple thing to create a work beautiful enough to be housed in an important nineteenth century theatre like the Ariosto ... For those who would like to know more about the project work and the creation of the curtain there is a book which recounts the story (Vecchi, 2002). But here I wish to underline ... that in order to receive a request of this nature, which I believe to be the only one of its kind in the world, Reggio schools, and in this particular case the atelier, had gained the trust of part of the city.
>
> (Vecchi, 2010, p. 156)

Accountability as shared responsibility

In arguing, as we are in this book, for the twin imperatives of educational renewal and public responsibility, we are nudging the notion of responsibility into a different philosophical and practical territory. Responsibility takes on a particular form here and connects with alternative understandings of accountability more suited to participatory rather than representative traditions of democracy (Fielding, 2001b).[4] 'High energy' notions of democratic accountability are better understood and enacted as forms of 'shared responsibility' – such as was vividly illustrated by the opening case of Reggio Emilia, where a large urban community has taken responsibility for the education of its young children. Understood in this democratic way, accountability is morally and politically situated, not merely technically and procedurally 'delivered'. It makes a claim on our ethical and civic responsibilities, which cannot be adequately understood or provided for by an entirely delegated mandate (to experts or managers), which provides too convenient and too corrosive an absolution. One important corollary of the democratic school is, thus, the requirement that we develop new forms of accountability better suited to a more engaged understanding of democratic living.

We cannot know what we are responsible for in anything other than a thin, box-ticking sense unless we return to shared educational purposes and from there co-author an account of core beliefs and the kinds of practices we believe will exemplify their realisation in an appropriately demanding and life-affirming way. Young people can and should be involved in such process, a good example being at Bishops Park College, Clacton, a school for 11- to 16-year-olds in England where, towards the end of its radical phase of development, it developed a Research Forum out of which emerged a framework of aspirations and practices that formed the basis of the College's accountability framework (Fielding *et al.*, 2006). The Research Forum comprised a core group of students, parents, governors, school staff and a small university research and development team.

What is particularly pertinent to this context is the way in which relationships between adults and young people changed over time. Both began to see each other with new eyes. The shared desire to explore matters of some significance and work in new ways led, in many instances and on a number of occasions, not only to respectful and appreciative encounters and new understandings, but also to mutual advocacy of and delight in inter-generational working. It also produced a remarkable document, which exemplified the kind of shared responsibility for which we are arguing.

Pedagogical documentation, as practised in Reggio Emilia (and many other places), which as we saw in Chapter 1 gives 'the possibility to discuss and dialogue "everything with everyone"', by making learning and learning processes visible and subject to deliberation, provides a further example of how the notion of a community taking responsibility for the education of its children can be pursued through to the level of the individual school and its everyday projects and practices. Such shared responsibility is not only a form of democratic accountability, but also a means of collective learning, as Carlina Rinaldi describes:

> By means of documenting, the thinking – or the interpretation – of the documenter thus becomes material, that is tangible and capable of being interpreted. The notes, the recordings, the slides and photographs represent fragments of a memory . . . [which are] offered to the interpretive subjectivity of others in order to be known or reknown, created and recreated, also as a collective knowledge-building event. The result is knowledge that is bountiful and enriched by the contribution of many . . . We are looking at a new concept of didactics: participatory didactics, didactics as procedures and processes that can be communicated and shared.
>
> (Rinaldi, 2006, p. 69)

Regional, national and global solidarities

Lastly, education in and for a radical democracy must learn the lessons of its own histories. Too often brave, imaginative and important work has been lost or weakened by the failure not just to connect with the local, but by the failure to take the strategic imperatives of the socialist tradition sufficiently seriously. Regional, national and global solidarities need to be made real and telling by building reciprocal ideological, material and interpersonal support through values-driven networks and alliances which draw on and contribute to the dynamic of radical social movements.

Over a ten-year-period, Alex Bloom was, in significant part, able to develop one of the most overtly democratic, radical secondary schools England has ever seen because of the multiple solidarities, alliances and networks to which he both belonged and contributed (Fielding, 2008b). In addition to huge support from his local community to which we have already referred, the school was used by a range of teacher training colleges. Despite some opposition at local office level, Bloom was supported by some key figures in the higher echelons of the London County Council e.g. Hubert Child, at the time their Chief Educational Psychologist and later an eminent head of Dartington Hall, one of England's most prestigious private progressive schools. Bloom also addressed national conferences on the potential of the, then, new secondary modern schools and was strongly supported by leading educational figures such as James Hemming who was at that time a research officer for the Association for Education in Citizenship. The school frequently hosted a huge number of overseas visitors from countries all across the world, largely through Bloom's long-standing, active membership of the New Education Fellowship and the articles on St George's that appeared in its journal, *New Era*.

The municipal schools and the whole educational project of Reggio Emilia provide an even more striking example of the possibilities of building regional, national and global solidarities to express and sustain radical education. Within Italy, the Reggio project was part of a wider movement – 'a municipal school revolution' (Catarsi, 2004, p. 8) – which led to many local authorities across Northern Italy creating their own services for young children in the 1960s and 1970s. Reggio Emilia is, Rinaldi observes, just 'one of many places which expresses the vitality, wealth and quality of Italian pedagogical research and courageous investment in services for early childhood' (Rinaldi, 2006, p. 102). And while each municipal project has its own distinct identity, differentiating it from others, enough is held in common to ensure the development of a network of supportive municipal relationships.

In the case of Reggio Emilia, as we saw in Chapter 1, this solidaristic network spreads beyond Italy, through a global community of individuals, centres and national 'Reggio networks', who are in active relationship with the Italian city. The network takes tangible form in the much-travelled Reggio exhibition, accompanied by speakers from the municipal schools; the numerous study visits by groups from around the world to Reggio; and in Reggio's Loris Malaguzzi International Centre, opened in 2006 and intended to represent and support international relationships and dissemination, and also to support developments and changes in Reggio itself (Vecchi, 2010). In such ways, Reggio Emilia provides a vivid example of how local projects can connect to form global social movements that can contest and resist dominant discourses.

3   The democratic common school

In the new public education system the school must be a place for everyone, a meeting place in the physical and also the social, cultural and political sense of the word. A forum or site for meeting and relating, where children and adults meet and commit to something, where they can dialogue, listen, and discuss in order to share meanings: it is a place of infinite cultural, linguistic, social, aesthetic, ethical, political and economic possibilities. A place of ethical and political praxis, a space for democratic learning. A place for research and creativity, coexistence and pleasure, critical thought and emancipation.

(Associació de Mestres Rosa Sensat, 2005, p. 10)

It is preferable for a state school admission system to be based on locality. Schools are cohering local institutions, for richer, for poorer, and that is how admission is determined across most of the globe. If aptitude or ability are to be criteria . . . let the tests be public and fair. It is not reasonable for admission to be based on parental class, background, faith or group affiliation. Those who want such schools can pay for them . . . Children should go to their local school, primary and secondary, warts and all.

(Jenkins, 2009)

In this chapter, we consider some implications for the school of adopting a radical democratic approach to education. In the last chapter, we considered some of radical education's images or understandings of the school: a public institution, a public space, a place of encounter, a collaborative workshop, a person-centred learning community and a place of democratic educational fellowship. We also looked at some ways in which a school might practise commitment to democracy, proposing indicators for the presence of a radical education. Now we turn to consider what form a school for radical education might take – at how it might be organised and structured, at how it might be staffed, at how admissions might be determined and at relationships with other schools and the local community.

We focus our attention on one possibility, which we believe is best-suited to and supportive of radical education: what we call the 'common school'. Others may have their contenders, and there is plenty of scope for further discussion, experimentation and evaluation. We shall start by explaining how we envisage a common school, to give the reader some initial idea of what we are talking about; for we are not just talking about existing schools with a different admission policy, we are envisaging a school that is very different from the commonplace in England today.

Although we have strong reasons for using the term 'common school', and an emotional attachment to the term, we also realise it can give rise to misunderstandings: for example, that a common school is an ordinary school, a 'common-or-garden' school that lacks identity or distinction; or that it is a standard, 'one size fits all' school or that it denies or tramples on diversity. None of these, we shall argue, need be the case. Indeed, our idea of the common school starts from a profound respect for otherness and singularity and a desire to experiment, to create new knowledge and new projects. A common school can – and indeed in our understanding, should – have a distinctive identity and be a place that welcomes and nourishes diversity. It is important, too, to emphasise from the start that, from the perspective of radical education, the common school is a *radical democratic* common school, and that this descriptor should always be read into our use of the term.

We will address some other issues raised by the concept. If, as we contend, a common school is a site for democratic practice, what does this mean in practice? What form of governance is suited to the common school and what should be the relationship between the democratic school and democratic political structures? What are the implications of the common school for equality and parental choice? Having wrestled with these questions, we will then suggest some signs that we think would be indicative of a school practising radical education.

We illustrate our ideas about the common school with a number of examples presented in boxes in the text. The first two boxes, we should make clear, are not accounts of actual children's centres or schools. Rather we have constructed vignettes, drawing on our experience of various centres and schools; we think this offers greater clarity about the potential of the types of service exemplified, as well as avoiding the problems of putting particular 'real live' places in the spotlight. So we offer imagined pictures of how these settings might work, but all grounded in actual experiences.

In defence of the school

But before we start on this exploration of the common school, and respond further to one of the libertarian critiques of progressivism, we need to make clear our belief in the continuing importance of the school itself as a unique and vital public institution, by which we mean a real school, a physical environment occupying a real public space, serving (as the quotation that starts this chapter puts it) as 'a meeting place in the physical but also the social, cultural and political sense of the word'. Our need to justify the school is also called for because we are aware of work on future scenarios for schooling (e.g. by OECD), which includes removing the existing school system, to a greater or lesser degree, for example 'the abandonment of schools in favour of a multitude of learning networks . . . The de-institutionalisation, even dismantling, of schools as part of an emerging "network society"' (OECD, 2003). We are also aware of movements to increase home-based education, undertaken by parents, which add further to our recognition that the school cannot be taken for granted.

As we have already made clear, our support for the future of 'real' schools is conditional. We do not offer a blank cheque and realise the potentially dangerous nature of the school as a place for the incessant surveillance and intensifying governing of children and indeed, their educators in ever more effective ways. As schools open longer hours, as they offer more services and projects, as they are offered more 'human technologies', so they become potentially more dangerous.

But the common school, as described later, practising radical education, as discussed in the previous chapter, does get our vote. For the school can and should represent something very special in modern societies: the only public institution to which nearly everyone is affiliated for a sustained period during part of their lives, whether as a child or parent – 'cohering local institutions' as Simon Jenkins puts it at the beginning of the chapter. In an increasingly fragmented world, this makes the school not only special but an invaluable site of encounter, exchange and relationship between citizens, both younger and older. Their near universal reach makes schools potentially dangerous places for exercising control and normalisation, places for governing children and adults alike: hence, the necessity of practising radical democratic education. But, they also have tremendous potential for good, as places for education-in-its-broadest-sense, as communities for the practice and sustenance of care and democracy, and as institutions for supporting solidarity and cooperation.

If, as Michael Apple argues, 'public institutions are the defining features of a caring and democratic society' (Apple, 2005, p. 18), then the school is the most important and ubiquitous of public institutions. But this key role of cohering public institution is under threat from what Tony Judt describes as 'a cult of privatisation [that] has mesmerised Western [and many non-Western] governments' (2009, p. 5) over the last 30 years, as education has become commodified, parents have been reconstituted as consumers and the school itself has been recast as a business. We turn the school into a private institution – a business selling a commodity to consumers in a competitive market – at our collective peril.

The common school: what do we mean?

At its most basic, we mean a school that is open to and attended by all citizens living in its local catchment area, children, young people and adults, without admission criteria, except residence, and without specialisms that enforce selective attendance. We mean a 'comprehensive school' – except that term has come to be associated, at least in England, with huge schools for a limited age range of children: a large-scale institution for secondary education. Strangely, in England, we have never referred to 'primary schools' as 'comprehensive schools', even though they often operate an open admission policy and are for all local children, their main difference being that they operate on a much smaller scale and with younger children than 'comprehensive' secondary schools. We use the term 'common school', therefore, to distinguish our concept of the comprehensive school from the form today's comprehensive school takes, because there are some distinctive differences in detail, and not because we reject the principles and aspirations of this important experience. We want to go beyond today's comprehensive school, and not turn our backs on it.

The common school is age integrated

For us, a common school would be 'comprehensive' not only in terms of admissions, being for everyone in its catchment area, but also because it broke down many of the age barriers that define children's education and separate educational institutions in England (but also many other countries) – typically at three, when 'nursery' education begins; then at five, or often earlier, when 'primary' education begins in 'reception class'; then at 11 or 12, when 'secondary' education begins. The common school would be more age-integrated than most current provision, with various options available. For example, there could be a common school for children below school age, both under and over three, along the lines of the imagined Children's Centre described in Box 3.1. Another example would be a common school for children across the compulsory school period, from 5 or 6 to 16 years. In Box 3.2 we offer a third option, using the example of a Swedish school covering the compulsory school period, but also responsible for 'pre-schools', centres for children from one to five years. Schools in Sweden increasingly include grades 1 to 9 plus pre-school classes (for six-year-olds), sharing the same site, resources and with the same *rektor* (or head teacher), and often too including one or more pre-schools; in 2008, these age-integrated schools took 35 per cent of all pupils (Skolverket, 2009).[5] We also note a recent English report that draws attention to 'a growing interest throughout the education community in the innovative re-organisation of schools', and adds that 'many heads are setting up all-age institutions'(Innovation Unit, 2006, p. 2).

Box 3.1 The Children's Centre in 2020

The Children's Centre is situated in an inner-city neighbourhood, and serves all families with children below compulsory school age (recently increased to six years) within a catchment area, defined as being within easy 'pram pushing' distance. It is run by a voluntary organisation, with public funding, while the neighbouring Children's Centre is run by the local authority; both have democratically chosen management committees with representation from parents, staff, local authority and the immediate community. These two Centres, plus a third nearby, cooperate closely and share the services of a *'pedagogista'*, or educational coordinator. The *pedagogista*, a former Children's Centre director herself and part of a local authority team of *pedagogistas*, provides support and critical friendship for each Centre, develops connections between Centres and other services, and contributes to the development of the local authority's educational project for young children. This coordination function emphasises dialogue and collaboration between local authority, Centres, staff and families.

At the heart of the Centre, and an integral part of it, is education for children from the earliest age, understood as being education in its broadest sense, combining learning, care and 'upbringing' and a concern for overall development

---

and well-being. Parents can decide when their children access this education and for how long, the Centre being open all day from 8 to 6. Attendance is free for a period equivalent to a school day, after which parents make an income-related contribution to costs. About half the staff engaged in this work at the Centre are qualified 'early years' teachers, with a graduate education and a specialisation in working with children from birth to six years, and their families.

Education is just one part of the Centre's remit. It offers a wide range of other projects, in response to the needs, conditions and interests of the community it serves. A child welfare clinic operates out of the centre, with a paediatrician and health visitor. There are various groups for parents – social, educational, cultural, health – including a parent and toddler group for parents who want to spend time with their children at the Centre before feeling ready to leave their children. Twice a month, a solicitor holds a session offering legal advice, and there is also advice and support for parents who want to re-enter education or employment. The Centre works hard to reach all parents in its catchment area, with staff visiting each new parent or newcomer to the area to tell them about the Centre and invite them to use its facilities.

This outreach work together with the responsive and welcoming services offered by the Centre have led to the Centre providing services for nearly all families with young children in its catchment area. Only a handful of parents choose to use alternative services, including a few local childminders (who receive support from the Centre).

Note on vignette: the Children's Centre envisaged earlier combines elements from a Children's Centre opened in London in the early 1970s (a time when a number of such integrated services were opened by people and organisations wanting to experiment with new forms of provision), from the former English government's Children's Centre programme, which aimed to provide multi-purpose Centres throughout the country by 2010, and hopes for the future. These hopes include increasing compulsory school age to six years; the offer of a 'school day' period of free attendance for children both under and over three years; and an integrated early years workforce based on graduate early years teachers. The original thinking behind the 1970s Centre was that this would become the main form of provision for all young children and their families across the country – a common school for young children. In its modern manifestation, however, the Children's Centre is just one form of provision in a market-based and fragmented mix of early childhood services, dominated by private for-profit nurseries focused on 'childcare for working parents'; and an array of playgroups and school-based nursery classes providing part-time education mainly for three- and four-year-olds. The vignette also envisages an important role for local authorities, both as major providers of Centres but also in the development and support of educational projects and services.

Box 3.2 The Swedish School

Lindgren school is situated in a suburban local authority, whose population of 28,000 (far smaller than comparable authorities in England but an average size for Sweden) is served by ten schools provided by the local authority and two private but publicly-funded schools. The school takes children from 1 to 16 years, all under one management and governing body. It includes three pre-schools, for children from 12 months to 6 years, though only one is on the school site, and has recently extended its upper age limit to include the top three year grades, i.e. from 13 to 15 years. This is part of the local authority policy that schools should be taking the full compulsory school age range. At 16, pupils move on to gymnasium, upper secondary school; 95 per cent of 16- to 19-year-olds in Sweden attend gymnasia.

Including its three pre-schools, the school has 550 children; 100 in the pre-schools, with the remaining 450 from pre-school class (6-year-olds) to grade 9 (15-year-olds). Young people leaving grade 9 go on to a separate gymnasium, or 'upper secondary school'. The school has been structured into four work units (*arbetslag*): (i) two of the three pre-schools; (ii) one pre-school + pre-school classes and grade 1 classes; (iii) grades 2 to 5 classes; and (iv) grades 6 to 9 classes. A fifth unit is being set up, organised around a newly built 'centre for aesthetics, domestic science and PE', equipped for woodwork, metal work, sewing, arts and crafts, domestic science and music; what might be thought of as a cluster of *ateliers* (though this term is not used). The staff working in this new unit were previously attached to the grades 6 to 9 unit, but are now forming a separate team with their own leader who sees this unit providing opportunities for doing cross-school project work.

The three existing and school-based units are staffed as follows:

- *Unit 1 (1 to 7 year olds)*: a work unit leader (*arbetslagsledare*) is responsible for a pre-school with 32 children and 93 other children in two pre-school classes and two grade 1 classes. The pre-school has 5.25 full-time equivalent (FTE) posts, 2 pre-school teachers and 4 *barnskotare*. A team of ten staff work with the 93 pre-school class and grade 1 children – two pre-school teachers, five free-time pedagogues and three school teachers, one of whom spends 0.6 of her time as unit leader, the remainder as a class teacher.
- *Unit 2 (8 to 11 years; grades 2 to 5)*: a work unit leader is responsible for 200 children, ranging from 32 in grade 3 to 65 in grade 5. There are 15 staff (14.3 FTE), including one assistant (one of only two in the school), three free-time pedagogues and ten teachers, one of whom works full-time as unit leader (along with school-wide responsibility for reading and writing). The smaller number of free-time pedagogues, compared to Unit 1,

reflects the fall off in children using free-time services after grade 3 (at which stage, children increasingly choose not to use the service).

- *Unit 3 (12 to 15 years; grades 6 to 9)*: a work unit leader is responsible for 150 children, with a staff of 16, comprising one assistant and the remainder teachers. The unit leader is introducing a new structure, dividing this unit into three smaller units: the first to consist of three classes (grades 7 to 9) with a group of teachers; the second of four classes (grades 6 to 9) with another group of teachers; the third of some specialist teachers, e.g. domestic science, music. The unit leader thinks the current work unit, with 15 teachers, is too big for making decisions and smaller groups could more easily work as teams.

There are only two classroom assistants throughout the whole school, and no midday or lunch-time assistants. Teachers or free-time pedagogues eat with the children from their work unit and supervise their play time. The school is open from 7 a.m. to 6 p.m. (and also during holidays), with a designated school period from 8 a.m. to 2 p.m. – though the *rektor* questions what sense this makes in an otherwise fully-integrated school. However, there is no separate 'wraparound care' with distinct staff and space; apart from a short period at the beginning and end of the day, when the relatively few children at the school are together in one group, free-time provision is based in and around the *arbetslag*. Pre-school teachers and free-time pedagogues are with the children outside the school period of the day but also work with children alongside teachers during school hours.

For example, a free-time pedagogue in one of the work units has a deep interest in art; she has her own art room, and, during the main school day, groups of children from the classes within the *arbetslag* came to her on a regular basis for art activities. She also takes groups out into local woods, 'to listen to the birds, to smell and feel nature' and assists teachers with project work. She offers woodwork and art activities during free-time hours. Another free-time pedagogue is a sports specialist within the main school day and during free-time hours; but he also contributes particular expertise in emotional and social support, through play and small-group work.

In addition to the work unit staff, the school has a school nurse, working four days a week, and a *kurator*, or counsellor, both employed by the school. The school *rektor*, the work unit leaders, school nurse and *kurator* constitute a 'pupil care team' (*elevvårdsteam, EVT*) which meets twice a week to discuss children who are causing concern and whose needs *arbetslag* teams feel unable to meet any longer.

Note on vignette: this vignette is based on one particular Swedish school, with examples of free-time pedagogues taken from a neighbouring school (for further discussion of this model, see Johansson and Moss, forthcoming).

Some age-integrated schools might provide sixth form and further education facilities. In most cases, however, we envisage the model of the separate sixth form college or (as in many other European countries) the gymnasium, catering to 16- to 19-year-olds. But age-integrated schools might well provide a range of adult education facilities, alongside a range of other providers.

The common school is small scale

So our common school would be age-integrated to a greater degree than many of today's schools, removing some of the transitions between schools that are currently required of children in England, especially the big move between relatively small primary schools and large secondary schools. Wouldn't such age-integrated common schools be even larger than many of today's comprehensive schools, with 1,000 or more pupils? No. Our Swedish example in Box 3.2 describes a school that is not only age-integrated, from 1 to 16 years, but also small in scale, a few hundred children, and this is not unusual in that country – in 2005, Swedish schools averaged 203 children and only 1.4 per cent had more than 700.

The same is true in other parts of the Nordic world. Wrigley notes that 'only one in ten secondary schools in Finland has more than 500, and half are smaller than 300, yet standards are clearly good . . . [While] there is a massive drive in the USA towards smaller schools and schools-within-schools' (Wrigley, 2007, p. 6). Arguing for 'alternative structures within comprehensive schools which provide a better sense of belonging, of community', Wrigley adds that the international research evidence 'shows convincingly that small schools have fewer drop-outs and evictions, fewer alienated young people, and are particularly more beneficial, including academically, for working class and ethnic minority pupils' (ibid.).

A small or human scale school is so for a reason: to create an environment that enables and deepens a particular concept of education. For the common school to function as the sort of public institution that we envisage, and as a site for radical education, it has to be organised on a scale that supports this functioning by being conducive to democratic practice and relationships and an ethics of care and encounter. These are not new arguments. Our earlier engagement with G. D. H. Cole's key notion of democratic fellowship (Cole 1950, p. 95) brings together the discourses and preoccupations of social justice and of care and insists that the arrangements of participatory democracy are best-suited to meeting both because they provide the means and the motivation for people to get to know each other and care for each other as persons. For Cole:

> [t]hat is why real democracies have either to be small, or broken up into small human groups in which men and women can know and love one another. If human societies get too big, and are not broken up in that way, the human spirit goes out of them; and the spirit of democracy goes out too.
>
> (Cole, 1950, p. 99)

Just as atomistic notions of representative democracy will forever and inevitably be compromised by the failure of their intellectual and historical conception so too will large schools, unless they are broken down into smaller units. A radical democratic common school is thus a school that takes seriously the challenge of size and the need for interpersonal and physical spaces for learning, for teaching, for the construction of identities and for the making of meaning.

This is an argument that has received renewed attention within education in the last 25 years, since the advent of Ted Sizer's *Horace's Compromise* (Sizer, 1984) and the development of the Coalition of Essential Schools in the US and the parallel English tradition that eventually became *Human Scale Education*. Human Scale Education (HSE), a UK organisation, calls in its *Practical Manifesto for Education on a Human Scale* for 'schools or learning communities of 250 to 300 students' (St George's, it will be recalled, was 260), organised around teams of four to six teachers and other staff. Their organisational proposal is based on what is needed to implement what they deem to be three core values: the primacy of human relationships, respect for the individual and the importance of community – specifically a democratic community. Mary Tasker, writing for HSE, argues that:

> [m]ost teachers would embrace these values and they feature in many school mission statements as desirable educational goals. It is, however, Human Scale Education's belief that they are difficult, almost impossible to achieve in a large school where young people are not known as individuals . . . The fundamental argument for small schools and a human scale approach to learning is that children and young people need to be known as individuals and not as part of a mass.
>
> (Tasker, 2008, pp. 7–8)

James Wetz, a former head teacher, concerned that large secondary schools contribute to many children leaving schools without qualifications, argues for 'urban village schools' on a human scale: 'based on a learning community of 350 pupils, where staff teach no more than 75 pupils a week, the urban village school will put relationships at the heart of its organisation and design' (http://www.gulbenkian.org.uk/publications/education/urban-village-schools). Similar arguments have persuaded another recent UK advocate of small (or smaller) schools. Writing about secondary schools, Charles Leadbeater has also come to the conclusion that 'learning should be organised around relationships'. From this basis, he too argues for smaller schools:

> There is no straightforward link between school size and attainment. But smaller schools within schools make it easier to personalise learning and build relationships . . . The average English secondary school has about 1000 pupils . . . The Government should announce the end of the large and monolithic secondary school. All pupils should be taught in schools within schools – no more than 500 pupils – which are small enough for them to form sustainable relationships for learning.
>
> (Leadbeater, 2008, pp. 55, 57)

Leadbeater's mention of 'schools-within-schools' (SWS) refers to a model that takes size and the centrality of certain kinds of human relationships seriously, and does so in ways which enable diversity within a common framework of democratic values and aspirations. There is still much work to be done in this area, in particular the necessity of revisiting the more overtly political and generally much more radical manifestation of SWS developed in the 1970s in the now largely forgotten work of John Watts (1977, 1980a, b), Michael Armstrong and Lesley King (1977), Richard Evans (1983), and Richard Martin and Jeni Smith (1979) at Countesthorpe Community College, Leicestershire; and in the US by Lawrence Kohlberg and his colleagues at Harvard University (see, for example, Mosher, 1980; Reed, 1997; also Box 3.3). More pragmatically, 'schools-within-schools' points to one solution to the dilemma of what to do with today's massive secondary schools in England if a 'small schools' policy were pursued. We offer examples of the model in Box 3.3, but there are many variants proposed and in existence.

Box 3.3 Schools-within-schools (SWS)

These schools can take many forms. In a paper for *Human Scale Education*, Mike Davies, a pioneer of schools-within-schools in England, outlines nine possible models, ranging from five autonomous schools sharing a building to a series of generic home base areas with access to a range of multi-provider, experiential centres. Although the models vary on a number of dimensions (e.g. curriculum, teacher organisation, sites of learning, etc), they have much in common:

> Throughout the range of schools there is a commitment to fewer hierarchical structures, more empowerment and the taking of decisions at the point and context of action – that is, decisions taken by those directly involved which frequently includes the students. It is, however, the commitment to relationships, to reducing alienation, to promoting identity and to recognising that personalisation will remain a seductive political slogan whilst in practice an empty concept which unites schools. This will not change until the learner is known and known well, otherwise we condone our 'impact' as being superficial, with students compliantly schooled, rather than educated as lifelong enthusiastic learners and citizens.
>
> (Davies, 2009, p. 11)

Human Scale Education has itself argued that the case for SWS and other small-scale schools rests on eight key principles, referred to on page 101.

But interest in SWSs is not confined to the UK, indeed has gone further in several other countries, including Australia and the US, from where we take our two examples.

Diversity, choice and unity: Morialta High School, Adelaide, Australia and the views of John Watts

Amongst the most interesting models for a SWS, from the standpoint of this chapter, is that developed at Morialta High School, Adelaide, Australia in the mid-1970s. Here, not only were there four different sub-schools operating as constituent parts of Morialta High, but their individual identities were deliberately distinct, thus offering choices of schools within the overall High School for parents and young people from the local community.

The following brief description of Morialta is by John Watts, the pioneering head teacher of Countesthorpe Community College, Leicestershire, arguably amongst the most innovative secondary schools in the radical democratic tradition in England and the spiritual and actual birthplace of English SWS, not as an organisational device, but as a means of learning, being and becoming.

> One sub-school offered a Formal Mode, with conventional classroom methods, teacher-directed, short term goals and regular testing. A second offered an Open Mode, with greater latitude of choice in both subject and style of work, flexibility of grouping and on-going assessment. The third was an Autonomous Mode, designed for independent study with staff as reference tutors, recruiting students who were well motivated to work in this way, but accepting the whole ability range. Fourth was an Alternative Mode for those who had already been at odds with school and needed a close relationship with a small number of trusted teachers with whom they could work out their own solutions to their own problems.
>
> Staff were at pains . . . to emphasise parity of esteem, to avoid hidden streaming. Admission to the last two modes [the Autonomous Mode and the Alternative Mode] required agreement between parent, child and staff after interview.
>
> (Watts, 1980, p. 16)

Two points are of particular interest. The first is Watts' additional observation that '[o]nce Morialta was established, greater numbers started to apply for Modes Three [Autonomous] and Four [Alternative], thus shifting the balance of cultures'. The second is his observation that these kinds of arrangement

> may well be one way forward for sub-school organisations that are seeking to avoid hidden streaming or embarrassment about emerging differences. They may also, as at Morialta, be the best answer in one school to the parental demand for choice of placement for their children.
>
> (Watts, 1980, p. 22)

While SWSs or sub-schools can provide an important way forward for the radical democratic common school in offering significant choice within the context
of overarching democratic values, there are dangers that without a fundamental,
pervasive rethinking of roles, relations, curriculum and pedagogy sub-schools
become 'merely a device for more effective control, social and epistemological'
(Watts, 1980, p. 20). Too many examples of the recent burgeoning of SWS in
England testify to the well-founded nature of his apprehensions.

Whilst the full realisation of the model for which Watts was arguing has yet
to be achieved, the new wave of SWS is gaining increasing momentum. How
fitting it would be, not only if it came nearer to the kinds of aspirations he and
others had over 30 years ago, but also if it embraced the extension of inter-
generational engagement with which he ends his visionary article.

> The sub-school also offers the potential for a learning centre that has suffi-
> cient security, by limiting its size, and continuity of contact, to attract more
> than a set age-group of students. Given reasonable resources, it should be
> possible to design a sociable physical setting where ages can meet without
> mutual threat, and with the conditions for conversation met. It is in such a
> context that adults may relax sufficiently to articulate their learning needs
> to sympathetic teachers and begin again to take up courses they never pur-
> sued at school, and where younger students still in full-time schooling may
> witness that learning is a rhythmic but lifelong occupation.
>
> (Watts, 1980, p. 23)

Choosing democracy: the Just Community School approach, School within a School, Brookline, USA, and the views of Lawrence Kohlberg

The kinds of internal choice within the common school illustrated by Morialta
High School were concerned predominantly with different approaches to
learning and curriculum. Another model is concerned with forms of participatory democracy and can be illustrated by a parallel development, also initiated
in the early 1970s. Here, Lawrence Kohlberg and his research team at Harvard
University developed the Just Community School (JCS) approach to moral and
citizenship education. Kohlberg's view was that

> [t]he most basic way in which the high school can promote experiences
> of civic participation is to govern itself through a process of participatory
> democracy . . . The only way school can help graduating students become
> persons who can make society a just community is to let them try experi-
> mentally to make the school themselves.
>
> (Kohlberg, 1980, p. 35)

At the heart of Just Community Schools lay the weekly Meeting (sometimes called a Town Meeting) attended by all students and staff who explored and decided on a one person one vote basis key educational issues, particularly to do with the development of the school as a just and fair community.

Given the marked absence of schools within the public sector run as participatory democracies and the difficulties of setting up radical democratic schools from scratch, the JCS project went for a school-within-a-school model, involving small numbers – usually four to five – of volunteer staff from social studies, English and mathematics departments and between 70 and 100 students in grades 9 to 12. Staff from the larger host school taught in SWS for part of their time. When not attending those classes, SWS students worked in the larger school on an appropriate range of curricular choices. In effect, what was created was an experimental/radical school operating with volunteer staff and students choosing to work in this innovative way housed within a more traditional secondary school.

One of the founding JCS schools – School Within a School, Brookline – is still pursuing a variant of the original approach. A short summary of its work appears on its website (http://bhs.brookline.k12.ma.us/Programs/SWS/). Here we have extracted a small number of key points which illustrate pertinent aspects of its manner of working.

> School Within A School [SWS] is a participatory democratic alternative program for approximately 115 sophomores, juniors, and seniors. It is located on the fourth floor of Brookline High School. SWS students take courses both in SWS and in the 'main' high school . . .

> *History* . . . In the spring of 1970, a small group of students, teachers, and parents began organizing an alternative school in Brookline where students would have a larger voice in their own education and a more personal, equal relationship with teachers. In the early years of SWS, students wanted to be as separate as possible from the High School. This attitude has changed. Students became interested in benefiting from the variety and scope of courses and activities in the high school. SWS became an alternative for all students who sought to participate in a democratic classroom and community.

> *Structure*

> SWS is a separate administrative unit for approximately 115 students . . . set up for each grade level as in the main high school. SWS is a voluntary program. Permission from a parent is required in order to enter. There is a lottery based on requirements set by SWS Town Meeting. Not all students can enter due to space considerations.

It is the goal of the staff in SWS to help students become responsible for their own education. To this end, the SWS Town Meeting serves as the major forum for shared decision-making in the areas of educational administration and educational policy. The weekly Town Meeting is mandatory for students and staff. Town Meeting serves as a forum for discussion and debate and for changes which are inevitable in a growing dynamic community. SWS gives students more freedom and more responsibility in directing their own education than is generally possible in the main school. Students have the chance to make their own education meaningful on their own terms, as long as they fulfill responsibilities to the SWS community. Students are responsible for their own attendance. They, not their parents, call in to report and explain an absence.

Six students and one staff member each quarter form The Agenda Committee which plans and runs SWS Town Meeting. Every student is eligible to serve on Agenda Committee which is chosen from a pool of volunteers.

The eight members of The Review Committee are responsible for reviewing the academic progress and well-being of students. The Committee meets with students referred by either staff or other students to discuss academic, social, and attendance problems. The Committee helps support students and ultimately decides whether or not a student should remain in SWS.

. . . Students take all non-SWS courses in the main school.

Town Meeting

Town Meeting, our mandatory community meeting, takes place during F-block, Wednesday, and is scheduled into students' programs along with their courses. Town Meeting is the governing body for SWS. All students and staff have one vote in decisions about the administrative and educational policies and practices of SWS. These decisions range from rules for attendance and admissions policies to the consequences for students who are not fulfilling their obligations to the community. Students form a majority on all Committees, including Hiring Committees for new staff.

Entrance to SWS

SWS is open to all students who attend Brookline High School and are in the 10th, 11th or 12th grade. A parent, dean, counselor and the SWS Coordinator must sign the approval form. There is a waiting list for entrance. Students are encouraged to sign up between January and March. The list closes by early March. Entrance is by lottery after fulfilling a few requirements. SWS has an affirmative action policy for minority and foreign born students.

Sadly, in England, the large-scale school rebuilding programme which started in 2005 – *Building Schools for the Future* – was embarked on without first considering what type of schools were needed, once again avoiding the critical questions of purpose and concepts, values and understandings before embarking on action. In England, therefore, whatever rebuilding emerges under the new government may well have to make the best of what we have through conversion of large units into schools-within-schools, and this may well hold true for many other countries. What the conditions may be for 'schools-within-schools' to function effectively as small schools, providing a 'human scale education', including whether there are upper limits to the overall size of the school, is one of the issues that is at the heart of developing radical education and the common school and which requires research, debate and experimentation. But there can also be a gradual development of small-scale, age-integrated common schools, along the lines of the Swedish school in Box 3.2, either by new builds or the renovation of primary or other existing smaller schools.

The common school offers depth over coverage

So we have a common school, a place for all members of its local community, which may very well be age-integrated (a primary-plus-secondary school, even a birth to 16 school) and will be on a modest scale, at least in terms of size, to be in tune with its democratic purpose, its caring ethos and pedagogy of relationships. But modest scale need not mean modest ambition. The thinking behind large schools has been, in part at least, that they can offer a wide range of separate subjects to children of all abilities. The smaller scale school does not try to compete in these terms; it does not set itself up as a miniature version of a big school, but works with a different approach to education, 'depth over coverage'.

Some parts of this approach are outlined in HSE's *Practical Manifesto for Education on a Human Scale*, whose 'eight key practices that schools might follow' include: small teams of educators working with 80–90 learners; a curriculum that is thematic, cross-disciplinary and holistic; a timetable that is flexible, making provision for whole class teaching, small-group teaching and individual learning; pedagogy that is inquiry-based, experiential and supported by ICT; assessment involving dialogue, negotiation and peer review, using methods such as portfolio, exhibition and performance; and student voice that involves students in learning arrangements and organisation of the school. This approach to education, primarily addressed by HSE to secondary schooling, has much in common with the educational approach of the municipal schools in Reggio Emilia working with children under six years, with which we began the book: a pedagogy of listening organised around interdisciplinary project work; team work by educators in small schools; pedagogical documentation for evaluation (and other purposes); and participation as a core value.

Work in Reggio Emilia highlights another potentially important feature of the small-scale common school, which supports depth of learning: the *atelier*. In their case, *ateliers* are workshops for visual arts and the *atelierista* is an educator (but not a teacher) with an arts background. The important point to emphasise here is the role of the *atelier* and *atelierista* in the whole school. They are not there to offer art lessons, but to make the arts – the aesthetic dimension or poetic languages – a central part of learning throughout the school, drawing in particular on the *atelierista*'s artistic sensibility, way of seeing and ability to facilitate connections and new perspectives. Vea Vecchi, one of Reggio's first *atelieristas*, describes the role:

> the atelier never organised children to take turns coming in; we [atelieristas] always did things in such a way that the atelier expanded out into the classes and school through enriched proposals in the classroom, above all as an approach. We always worked on projects and it was the progress of these that determined children's presence in the atelier. It would be difficult to say exactly how because the organisation was not defined beforehand. . . . Another important task for atelieristas in work carried out in school, is maintaining a certain way of seeing among both children and adults – how to define this? aesthetic, poetic? – highlighting the role of poetics in learning processes, or better still, appreciating the dance constructed together by cognition and emotion in all fields of knowledge. . . . atelieristas as *guarantors* that the dance between cognitive, expressive, rational and imaginative would always happen, or at least that it would be present as often as possible in processes of learning.
>
> (Vecchi, 2010, pp. 127, 128, 131; original emphasis)

Schools need not be confined to one *atelier* nor need *ateliers* only be for visual arts. One school in Reggio Emilia for around 70 three- to six-year-olds houses one *atelier* and employs one *atelierista*. A common school of several hundred children could have two, three or more *ateliers*, each 'expanded out into the classes and school' through the work of their accompanying *atelieristas*. There are, too, many 'languages' that *ateliers* can offer: music, drama, mathematics, science and so on (see, for example, the range of *ateliers* in the Swedish school in Box 3.2). Specialist *ateliers* can also be shared by a group of schools or be housed in another setting, with children coming in to the *atelier* to use its specialised facilities and *atelieristas* doing outreach work within the group.

But specialist input to learning need not be limited to *ateliers* and *atelieristas*, whatever their disciplinary backgrounds. We described earlier and discuss in more detail later the profession of pedagogue, which can bring a range of particular interests, capabilities and languages to the school. A reformed teacher education can include certain specialisms giving each teacher a particular profile on graduation. As well as specialisms related to particular groups of children (e.g. younger/older; with additional needs) and particular pedagogical approaches (e.g. Reggio Emilian pedagogy), others could be related to disciplines or languages, for those working with younger and older children, but usually not confined to just one but perhaps to two or three related disciplines.

Combine pedagogues and teachers working in teams and with mixed-age groups of children, as we advocate later, add in *atelieristas*, and the common, small-scale school can offer a wider range of knowledges and expertises: it can be a multi-lingual and resource-rich environment for all ages of children. But in our thinking of education and knowledge, the point of this diversity, this broad repertoire of educational roles, is to contribute to an education that connects – is interdisciplinary, inquiry-based, experiential and often, project-oriented, rather than an education that cuts life into slices through specialised and disconnected subject teaching. The question, therefore, is not whether or not to have educators with specialised disciplinary experience and knowledge. The question is how they are used and how they relate to other educators, children and young people to deepen understanding of the world rather than covering many subject headings at the expense of depth and connections.

The common school is based on team work

Within the age-integrated, small-scale common school, we envisage organisation of children and educators similar to that of the Swedish school (Box 3.2). This is based on mixed age groups of children (for example, 5- to 8-year-olds; 8- to 10-year-olds; 11- to 13-year-olds; and 14- to 16-year-olds) and multidisciplinary teams of 'educators', the group and its team being together throughout a whole school day from 8 to 6. The teams consist of a variety of group-based educators, including teachers and pedagogues, supplemented by *atelieristas* working out from the school's stock of *ateliers*.

We have already introduced, in Chapter 2, the theory and practice of social pedagogy, and its affinity with the concept of education-in-its-broadest-sense. We now need to introduce the profession and role of 'pedagogue'. For although common in Continental Europe, working in a wide range of children's and (sometimes) adult services, and with a tradition going back to the nineteenth century, the pedagogue is little known or understood in the English-speaking world; she or he, as we noted in Chapter 2, has often been rendered invisible when 'pedagogue' has been wrongly translated as 'teacher'.

As already introduced in the previous chapter, the theory and practice of 'social pedagogy' and the profession of 'pedagogue' are concerned, broadly, with supporting the overall development of individuals and their integration or socialisation into the human collective (community or society). 'Upbringing' is a very important pedagogical concept that captures the holistic and integrative concerns at the heart of social pedagogy; Paul Stephens, for example, defines social pedagogy as 'the study and practice of deliberative care, education and upbringing, viewed holistically rather than as separate entities, and with an emphasis on finding pedagogical ways of nurturing and supporting positive social development' (Stephens, 2009, p. 347).

What are these 'pedagogical ways'? What are the basic values and principles of the pedagogue? The pedagogue adopts a holistic approach to working with children (or adults) in which learning, care, health, general well-being and development are viewed as totally inseparable:

> The pedagogue sets out to address the whole child, the child with body, mind, emotions, creativity, history and social identity. This is not the child only of emotions, the psychotherapeutical approach, nor only of the body, the medical approach, nor only of the mind, the traditional teaching approach.
>
> (Moss and Petrie, 2002, p. 143)

The 'social' in social pedagogy is highly significant: it is a holistic approach not only in its recognition of the need to work with the whole child, but also in its recognition of the child in the social context and the centrality of relationships. As Pat Petrie puts it, for pedagogues:

> it is very difficult to abstract the social from human activity . . . [T]he child is seen as social both in their immediate relationships and as members of the larger society. Association, community and society are all keywords for social pedagogy. Social pedagogy is deeply concerned with the connectedness of human beings . . . social pedagogy is a form of education in which the intrinsic social nature of human beings is fully acknowledged and prioritised.
>
> (Petrie, forthcoming)

Other important principles of the pedagogue's practice include:

- Paying attention to the quality of the relationship with the child or young person, communication skills being crucial;
- Sharing the same social life spaces and many aspects of the daily lives of children or young people, rather than occupying discrete hierarchical settings;
- Working with heart, head and hands, including a strong emphasis on creative activities;
- Valuing children's associative life – the group as well as the individual;
- Supporting the rights of children, including the right to social inclusion; Engaging in professional reflection and basing practice on theoretical understanding and self-knowledge;
- Valuing team-working, dialogue and democracy.

(Stephens, 2009)

Such principles may not seem foreign to some coming from a certain tradition of education to which we have already referred, what may be termed the 'person-centred' tradition, illustrating how although social pedagogy and the pedagogue may be mostly found today in Continental Europe, they are not totally foreign to education and teaching in English-speaking countries. So we can see both teachers and pedagogues as 'educators', a generic term for practitioners of education-in-its-broadest-sense, each with distinct but complementary roles working together in teams. The teacher, perhaps, would be more expert in formal educational contexts and in certain disciplines or – to use the term from Reggio Emilia – languages; the pedagogue more expert with informal learning and in some other languages, especially the aesthetic ones such as arts and drama, and with a particular strength in relationships. The two professions, between them, would bring a wide range of disciplines both to the school in general and to the team in which they work together. This team is a broad-based and interdisciplinary partnership of equals, with both teachers and pedagogues educated to at least graduate level.

To digress briefly, a more radical development would be to move beyond a division between teacher and pedagogue, to a new profession of 'educator', combining elements of both professions and re-connecting with the person-centred tradition in England that emphasised the importance of relationships and a holistic approach as part of what it means to be a teacher. The argument for this integration of professions is that a division between teacher and pedagogue – between more formal and more informal concepts of learning, between education more in its narrower sense and more in its broader sense – splits what should be holistic. Moreover, the existing division places too much faith in the possibility of a strong and equal partnership between teacher and pedagogue, which may be liable to give way to produce a hierarchical relationship in which one profession dominates the other, for example the teacher viewing and treating the pedagogue as assistant.

In some Nordic countries, at least, the border between teacher and pedagogue might not be so difficult to remove. Stephens comments that 'there is a lot of implicit social pedagogy [in the sense of an emphasis on affective relational focus] in the education of schoolteachers in Norway . . . [envisaging] teaching as a caring profession' (2009, p. 346). While for one of us, when researching in Swedish schools, it became commonplace to hear teachers describe themselves as 'pedagogues' when asked how they think of themselves. During the same fieldwork stint, the Director of Education of a local authority said that he often used 'pedagogue' instead of 'teacher', for example when writing about schools or talking with politicians. He did this to stress:

> an idea about learning, the role of the pedagogue as creating learning environments. Pedagogue implies working socially and emotionally as well as with learning. They try and look at the child as a whole person, they want pupils to leave school with values, social abilities, curiosity.

This is a complex but important issue, which all we can do at present is raise. For now, we will stick with the concept of a 'core' team of teachers *and* pedagogues in the common school, which is with its group of children throughout the school's day, potentially from 8 a.m. to 6 p.m., though few if any children would attend for the full ten hours. The team organises a day that combines formal and informal learning, leisure and other activities – and leaves spaces where children can do nothing in particular, just hang out or have time for themselves that no one else organises or intrudes into.

In this structure, the distinction between 'education' and 'childcare' would be broken down; no more 'wraparound care', no separate group of 'childcare workers' in a separate 'childcare' service. Care instead would be viewed as an ethic and practice applied by all educators throughout the day, with the school, in its opening hours and organisation, recognising the reality of most parents being employed and needing 'childcare' (i.e. in the sense of a safe and secure environment) throughout the working day. The team of equals would replace the hierarchical, Taylorist team found in English schools, in which the class teacher manages various grades of assistants. Indeed, like the Swedish school (see Box 3.2), assistants in the 'common school' would be few and far between, radical education requiring well-educated and reflective practitioners, while there would be no separate and lower status group of 'childcare workers'.

This model of multidisciplinary team work is very similar to the practice developing in Swedish schools, which we exemplify in Box 3.2 to give the reader a better sense of how the approach would work in practice and how teachers and pedagogues can work in complementary ways. These core teams of educators would be supplemented by other workers who would not be a permanent part of any one group of children and team of educators, but would work with both from time to time: as already noted, an *atelierista* responsible for an arts *atelier*, or workshop, another educator whose particular contribution is providing an aesthetic dimension that we think is central to learning; other *ateliers* and *atelieristas*, contributing their 'languages' to the learning process, for example in science or maths; a school nurse, in at least part-time attendance in every school; a counsellor, providing more general social and emotional support to members of the school community; and a range of other staff supporting the other purposes of the common school as they emerge through democratic processes. It is to these other purposes that we now turn.

The common school has a project identity

A common school is also a school of many different projects, not just projects for learning, but also projects with the local community that the school serves. It is, as we quoted at the start of the chapter, 'a place of infinite cultural, linguistic, social, aesthetic, political and economic possibilities'. This means the common school operates as a 'multi-purpose' institution providing education-in-its-broadest-sense and acting as a social resource to its local community, responding to the needs, the ideas and the desire to experiment of that community. We return to this theme of community projects and experimentation later in the chapter.

By proposing this idea of the multi-purpose, multi-project 'common school', we make some connections to school policy in England, namely the goal of every school being an 'extended school' by 2010. The defining features of these schools, according to the last Labour government, are that they will be open from 8 a.m. to 6 p.m., and ensure for all children under 14 years access to a range of services:

- a varied menu of activities, combined with childcare in primary schools. These activities 'might include academically-focused activities (from extra tuition for those who have fallen behind to more challenging opportunities for the most able), homework clubs, arts and creative activities, sports activities, and other recreational activities, including play';
- parenting support, including 'structured evidence-based parenting programmes', 'family learning sessions', and the provision of various types of information;
- community access to school facilities 'where a school has facilities suitable for use by the wider community (e.g. playing fields, sports facilities, IT facilities, halls)';
- swift and easy access to targeted and specialist services, with 'a focus on early identification of, and support for, children and young people who have additional needs or who are at risk of poor outcomes'.

(http://www.teachernet.gov.uk/_doc/13061/esp2008.pdf)

According to the policy, ensuring access does not mean that schools need to provide such services directly or on site; they can, and often do, work in partnership with local providers. Childcare could, for example, be available from a private provider in another setting, as long as children from the school can be assured safe transit. In practice, most 'school-age childcare' (as out of school hours provision is termed), and 'childcare' for children under five years, is delivered by private providers, often for-profit businesses (English Department for Education and Skills, 2005).

We have some reservations about aspects of this official concept. It is a prescriptive approach, offering a sort of standardised model kit to be built following the instructions provided: the school as provider of specified services rather than creator of emergent projects. And it pays little attention to identifying or discussing critical questions. What concept of education might underpin the extended school? What other concepts, understandings, values and ethics? What, for example, is the relationship between education and care, with the idea of 'childcare' as something apart from the school – 'wraparound' as it is sometimes referred to – seeming to imply the continued separation of education and care, with care as a discrete activity applied to younger children, not an ethic for all embedded in the full life of the school? How does the extended school reconcile a standards agenda with a holistic approach? As a community facility, what place, if any, should democracy and democratic practice have? How does the idea of an accessible extended school serving a community square with the idea of the school as business competing for consumers in an education market?

Without tackling these and other questions, an extended school programme may simply lead to unreformed schools continuing as before but with the various bits and pieces bolted on, in the same way as new subjects get bolted on to the curriculum, rather than a fundamental rethinking and reforming of the image, purpose and form of the school. Still, despite these reservations, the programme does recognise that schools are 'at the heart of our communities' and that they should 'extend the services they offer beyond the traditional school day'. It does provide another point of contact between our thinking and the way schools (and not only in England) are moving.

So our common school is a place for all members of its local community, but it is not simply a renaissance of the large, subject-based and narrow age-ranged comprehensive school. It is a comprehensive school, but re-conceptualised. It is age-integrated, it is relatively small in scale, it is a 'multi-purpose' or multi-project public institution, and has a multidisciplinary workforce that emphasises team work. But having introduced our concept of the common school, we need now to turn to why we place such importance on this concept.

Why the common school?

> For Dewey, individuals can only learn to understand themselves as democratic individuals by becoming members of a community in which the problems of communal life are resolved through collective deliberation and a shared concern for the common good. For this reason, a democratic school is a common school providing a broad social community to which children of different race, class, gender and religion can belong. Democratic schools thus offer a 'mode of associated living'.
>
> (Carr and Hartnett, 1996, p. 63)

Those who advocate 'uncommon' schools, schools based on selection on grounds of intelligence, aptitude, religious belief or parental choice have a clear image of the school. The school is primarily concerned with the effective reproduction of predetermined outcomes and with either selling on performance to consumer parents or selecting children who will best enable it to enhance its own performance by producing outcomes effectively. The school is akin to a commercial enterprise, applying technologies to achieve output and a business whose success is measured by output, sales and profit; selection is important for effective performance (getting the right raw materials) and market share (finding a niche where it can successfully sell its services).

In contrast, the common school, as we envisage here, is very different, and closely linked to our understanding of radical education. It is designed to provide an environment conducive to such an education. More broadly, we see the common school as epitomising our understanding or image of the school that we offered in the previous chapter: as a public institution and a public space, a forum or place of encounter and connection, interaction and dialogue open to all citizens, young and old. As a public space it is a capable of many collective projects, democratically determined and implemented. These will, of course, include education and learning, though as we have argued earlier, how we understand education and learning and the knowledge it gives rise to is a contentious issue. Two other important projects are the exercise of ethical and political practice.

The school as public space is, first and foremost, a place for ethical and political practice, not of technical practice driven by an instrumental rationality of means/ ends. In previous chapters, we discussed possibilities for ethical practice around the ideas of care and encounter. Political practice means democratic politics, and the radical 'common school' is both democratic in its practice – offering a 'mode of associated living' – and plays an important part in the democratic politics of the wider society. So it is a place where a common democratic identity is formed and constantly validated and expressed, both amongst members of the school community itself and in the community that the school serves. Michael Sandel develops this theme when he speaks about public institutions being

> traditionally sites for the cultivation of common citizenship, so that people from different walks of life encounter one another and so acquire enough of a shared life that we can meaningfully think of one another as citizens in a common venture.
>
> (Sandel, 2009a, p. 9)

As such, the common school becomes one of the places needed for widening, deepening and recreating democracy in society, one of the 'everyday institutions' that Bentley views as necessary for a flourishing democracy:

> Building everyday democracy therefore depends on applying its principles to everyday institutions through which people make their choices and develop their identities. Its basis is the idea that power and responsibility must be aligned with

each other – and widely distributed – if societies are to exercise shared responsibility through social, economic and institutional diversity.

(Bentley, 2005, p. 21)

As we have discussed in Chapter 2, democratic practice permeates the approach taken towards learning and knowledge creation in the common school practising radical education. It also shapes the other projects that the common school embarks on. Which projects? How to proceed with them? How are they evaluated? All these questions should be democratically determined. We have indicated some possibilities for the projects of the common school in Chapter 2, but the possibilities for projects are endless, especially once we can free ourselves from the constraining idea that the school is simply a service delivering a particular function or even two or three functions and see it instead as a limitless potential, a constant becoming.

This way of thinking about schools creates our image of the school in a radical education: of the school not only as a public space but also as a public or collective workshop or laboratory, an invaluable potential for collective deliberation, choice and action, involving children and adults, pupils, educators, parents and other interested citizens. As a workshop or laboratory, the school becomes a place for public research and experimentation, and therefore a place that can bring about new thinking, new practice and change. Reggio Emilia has adopted these images of their municipal schools, speaking of them both as public spaces and 'as one big laboratory, a workshop of learning and knowledge'. Their schools, as we have seen, include arts workshops (*ateliers*) – a workshop in a workshop we might say – and these comments by an *atelierista* about why Reggio chose the name of '*atelier*' can stand also for our image of the school-as-workshop: 'we felt it was the most suitable metaphor for a place of research where imagination, rigour, experiment, creativity and expression would interweave and complete each other' (Vecchi, 2010, p. 176).

The municipal schools in Reggio Emilia offer an example of schools as workshops for *learning* projects. Another example, the Sheffield Children's Centre, is outlined in Box 3.4. It illustrates the potential of an early childhood centre or school to act as a workshop of *community* projects, going beyond learning and knowledge into many other areas important to the well-being of a local community; and also to serve as a locus of democratic political practice. Working alongside its local community to resist the oppressive conditions under which its members live, the Centre has created new possibilities by welcoming diversity, building solidarities and a willingness to experiment.

A point to be emphasised here, and clearly exemplified by the Sheffield Children's Centre, is that the potential for projects of the common school is open to adults as well as children; the common school welcomes participation by all, not just children, not just parents. In this emphasis on the relationship between the school and its community, we are, once again, connecting with a tradition of English, and other, education: the school as community centre and resource for both young and old.

As a public space, a place of encounter and a collective workshop, the common school can be an important site of what Michael Hardt and Antonio Negri call

Box 3.4 Sheffield Children's Centre

The Sheffield Children's Centre started in a northern English city in the early 1980s as a local community initiative. Since then, it has grown to provide a wide range of services for hundreds of children and young people, from infancy to 18 years, as well as their families, serving an inner-city area of economic disadvantage with many minority ethnic families; its work has also extended to initiating projects in Ethiopia, Jordan, Pakistan and Zimbabwe. The Centre, run as a cooperative, provides a range of 'core' services, including early childhood education and care and free-time and play services for school-age children. But the Centre has also created multiple projects for families in its local community and beyond. These include: assistance with translation and interpretation; adult education; dance and other workshops; access to legal, health, housing and other services; counselling, advocacy and advice; home care and other domiciliary support workers; respite care for seriously ill parents; support for various groups, including terminally ill children and parents, adult survivors of child sexual abuse, domestic violence and female genital mutilation; and a range of inter-generational activities.

As well as more formalised services, the Centre's workers provide important support by 'walking alongside' families in difficulty, as this family vignette illustrates:

> I came to the centre for help with domestic violence. They found us a refuge and went back to the house to get our things. My husband left the country after this and they found us a house in Sheffield and helped us furnish it. They got us school placements and gave us a baby place at their nursery and got me a place on an access course in college. My children go to the violence support group. Everyone knows it's the place to go for help. They never turn anyone away. The centre has kept us alive and safe and it has helped get over the violence. He would have killed us. In our community there is no escape and it is expected women stay with their husbands. The centre gave us a different path to escape and the centre's cultural workers made it ok with our community.
>
> (Broadhead, Meleady and Delgado, 2008; see this reference for many other family vignettes and a fuller description and analysis of the work of the Centre).

The Centre identifies closely with its diverse community, many of whose members have felt alienated from and excluded by mainstream society and its services. It has sought to develop work that emerges 'from local demands struggling to change perceived conditions of exclusion and existing power relations' (Broadhead, Meleady and Delgado, 2008, p. 21). It describes itself as developing a 'project identity', following Manuel Castells who defines a project identity as 'when social actors, on the basis of whichever cultural materials are available to them, build a new identity that redefines their position in society and, by so doing, seek the transformation of overall social structure' (1997, p. 8).

Underpinning this work is a strong ethical and political commitment to diversity (most unusually, it has a gender mixed workforce, with almost equal numbers of men and women, but diversity covers many other dimensions including ethnicity, language, sexual orientation, age and disability); to children's rights; to equal opportunities; and to democracy, building on its original and continuing cooperative status.

> [The Centre's identity] reflects the desire of ordinary people to influence social change based on local demands. The centre began because local people expressed concerns about the cultural inappropriateness of a mainstream provision close by and it grew because its aim was to reflect diversity in all its practices. This aspiration has been its strength and its greatest challenge and locates the centre, as described by Dahlberg and Moss (2005: 171) as 'a site for democratic practice and minor politics'.
>
> (Broadhead, Meleady and Delgado, 2008, p. 3)

For more about Sheffield Children's Centre, see Delgado, 2009.

'immaterial production': this includes the 'production of ideas, images, knowledge, communication, cooperation, and affective relations, [which] tends to create not the means of social life but social life itself'. They emphasise that this production, including knowledge but much else besides, is 'produced not by individuals but collectively in collaboration . . . [creating] a common, social nature of production' (Hardt and Negri, 2005, pp. 146, 187). If we view the school in this light, as a site of collective immaterial production, then the 'common school' ensures that the benefits of this production – the school's output as a public space, a workshop of projects and a creator of new knowledges – are secured for the whole community and for the common good.

The common school serving a defined catchment area also enables cooperation to replace competition between schools, creating genuine learning communities and support networks between schools serving wider areas and a generous attitude to sharing the benefits of immaterial production. It nurtures what Dewey called 'social intelligence', the capacity of humans to develop their capacity collectively to enlarge freedom, create more desirable forms of social life and realise the common good. Today, we might want to add nurturing the capacity collectively to reduce the dangers confronting our species and to create sustainable and equitable conditions for survival, prosperity and flourishing. The common school provides a microcosm of the cooperation that is needed if there is to be any hope of lifting the Damocletian threat from the planet: a prefigurative practice for a sustainable, inclusive and democratic world.

Working together, an ethos and practice of cooperation to replace the driving force of competition is such an important principle, yet so difficult to practise, that it is worth expanding on briefly and in particular on the ways in which colleagues – whether in the same school or from different schools – can learn with and from each other (see Fielding *et al.*, 2005). There is, of course, a huge literature on this field and on the rise of networks as a social and political phenomenon. There are two main points that are particularly pertinent to the kinds of exchange we think are likely to be helpful, particularly amongst pioneers and radicals who by definition are in the minority and whose practices go substantially against the grain.

The first point to make is that the manner and purpose of joint activities between human beings will both open up and close down possibilities. Enthusiastic advocacy of, for example, collaboration and collegiality is often much less fruitful than it might be because it fails to attend to theoretical and philosophical distinctions and differences that underpin the kinds of partnership and exchange being proposed (see Fielding (1999), Hargreaves (1999) and Little (1999) for a lively, if rather tetchy, exchange of views on these matters). 'Collaboration' and 'collegiality' are not the same and to presume they are is to invite failure and disillusion. One typology (Fielding, 2007b) argues for four interrelated forms of joint-teacher activity – co-existence/ collaboration/collegiality/community – each typifying a particular way of working with others.

Within the 'co-existence' mode, those involved (whether within or across schools) would, in truth, rather be working on their own. Joint work is seen as an intrusion and if required by those in authority, becomes a pretence or a thin conformity. 'Collaboration' is quite different. The prospect of working with others is welcomed. The focus is typically clear and anticipated outcomes seen as worthwhile. The joint work and the relationship are defined by the task. 'Collegiality' also involves tasks and joint undertaking, but the spirit in which they are approached goes beyond the mere accomplishment of stated objectives. The unity draws on shared moral and professional expectations, which give the partnerships richness and strength through a shared commitment to wider social ends that contribute to the common good. These in turn legitimate levels of trust and risk-taking, not usually available with the predominantly instrumental rubric of collaboration.

Finally, within the rarely achieved Macmurrayian 'community' mode people do, of course, undertake tasks and aim to achieve often very demanding aspirations. However, what they choose to work on with others will emerge from a relationship of care informed by the principles of freedom and equality. Rather than defining the relationship (as they do in the case of collaboration), the joint work will be expressive of it. Within a community thus conceived, the boundaries of the personal and the professional begin to blur. Members are keen to learn from others, not just as respected professionals but as interesting and wise persons, and are thus willing to take risks grounded on personal and professional trust. What is clear from recent small-scale research (Fielding and Cunningham, 2009) and from wider engagement with innovative head teachers in the field is that those who are committed to ways of working that rupture the presumptions of the *status quo* need and find support in the last of these working modes, i.e. within rich partnerships of Macmurrayian community.

This links to our second point, which is that whilst networks have their place and have an important function to perform, because they are often geographically-determined, externally-imposed or administratively-driven they cannot provide the secure environment for exploratory dialogue that so many contemporary head teachers (and others) both need and want. Furthermore, and of special importance for the core arguments put forward in this book, they do not and cannot provide the necessary contexts of solidarity and values-driven challenge that pioneers of radical education would find so sustaining and so liberating within the largely hostile macro-environment of performativity and myopically-instrumental schooling. Our positive suggestion, therefore, is that the richness and range of practice within the geographical parameters of the local clusters of common schools are enriched by all three positive professional forms of partnership; that the differences of form, intention and possibility are genuinely understood and appropriate, diverse provision made available; and, finally, and to return to a theme in Chapter 2, that the opportunity to form values-based alliances and companion forms of professional learning are encouraged, not only locally, but also regionally, nationally and internationally (as, for example in Human Scale Education in the UK, the Coalition of Essential Schools in the US, the Freinet Movement in France or the many early childhood centres across the world working with inspiration from Reggio Emilia).

The singularity of the common school

The application of pejorative and unjustified terms such as 'bog standard' to existing comprehensive secondary schools (the insulting reference of an English Education Minister) and the grandiose names given to proliferating selective schools – 'academies', 'charter schools', 'foundation schools' and so on – may encourage the view that a 'common school' as we envisage here must be a mediocre and standardised place, offering a 'lowest common denominator' and 'one size fits all' experience to all children who are treated similarly without regard to diversity of identity, need or interest. This is very far from the case. The 'common' in the common school does *not* mean uniform, standard, homogeneous. It stands for common citizenship reflected in inclusive access and a common educational project, based on a shared commitment to the values, ethics, concepts and understandings we have outlined as defining 'radical education': values such as democracy and justice; the ethics of care and of encounter; the concepts of education-in-its-broadest-sense and person-centred education; and images such as the rich child and the school as public space, collective workshop and person-centred learning community. What we envisage, therefore, is a radical democratic common school premised not on uniformity but on diversity and plurality, expressed in two ways: first, through a personalist approach with deep respect for otherness and the absolute singularity of the individual within the relational context of a restlessly inclusive community; second, through a desire and readiness to experiment, to explore new possibilities that emerge from democratic processes.

The individual and the common school

In our thinking here we are influenced by the ideas of John Dewey on democracy and, more recently, of Michael Hardt and Antonio Negri on 'the multitude', of Bill Readings on the university and the pedagogical relationship, and of Carlina Rinaldi on early childhood education. All share a belief in the importance of both the individual and the communal. All recognise the interrelationship of singularity and the common, the personal and the communal.

For Dewey, the democratic common school was a source of integration, 'not via creating uniformity but enabling citizens to understand and learn from each other, to respect others, to work cooperatively'. It creates a greater sense of community and develops the capacities of individuals to work together to find collective ways of meeting common concerns. So the common school that he advocated was to provide a unique place 'where diversity could be turned into a community of mutual respect that embraced and learned from diversity' (Pring, 2007, p. 171). Starting from diversity, therefore, a key purpose and project of the school is to create solidarities and shared identities, including a common citizenship, and to enable individuals to learn how to work collaboratively, both in school and the wider community.

This sense of community neither requires nor strives for consensus. Within a broad framework of agreed values and ethics, the common school does not call for sameness of opinion or perspective. Indeed, a democratic common school expects and values differences of view, conflicts and confrontations. Democracy, Morin insists, feeds on conflicts and lives on plurality; to remain healthy, it needs what Mouffe (2000) terms 'agonistic' relationships that do not believe it is possible to eradicate differences, or even desirable to try.

Hardt and Negri work with a similar idea, though not specifically in relation to education and schooling; their thinking also relates to the ethics of an encounter with its attention to alterity. In the book *Multitude*, they make some important points about the possibility, indeed necessity, of a relationship between singularity (absolute otherness) and commonality. They begin by asserting the singularity – the absolute otherness – of individuals:

> The multitude is composed of a set of singularities – and by singularity here we mean a social subject whose difference cannot be reduced to sameness . . . The multitude, although it remains multiple and internally different, is able to act in common and thus rule itself . . . The multitude is the only social subject capable of realizing democracy, that is the rule of everyone by everyone . . .
>
> A multitude is an irreducible multiplicity; the singular social differences that constitute the multitude must always be expressed and can never be flattened into sameness, unity, identity or indifference . . . *The fracturing of modern identities, however, does not prevent the singularities from acting in common. That is the definition of the multitude we started from above: singularities that act in common.*
>
> (Hardt and Negri, 2005, pp. 99, 100, 105; emphasis added)

So once this singularity is recognised and valued, the common can begin to be built, with no contradiction between this singularity and commonality:

Singularities do communicate, and they are able to do so because of the common they share. We share bodies with two eyes, ten fingers, ten toes; we share life on this earth; we share capitalist regimes of production and exploitation; we share common dreams of a better future. Our communication, collaboration, and cooperation, furthermore, not only are based on the common that exists but also in turn produce the common. We make and remake the common we share every day.

(Hardt and Negri, 2005, p. 128)

The common is not, therefore, about the imposition of supposedly essential and shared identities (e.g. national, ethnic or religious), nor about autonomous subjects entering into contractual relations with each other. Rather, it is a process of individuals co-constructing the common, based on what we share and on relationships, communication and collaboration:

> The common does not refer to traditional notions of either the community or the public; it is based on the communication among singularities and emerges through the collaborative social processes of production. Whereas the individual dissolves in the unity of the community, singularities are not diminished but express themselves freely in the common.

(Hardt and Negri, 2005, p. 204)

In a later interview, Michael Hardt again emphasises the constructed, rather than essential, character of the common emerging from the singular:

> We think of the multitude as formed by an assemblage of singularities . . . and the most important thing is that these singularities are not fixed identities, they are always and each becoming different. And they are always and each multiplicities.

(Hardt, 2008, p. 5)

What Hardt and Negri contest is a binary with its two opposites: either atomised individuality or an aggregate that subsumes all difference into a faceless and standardised mass or a chaotic and incoherent mob. They recognise the singularity, the alterity of the individual, but envisage the reconciliation of singularity with a plurality, a multitude which coheres by individuals finding common cause: 'the multitude is an internally different, multiple social subject whose constitution and action is based not on identity or unity [or, much less, indifference] but on what it has in common' (Hardt and Negri, 2005, p. 100).

Bill Readings, in *The University in Ruins*, his enquiry into the university and pedagogical relationships, develops a critique of the 'enlightenment narrative' of education as a search for truth that produces an autonomous subject – an individual learner – made free of obligations by what they learn and the development of reason; and of the neoliberal narrative of education as a project of self-accreditation and entrepreneurship, a process of consuming knowledge in preparation for the market. Rather, he seeks to rebuild a notion of pedagogy as first and foremost an ethical practice that recognises and values both our absolute otherness – our singularity – and relationships, in particular our 'obligation to the existence of otherness', understanding community on 'the model of dependency' (Readings, 1996, p. 190). Education is 'not primarily a matter of communication between autonomous subjects functioning as senders and receivers', and teaching 'should cease to be about merely the transmission of information and the emancipation of the autonomous subject'. Instead education is about 'the drawing out of the otherness of thought' and is in Blanchot's words, 'an infinite attention to the other' (ibid., pp. 156, 160).

The scene of teaching

> belongs to the sphere of justice rather than truth: the relation of student to teacher and teacher to student is one of asymmetrical obligation . . . Justice involves respect for the absolute Other, a respect that must precede any knowledge about the other.
>
> (Readings, 1996, p. 162)

We recognise otherness and respect otherness, but can still work with otherness in an overtly ethical relationship:

> Listening to thought is not the spending of time in the production of an autonomous subject or an autonomous body of knowledge. Rather, to listen to Thought, to think beside each other and beside ourselves is to explore an open network of obligation that keeps the question of meaning open as a locus of debate. Doing justice to Thought, listening to our interlocutors, means trying to hear what cannot be said but that which tries to make itself heard. And this is a process incompatible with the production of [even relatively] stable and exchangeable knowledge.
>
> (Readings, 1996, p. 165)

Readings' ideas resonate with some of our earlier discussions of an ethics of an encounter (he acknowledges the relationship with Levinas), a pedagogy of listening, education as ethical practice, education as an open-ended network of obligation, education as openness rather than closure. But in terms of our discussion here, he sketches out important ideas about the relationship of the singular and the common. He contests the need to equate singularity with the concept of the autonomous, independent subject, the icon of neoliberalism, proposing instead that singularity can go with (inter) dependency and obligation based on relationships of listening and strong social bonds: for we are, Readings believes,

> addicted to others, and no amount of twelve-stepping will allow us to overcome that dependence, to make it the object of a fully autonomous subjective consciousness . . . there is no freeing ourselves of the social bond, precisely because we do not come to the end of it.
>
> (Readings, 1996, p. 190)

From her work in Reggio Emilia, Carlina Rinaldi is drawn to a similar relationship between the singular and the collective. She rejects the current trend towards individualisation, with its emphasis on the individual and individual educational actions, since it fails to recognise not only how the individual learns within the group, but also the possibility of the group itself learning, building collective knowledge, becoming a learning group. Both individual and group thought grows and advances through interrelationships involving difference and confrontation (using the term in its Italian sense[6]):

> Controversy and the conflict of ideas play a fundamental role in this system, bringing out the significant aspects of individual thought and at the same time giving new meaning to the knowledge-building process. This is because knowledge develops much more within a context of diversity rather than in one of homogeneity, and also because in situations of conflicting interpretations, the need to argue your own point of view is the catalyst for the fundamental process of metacognition (knowledge of knowledge), providing an opportunity for 're-knowing' your knowledge in a different light, enriched by the new and different opinions offered by others.
>
> (Rinaldi, 2006, p. 127)

Singularity and its construction depends on social processes of learning and communication; we need, she argues, to 'promote a singularity which does not simply open up to exchange in a process of self growth, but rather "negotiates" its structure and identity in a permanent process taking place inside contexts' (Dahlberg *et al.*, 2007, p. xxi). In short, it is as mistaken to focus on individual performance and achievement in isolation as to dwell excessively on the group; individuals learn in group settings, singularities form in social contexts.

The common school, therefore, starts with singularities, which are themselves in a state of flux, or becoming, and provides a space for these singularities making and remaking both themselves and the common. Within the common school individuals or singularities can form collectivities and multitudes, which in their turn are highly productive. The common school (to return to Dewey's language) creates a context where diversity can produce community.

This way of approaching the question of the common school's response to diversity has some radical implications. It supports the importance of working with the ethics of an encounter, with its concern for alterity and its resistance to the grasping of the Other and making them into the Same. It questions selective schools that presume the primacy and stasis of a particular value or identity, so constraining the possibility of children and adults forming new and different values and identities and creating new solidarities – unexpected assemblages of singularities; the school is a place primarily for co-construction, not reproduction. It assumes that identity is not prior to society, nor innate, but is formed in and through relationships, so that the relational environment, in which the school has an important part, becomes a matter of great importance. Dewey, once again, provides an important reference point, since he argued 'that the individual, far from being some kind of preformed entity that existed prior to society, was always a product of its social relationships' (Carr and Hartnett, 1996, p. 58). Last but not the least, through providing a pedagogical space 'for original thinking, without rushing to restrict it with predetermined schemes that define what is *correct* according to a school culture' (Vecchi, 2010, p. 138; original emphasis), the common school offers children opportunities to create new and diverse forms of knowledge rather than reproducing pre-existing and standardised knowledge.

Experimentation and the common school

There is another feature of the common school in the radical education system that we envisage, that makes for singularity and diversity: experimentation. Experimentation, as we described in Chapter 2, is an important value in a radical education. It is about bringing something new to life, whether that something is a thought, knowledge, a project, a service or a tangible product. It expresses a willingness, a desire in fact, to invent, to think differently, to imagine and try out different ways of doing things: 'experimentation is always that which is in the process of coming about – the new, remarkable, and interesting that replace the appearance of truth and are more demanding than it is' (Deleuze and Guattari, 1994, p. 111). Experimentation calls for being open-ended (avoiding closure), open-minded (welcoming the unexpected) and open-hearted (valuing difference).

Experimentation can mark the way learning takes place in the common school: indeed, experimentation is the hallmark of a pedagogy for radical education. There are important examples of pedagogical practice inscribed with the value of experimentation, avid to create new knowledge. John Dewey's approach to pedagogy has been described by a recent biographer as 'essentially experimental', expressed in his establishment of a school for testing out ideas, the 'Laboratory School' (Pring, 2007). Gert Biesta and Deborah Osberg also point to the example of Dewey, whose pedagogical approach they describe as 'strongly rooted in the idea that knowledge is not a reflection of the static world but emerges as we engage with or "experience" reality' and whose goal was to make schools 'into places where children could learn directly by experiment and discovery' (Biesta and Osberg, 2007, pp. 25–26).

In another article, Biesta explores further the pedagogical ideas of Dewey and in particular, his view of the centrality of experimentation:

> We basically acquire our habits through processes of trial and error – or, in more theoretical languages, through experimentation. In a very fundamental sense, experimentation is the only way in which we can learn anything at all: we learn because we do and subsequently undergo the consequences of doing. Yet for Dewey, there is a crucial difference between blind trial and error – experimentation without deliberation and direction – and what he calls intelligent action. The difference between the two has to do with the intervention of thinking or reflection.
>
> (Biesta, 2007, p. 14)

Dewey contrasted this 'transactional theory of knowing' with what he called the 'spectator theory of knowledge', which assumes 'an immaterial mind looking at the material world and registering what goes on in it' (Biesta, 2007, p. 13). Dewey also argued that we should be experimental with respect not only to means but also to ends and the interpretation of the problems we address. Such experimentation includes creating new understandings and imagining innovative practices, similar perhaps to what Halpin describes as 'utopian thought experiments', which start from the question '[h]ow would social reality look if we configured it in radically different and improved terms and from different positions than is normally adopted?' (Halpin, 2003, pp. 53–54).

More recently, experimentation can be seen as an important influence in the municipal schools of Reggio Emilia, in particular through what they term a 'pedagogy of listening', with its process of theory-building (meaning-making), active listening to theories, dialogue and confrontation (in its Italian sense, see note 6), then further theory-building. This process provides active encouragement to children to experiment as part of a 'community of inquirers':

> To construct a community of inquirers with an experimental spirit requires listening and a radical dialogue. In 'real' listening children become partners in a process of experimentation and research by inventing problems and by listening to and negotiating what other children, as well as the teacher, are saying and doing. In this process the co-constructing pedagogue has to open her/him self to the unexpected and experiment together with the children – in the here and now event. S/he challenges the children by augmenting connections through enlarging the number of concepts, hypotheses and theories, as well as through new material and through challenging children's more technical work. Besides getting a responsible relation to other children by listening, they also are negotiating in between each other, enlarging the choices that can be made, instead of bringing choice down to universal trivializations.
>
> (Dahlberg and Bloch, 2006, p. 114)

Experimentation in Reggio Emilia is actively pursued through their ways of working. Project work, introduced in Chapter 1, encourages and supports experimentation, by offering opportunities to hypothesise, test out theories, explore new meanings, take off in unexpected directions; but to do so, to be experimental, project work must be able to grow 'in many directions, with no predefined progression, no outcomes decided before the journey begins' (Rinaldi, 2005, p. 19). The idea of the project-as-experiment, creating possibilities for exploring and making meaning, and how it can contrast strongly with learning as the transmission of meaningless information, is caught in these reflections from Ann Åberg, a Swedish pre-school teacher working with inspiration from Reggio Emilia, on a project about crows undertaken with four- and five-year-olds:

> When I think back on previous bird-related projects, I recall that we teachers focused on teaching children basic facts about birds, such as the names of the most common birds. In retrospect I ask myself: For whom were these names so important? And I wonder how meaningful it was for the children. Did they actually learn something about birds that they found exciting? Nor do I

remember choosing birds as a theme because the children actually showed interest in birds. Birds were just one of many topics that we were supposed to look at with children.

We called this project Crow. But the project did not deal only with crows. If it had, it would have become tedious. For children and teachers alike the project dealt with so much more – discovering the joy of learning together and the dialogue with other investigators, thinkers and researchers. It was about experimenting with different languages; listening, discussing, imagining and asking ourselves questions; examining and questioning the teacher's role in enabling children to participate more in their own learning processes. It dealt with learning to feel and shape an intimate relation with animals and nature and to challenge and question scientific truths.

(Åberg, 2005, p. 21)

Experimentation is enabled through working with and making connections between multiple languages, facilitated by *ateliers* and *atelieristas*, such as Vea Vecchi. We reiterate their central part in the creation of an experimenting common school, in particular through their role in making connections: 'thinking is, above all else, experimentation, and can only be understood through the connections it invites', since through making connections 'something unexpected, surprising, provoking may happen' (Dahlberg, 2004, p. 22).

The final example of experimentation as a value in pedagogical practice comes from a recent book by Liselott Marriet Olsson, *Movement and Experimentation in Young Children's Learning*. Starting from the premise that young children and learning are today often tamed, predicted, supervised, controlled and evaluated according to pre-determined standards, the book argues that the challenge to practise and research is to find ways of regaining movement and experimentation in learning. Inspired by the work of Gilles Deleuze and his colleague Feliz Guattari and also by Reggio Emilia, Olsson demonstrates the possibilities for experimentation in the classroom through documenting and analysis of extensive experience in Swedish pre-schools:

In many of the preschools in the city of Stockholm and its suburbs and at the Stockholm Institute of Education, 'every day magical moments' take place. Children, preschool teachers, teacher students, teacher educators and research-ers come together and are literally caught up in the desire to experiment with subjectivity and learning. In these practices experimentations and intense, unpre-dictable events are taking place, concerning the idea of what a child is, what a teacher should do, the purpose of a preschool and its organisation, contents and forms.

(Olsson, 2009, p. 11)

Experimentation in learning is not just about experimentation as an intrinsic part of learning processes in school; it can also involve experimenting in schools with different theories and practices to enrich and deepen these processes. Early child-hood education provides important examples. We have just mentioned Swedish early childhood educators working with the theoretical perspectives of French poststructural philosophers, Deleuze and Guattari. But such experimentation has been underway for some time now. Joseph Tobin, one of the American founders in the 1980s of the Reconceptualizing Early Childhood Education movement, which contests the positivist mainstream, has noted that

> although post-structural theorists such as Michel Foucault, Mikhail Bakhtin, Judith Butler, Frederic Jameson, Michel de Certeau, Jean Baudrillard, Jacques Derrida, Gayatri Spivak, and Homi Bhabba have written little or nothing about young children, their theories beg to be applied to early childhood education.
>
> (Tobin, 2007, pp. 28–29)

Not only do their theories beg to be applied, they are being so: early childhood researchers and practitioners, in universities and pre-schools, are experimenting with their use in practice. Today, you can read the experiences of academic and early years educators who are 'doing' not only Deleuze and Guattari in everyday early childhood education, but Foucault, Derrida, Bakhtin and others (cf. Dahlberg and Moss, 2005; Mac Naughton, 2005; Edmiston, 2007; Lenz Taguchi, 2009). Such experimentation in what are, in effect, common schools for young children make early childhood arguably the most innovative branch of education today.

But experimentation need not be confined to learning; it can also be expressed in the projects initiated by the common school, working with families and, indeed, the whole local community, what we termed earlier as 'community projects'. Schools can keep to the stated goals and tasks, the prescribed menu of activities for 'extended schools'. Or they can experiment, generating new activities that emerge from participation by citizens and their engagement with the school. Working in this way, like the Sheffield Children's Centre (see Box 3.4), they can be 'extended experimental schools', from which new projects are created from the school's sense of responsibility and a desire of all concerned to try something new. Experimentation here may involve further learning, for example with adults, but also for many other purposes: family support, building solidarities, supporting resistance to injustice and exclusion, sustaining culture, generating the local economy, strengthening democracy, etc.

Like democracy, therefore, experimentation can have its more formal side, which involves deciding upon and implementing new projects in a service or community. But it also represents a way of living and relating, expressed for example in educational relationships within the school that are open for experimentation by adults and children alike. It can be a new take on an old subject, bringing to bear new perspectives and methods; or responding to a new subject, one that has emerged because of changing conditions or new understandings.

Responsibility of and for the common school

We have proposed a radical education based on democracy as a fundamental value. The common school is a place for children and adults, educators, parents and others, to practise democracy. At the institutional level, we envisage schools that are democratically governed, by a governing board elected by the school *and* its local community, and by various representative school bodies, such as the mix of Panels and Meetings that played such an active and central role in the life of St George-in-the-East school. Formal democratic management is complemented by democratic practice permeating, as we have seen, into the common school's everyday practices and relationships; it is lived not taught democracy. But what is the relationship between the democratic school and the democratic local community – the democratically-elected and democratically-run municipality, commune, council or local authority?

In recent years, the key axis in English education has shifted from the local authority – the political expression of community – and the school, to national government (and its agencies) – the political expression of the nation state – and the school. Increasingly, the relationship between school and political community has been weakened and, in an increasing number of cases, such as 'academies', severed altogether. In the process, democracy and the potential for democratic participation by the community in the education of its children has been eroded; this must, in our view, be reversed if the kind of education and school we envisage are to flourish.

Our starting point is that education is not just a market relationship between parents and schools and a regulatory relationship between schools and national government. Nor is it acceptable to hand over public schooling to closed groups to run, whether wealthy sponsors, parent groups or companies. It is undemocratic, severing a school from the community as a whole and from public responsibility for children and their education; and it privatises what should be a public space and institution. Today's wealthy sponsors, the parents of today's children and the management of today's companies all have a legitimate interest in and responsibility for education – but so too does everyone else. A radical democratic education resists the exclusion of anyone, today or tomorrow, from active participation in education and schools and the privileging of one group over other citizens.

All citizens, we repeat, have an interest in and responsibility for the education of children. It is a public responsibility, involving the national political community – the nation state – and the local political community – or local authority. The state, of which children and adults are citizens, expresses its responsibility for children's education through certain common and democratically-determined values, goals, entitlements and structures. In our scenario, it would collectively decide for radical education and the common school, based on adoption of certain key values, notably democracy, ethics, concepts and images. It would support the development of structures to enable them, for example a re-formed workforce suited to the common school. It would define entitlements to education, not only a compulsory phase of attendance but also an entitlement to voluntary attendance at either side of compulsory education, for example from birth or soon after (as in the Nordic countries) and to higher education. It would define certain goals for education, probably expressed in the form of a curriculum, and some system for evaluating how these goals were being addressed and with what success. In short, radical education and the common school are compatible with a national framework that applies a degree of coherence across the territory of the nation state and expresses a view about what all citizens share in common.

The framework would consciously allow space for diversity, indeed would positively support diversity by assuming experimentation as a shared national value and providing support for experimentation – it would be a state that valued, welcomed and guaranteed experimentation. It would be a state that similarly valued, welcomed and guaranteed democracy throughout the educational system, acknowledging democracy as a fundamental educational value and positively supporting democracy not only in national decision-making but in local decision-making and practice, whether in local communities or schools. Indeed, one facet of national evaluation of education would be the health of both democracy and experimentation in schools. And it would be a state that ensured that local bodies adhered to the values, entitlements and goals of the national framework, so placing some limits on decentralisation, autonomy and diversity: so our advocacy for decentralisation, diversity and democracy does not mean 'anything goes' as long as people freely choose it.

But the local and democratic political community – the local authority – also should have responsibility for the education of its children, indeed more broadly for the relationship between its children and the community. This does not mean going back to a situation where local authorities manage schools directly. Schools should be democratically managed in a system of governance marked by decentralisation and widespread participation, by children and adults, teachers and parents, school and local communities. Nor does it mean excluding more local communities, within each local authority. A radical education calls for local authorities to work closely with both communities and schools. We agree with Alan Dyson and his colleagues that the current marketised model must change so that 'communities have an active voice in shaping local education provision' and that this requires mechanisms to be 'developed to enable communities to be actively engaged in shaping education in their area' (Dyson *et al.*, 2010, pp. 11, 15). Moreover, our image of the common school as a public space, a forum and a collaborative workshop also envisages a close, inclusive and democratic relationship between local community and local school.

But this still means an important role for the local authority (or council, commune, municipality or whatever other name elected local government goes under) in education, as a democratic partner to the democratically-run school; no school that is publicly funded, and therefore a responsibility of the public, should be outside this central democratic relationship, no school should just be an autonomous institution. The local authority has responsibility for the education and schools of its children, and those schools have responsibilities towards the local authority.

We use the term 'responsibility' here in preference to accountability. As we argued in Chapter 2, there is such a thing as democratic accountability, which we equate with shared responsibility. But in today's neoliberal climate, 'accountability' is widely understood in a predominantly contractual and legal sense as 'a largely negative instrument of social and political control' (Fielding, 2001b, p. 699); it is the language of the market, commodification and exchange between trading partners. 'Responsibility' on the other hand is primarily an ethical concept, and 'elicits and requires a felt and binding mutuality . . . [it] tends to be a largely positive, morally resonant means of encouraging mutually supportive endeavour to which both, or all parties feel reciprocally and interdependently committed' (ibid., p. 700). 'Responsibility' is also the language of care – we feel responsible *for* the other. Given current associations, therefore, we prefer to stick with the term responsibility in this discussion.

The relationship between a local authority and its common schools is defined, therefore, by democracy and responsibility. This means, we think, that local authorities – as the political expression of the larger local community within which common schools are situated – assume three main roles. First, *they participate in the democratic self-government of common schools*, through (as is currently the case in England) some members of the governing body representing the local authority, as well as providing one conduit for dialogue and exchange between local authority and school.

Second, *local authorities define a local cultural project of education for their community*, a collective vision for the area, in relationship with schools, local communities and citizens, and also in relationship with a common national policy that defines radical democratic education and the common school as two of its broad aims. Supporting democracy at all levels includes strong decentralisation of responsibility and decision-making, from central to local government and from local government to local communities and individual institutions. This would include, for example, what have been termed framework curricula (OECD, 2006, p. 209), broad national guidelines that allow extensive scope for local interpretation – by local authorities and schools – of the constituents that make up the framework, as well as space for the expression of a local educational identity expressing locally determined values and objectives. You can see such a relationship expressed in the Swedish pre-school curriculum, a relatively short document (19 pages in the English version) (Swedish Ministry for Education, 1998), setting out broad fundamental values and tasks for the pre-school and general goals and guidelines, but leaving plenty of room for local meaning-making and variations. Nearer home, the Cambridge Primary Review (2009) for England proposes a curriculum divided between nationally determined and local determined components, to account for 70 and 30 per cent of teaching time respectively. While Alan Dyson and his colleagues call for 'an element of local determinism over the curriculum and scope for locally created learning opportunities' (Dyson *et al.*, 2010, p. 9).

Local government has a responsibility to work with national government and within the context of the national education framework. But local government is not just the agent of national government: it should be an active subject, not just a local interpreter of the national framework. It should be a vigorous participant in education, in its own right, with the capacity to undertake its own collective and political process of thought and deliberation leading to local action: in short, to create a local cultural project of childhood or education. In the past a number of Chief Education Officers in English Local Authorities – for example, Henry Morris in Cambridgeshire, Alec Clegg in the West Riding of Yorkshire, Stewart Mason in Leicestershire, and Tim Brighouse in Oxfordshire and in Birmingham – have not only developed such a role locally, but exerted significant national influence through the depth and integrity of their thought and the symbiotic vibrancy of its lived practice. The city of Reggio Emilia provides another vivid example, where the municipality has taken responsibility for fostering local pedagogical thought and practice, resulting in a distinct pedagogical project, a Reggio Emilia 'approach' to the education of its young citizens, involving participation by municipal schools, educators, administrators, local politicians and other citizens.

Such local educational identities may not always be very different to those in other areas; for example, in Northern Italy, as we have already seen, there has been much exchange and dialogue between active local authorities that participated in 'the municipal school revolution', places such as Parma, Pistoia, Bologna, Modena, San Miniato, to name a few (Catarsi, 2004). This has led to some broad similarities of approach, but has also left some important differences of opinion and perspective. Some local authorities will be better at developing local cultural projects, more able to work democratically and innovatively. Moreover, the national educational framework will define some common strands with which all local authorities will have to work.

So, the second role of the local authority in relation to schools is as a leader and facilitator of the development of a local educational project, a shared and democratic exploration of the meaning and practice of education and the potential of the school. This project provides an educational context and ethos, as well as a forum for exchange, confrontation, dialogue and learning between schools.

Third, *the local authority engages with schools in the implementation of a local educational project developed within the framework of a national policy for radical democratic education and the common school.* This will not be easy; too many past attempts at experimentation and innovation have faltered or failed after a short time, often for lack of sustained political and organisational support. There is no guarantee of success, but the best chances for successful transformation, and for the experimentation that goes with it, will arise in a supportive political climate and with great attention being paid to building a strong supportive infrastructure. The local authority has a key role to play in both.

It does this by adopting a political commitment to pursuing radical education and the common school, and to developing a local educational project that incorporates these goals whilst taking account of local conditions and complexities, local needs and desires, and local ideas and projects. The local authority should be well-placed to understand and respond to this singular context.

It does this through promoting and supporting cooperation between schools, and indeed other services – ideally collegial or communal, but at least collaborative. The English education policy is currently premised on promoting competition between schools, and in early childhood the Childcare Act 2006 actually requires local authorities to actively manage the 'childcare' market. In our thinking about local political responsibility for education, there would be no place for managing markets or promoting competition. Instead, the task for local authorities, indeed the duty placed on them, would be that of promoting connectedness and collegiality within networks of municipal schools and other services to further the goal of a radical democratic education.

Last but not least, it does this by creating a local infrastructure to support the development of the local educational project, both in individual schools and through building and invigorating networks between schools, and between schools, communities and the local authority. This infrastructure would consist of a variety of shared resources, at the centre of which would be a team of educational coordinators, what are termed *pedagogistas* in Reggio Emilia.

Carlina Rinaldi describes the crucial role played by the local authority team of *pedagogistas* in Reggio Emilia, within schools, between schools, and between schools and their communities and the city itself; they listen, they dialogue, they make links, and they connect theory with practice, the work and organisation of the school with the project of the municipality. They are, Rinaldi says, 'responsible for the relationship between the inside and the outside world' (2006, p. 167), making connections, crossing borders, improving flows, offering new perspectives, etc. By doing so, they can foster participation in the local educational project and cultivate a shared educational identity.

Annalia Galardini, the head of early childhood education in Pistoia, another Italian city which has taken responsibility for the education of its young children by creating its own local educational project, describes the team of *pedagogistas* in that local authority as 'a decisive factor in the quality of local networks of services' and develops Rinaldi's discussion of the *pedagogista* role:

> [The *pedagogista*'s role] is to nurture and improve the quality of educational policies for children . . . One of the *pedagogista*'s strategic functions has been to guarantee a link between the various services in order to develop a unified educational identity and a shared perception of children's needs. This coordination function emphasises dialogue and collaboration between educators, schools and families . . . [The role] has meant giving visibility to good practices, guiding individual services away from a self-referential educational style, and, above all, the opportunity to project the identity of the nurseries and nursery schools to the outside community . . . This has been the *pedagogista*'s task: to ensure that there are links between the services in order to create networks and to set down roots in the local area; and to foster a spirit of collaboration and open-mindedness in order to raise awareness and sensitivity in the local community about children's rights and the function of nurseries and nursery schools.
>
> (Galardini, 2008, p. 18)

There can be many other parts to the local authority's infrastructure for promoting and supporting the local educational project, in addition to the team of *pedagogistas*. Reggio Emilia, again, provides an interesting model of this implementation role of the local authority. The city's municipal schools each have their own distinct identities and manage themselves, either through the staff acting as a cooperative, along with management committees drawn from staff, parents and local citizens, or as services privately run by other cooperatives but with an agreement signed with the city. But the schools also have a clear municipal identity, they are engaged in a common project, and the city provides a key role in the construction of that project.

In addition to the work of the *pedagogistas*, that project finds collective and public expression in a range of project work, displays, seminars and conferences, publications and two public travelling exhibitions. The first, *The Hundred Languages of Children*, has been produced in six different versions since 1981, for Italy and the rest of Europe, North America, Australia, France, Holland and Japan. The second new travelling exhibition is called *The Wonder of Learning*, and has been authored by children, *atelieristas*, teachers and *pedagogistas* in Reggio Emilia's schools and two schools in a small nearby town. What these exhibitions offer, and what all local authorities could work towards, is documentation of how that political community has developed its thinking and practice and with what results in terms of children's learning and knowledge production.

Before moving away from this topic, we should add one last component to the responsibility of elected local authorities towards the common school. They should be the admissions authority for their area, being responsible for the process of allocating children to schools. For the common school, this means defining (and keeping under review) the catchment areas of each school or cluster of schools.

But the relationship of responsibility between local authority and school is not one way. What is the responsibility of the common school towards the democratically elected political community? First and foremost, to be active in the development and implementation of local educational projects, contributing towards their construction, practice, evaluation and reconstruction. Schools share their perspectives, experiences and knowledges with each other and with the local authority; their work, including their *ateliers* and pedagogical documentation, is invaluable to the wider community for deepening its understanding of education. They actively participate in shared projects with other schools and with other parts of the local authority and other organisations and groups in the local authority. They cross borders and experiment, and share the resultant 'immaterial production' to the common good.

But common schools are also responsible to the local authority for their work, including how they are working with the national framework and the local educational project. Through political representation on governing bodies, through the involvement of *pedagogistas*, through processes such as pedagogical documentation, common schools must make their pedagogical work and the learning it is producing visible and subject to evaluation by the wider community.

Before leaving the relationship between the local authority and the school, we should acknowledge that, in England at least, some will view any hint of closer relations with concern, if not horror. In some quarters, local authority involvement in education has a bad name, and cases can be cited in support of this. As with much else in this book, we have no magic solutions or cast iron guarantees to offer: everything is dangerous and every proposal has downsides.

We would, however, make four points. First, as we have indicated earlier, there are examples of local authorities that have been innovative, supportive and democratic in their relationship with schools, and we should learn from them in a study of how to strengthen the role of local authorities. Second, everything connects, so the development of radical education and the common school needs to go hand-in-hand with the renewal and development of democratic local government, which in our view has to include an active and innovative role in education. Third, the relationship of schools and education with any wider democratic body is bound to be fraught, but is also bound to be pursued if education is acknowledged to be a public responsibility; cutting schools off from the wider community, handing them over to closed bodies to govern (be they businesses, parent groups or other unrepresentative organisations) is no answer to the issue of democratic responsibility and is incompatible with a radical education. Fourth, get the relationship right and schools have much to gain from membership of a thriving local education system, gains that are not available from central government or from being autonomous institutions. So we are left with working on and working through the relationship between schools and local authorities, a necessity we face both with trepidation but also with considerable hope since a successful relationship has much to offer both partners.

But we should see the relationship between schools and local authorities as part of a bigger picture: relationships of responsibility between national and local governments and between local governments and common schools, democratic relationships between democratic bodies. Like any relationship, these relationships are full of potential and actual tensions and even conflicts and are always in movement. In particular, there will often be the desire on one side to be more controlling and to press for more coherence and uniformity, in tension with the desire from others for more freedom and diversity. This tension goes back forever and there is no final solution to it – no perfect point of balance which once found can remove all future tension and need for change.

So we have no magic solution to this tension, just some thoughts about how its positive aspects might be enhanced and its destructive tendencies reduced. The adoption of democracy as a fundamental value and reference point by all concerned is essential, since it provides a means for confronting and negotiating the issue of diversity and coherence. This in turn means decentralisation and redistribution from national to local and from local to individual school, which must be based on mutual trust and a mutual sense of responsibility; all is lost if the relationship degenerates into that of management, with each layer trying to control and exploit the next level down.

Finally, we wonder – and this is pure speculation – whether size matters in government, just as in schools. England is a large centralised state with a relatively small number of local authorities, averaging a third of a million people (the average size of Swedish local authorities is 28,000). Does this, perhaps, militate against democratic relations of mutual responsibility? Does this instead encourage managerial relations of control and command? Of course other influences play their part, for example in the case of England a very long history of highly centralised administration. But large units of government smack rather of the days when the task was to administer the population, mould it to a common sense of national identity, and ensure the inculcation of certain common skills and allegiances. That notion of governance may not be conducive to radical education and the common school.

Inequality and choice: two thorny issues

Our concept of the common school providing radical education raises many issues. Some concern implementation, more technical in nature though never without political elements – how would you take the idea forward and transform the scene of education? We address some of these points in the next chapter. Others are more fundamentally and intrinsically political, involving conflicting principles and goals and making choices as between them, choices which are not without drawback and cost.

We consider here two of these thorny issues, which are difficult to resolve without some pain.

Education in an unequal society

Education would be so much easier in a society with low levels of income inequality, few very poor or very rich families and socially mixed and cohesive communities. So much of educational policy in many countries has been driven and constrained by the consequences of not having produced such societies. Instead, inequality goes hand-in-hand with segregated communities, differentiated by class, income and, often, ethnicity and religion. A major argument against the common school is that in such unequal and divided societies, where richer and poorer are often segregated into different localities, for a school to serve a local community will consign some schools and children to certain failure (at least in conventional academic standards). Schools, the argument runs, function best when they have a mix of children from different social and economic backgrounds, and schools with large intakes of children from poor families are seen to face an uphill task. A concentration of 'low ability' children will produce a 'low performance' school, bad for school and children alike.

There are several points to make in response to this concern. First, we must be wary of the concept of 'ability', with its corollary that children vary in ability. While this may be true if ability is thought of in narrow academic terms, if we adopt the image of the 'rich child', born with a hundred languages, then the picture may be more complex and variations in ability less clear-cut – that is if we treat ability as multidimensional.

As we suggested in Chapter 1, it is important to remind ourselves of a long tradition of radical practice and rigorous research that questions the intellectual legitimacy as well as the moral and educational defensibility of ability grouping. Particularly compelling is the work of Alison Peacock (2005, 2006) whose leadership of the Wroxham School, a primary school in Hertfordshire (England), not only confronts the juggernaut of largely ignorant, predominantly visceral support for setting and streaming/tracking, but also demonstrates the success of creative alternatives. At its latest inspection, the school was again judged by OFSTED (the national schools inspection agency in England) to be 'Grade 1 outstanding' in all respects.

All children have potential, and the educational task is to resist an overly narrow understanding of potential (focusing, typically, on a handful of languages at the expense of many others), but also to realise that potential through supporting learning processes that build on new understandings of learning and knowledge. The concept of 'ability' seems apt for an education and school whose task is purely to produce pupils trained and graded for a hierarchical labour market – 'low ability' for the unskilled end, 'high ability' for lawyers, accountants and bankers. It is not so apt for an education and school whose aim is an education in its broadest sense and to develop the many languages that children bring to the formal education process. This is not to deny that a significant proportion of children struggle to gain fluency in certain highly-valued languages, such as reading, writing, maths, or that these children and their schools need resources to help gain that fluency. But it is a reminder of the multiplicity of languages available, of how fluency in one language can aid fluency in others and of the dangers of expectations that are both too low and too narrowly framed – the image of the 'poor' child.

Second, the dilemma about school intake remains the classic example of an education system having to deal with the fallout from a deeply unequal and socially segregated society. The more unequal and segregated the society, the more difficult, if not impossible, it becomes to have schools with a 'socially mixed' intake, especially in larger urban areas. The basic problem of income inequality and residential segregation is exacerbated not only by a marketised public education, but by a school system that includes a significant private sector reliant on parents able to pay high fees and that serves the interests of those at the top of the social and economic hierarchy, and whose purpose (all too successfully achieved) is to reproduce privilege and inequality.

To reaffirm our position: whilst abolishing private, fee-paying, so-called 'public' schools (what private schools are, misleadingly, called in England) may be politically unachievable in the UK and many other countries across the world at the present time, the ethical case for and the political desirability of doing so remain as compelling as ever. We would do well to remember that revered figures in the tradition of British ethical socialism such as R. H. Tawney and such contemporary icons of good sense and humanity as the playwright Alan Bennett, have been less equivocal than today's politicians on the matter. For Tawney, who was himself educated at Rugby (public school) and at Balliol College Oxford, public schools were monuments to inequality and snobbery. As Hywel Williams reminds us

> Towards the end of the 1945 Labour government, R. H. Tawney said that the failure to abolish public schools would undermine everything the Labour movement had achieved in other areas. It was the one reform that mattered – the profound one from which all other changes in the way the English treated each other and looked at the world would flow.
>
> (Williams, 2000)

For Bennett, 'quite plainly the public school should be abolished'. Whilst acknowledging its inevitable unpopularity his firm view was that it would, nonetheless, be worth it because such schools cause 'a fissure running through British society' (BBC, 2008). We concur with such sentiments: whilst from the standpoint of a pragmatic politics fee-paying schools cannot be abolished, they really have no place in and only serve to undermine a society committed to democracy, justice and solidarity and are quite incompatible with radical education.

We are back here to the conclusions of Wilkinson and Pickett, whose work on inequality we introduced in the first chapter, and which Peter Wilby (2009) succinctly summarises: 'we have a social and economic problem, and we have to tackle that before we have a hope of curing educational problems'. If we want a better functioning and healthier society, then we need to pay serious attention to reducing inequality; and you do not do that primarily via educational policies, though you need to design them so they support, rather than work against, the goal of a more equal society. You do not do it by a policy of marketisation and parental choice, which works, as we have seen, against those at the bottom end of the hierarchy and further fragments an already badly divided society, a theme to which we return later. In the meantime, the issue of social mix in school admission remains fraught in unequal societies under any system.

Our third and final point is that perhaps, to mitigate some of the worst educational effects of highly segregated communities, especially in cities, the common school could have a variant. In most cases, it will simply serve its very local catchment area. But in some others it might serve a rather wider catchment area, but on the basis of banding by academic ability, so each school serving this extended area gets a mix of a certain kind of academic ability by band from its larger catchment area; this is not original and untried, for example forming the basis for school admissions for some years in London. Yet, we see problems with this – as with any system. Apart from our ambivalence about the concept 'ability', how would this work in age-integrated schools? When banding was applied in London, so that each school got a cross section of children classified by academic ability, this was for children assessed at 11, prior to secondary school entrance. But how would banding work if the key admission point was at five or six years, or even younger? Again, this and other variants should be high on the agenda for research, debate and experimentation.

Parental choice

Our proposal of radical education and the common school does attach strong value to parental choice, but to a particular understanding of this choice: parents participating in the democratic life of a common school, including *collective* choice or decision-making, as opposed to the *individual* choice of the market model. A recent report into democracy in the UK draws the distinction:

> We do not believe that the consumer and the citizen are one and the same, as the new market-driven technocracy seems to assume. Consumers act as individuals, making decisions largely on how an issue will affect themselves and their families. Citizenship implies membership of a collective where decisions are taken not just in the interest of the individual but for the collective as a whole or for a significant part of that collective.
>
> (Power Inquiry, 2006, p. 169)

Both kinds of choice – consumer and collective decisions – have value, but we must decide the relative value we attach to each kind in any given context. So when it comes to doing the weekly shopping, individual choice might be predominant (though does that mean we should be free to choose meat from animals that have been cruelly raised? Or products brought to us at high environmental cost?). But when it comes to education, viewed as a public responsibility, then we would argue that collective choice is more important. Indeed, we would agree with Tom Bentley who blames a shift from collective to individual choice-making for the contemporary crisis of democracy:

Liberal democracy combined with market capitalism has reinforced the tendency of individuals to act in ways that reduce our ability to make collective choices. This is the underlying reason for the crisis in democracy . . . Not enough people see democratic politics as part of their own personal identity to sustain the cultures and institutions through which political legitimacy is created. The result is that our preoccupation with making individual choices is undermining our ability to make collective choices. Our democracy is suffocating itself.

(Bentley, 2005, pp. 9, 19)

Sadly, education offers an all too clear example of this shift.

Parents, but also children, in a radical education system and attending common schools engage in democratic activities and practices that enable them to make public and collective choices taking the common good into account. They are all citizens able to participate in the co-construction of person-centred learning, in the evaluative and other purposes of pedagogical documentation, and the projects of the school as collaborative workshop. This does not preclude opportunities for the expression of individual choice. Indeed, we would argue that our conception of radical education pays far more attention to individuality by recognising, for example, the centrality of meaning-making and the significance of the hundred languages in the educational process; in present circumstances, children have little individual choice in an educational process in which outcomes are not only predetermined – what is wanted is what has been pre-specified – but also expressed and assessed in terms of standardised and universal norms, such as learning or developmental goals.

But at the same time as building up collective choice, our direction calls for a questioning of instances of individual choice, to ensure they are not at the expense of more important values. Take individual parental choice of school, a central tenet of the current dominant educational discourse. The underlying rationality for pursuing these market policies is set out in a UNESCO report:

In standard economic theory, choice and competition are two of the most powerful drivers of efficiency, with the spur of the market acting to raise productivity and enhance welfare. Few people see education provision as directly comparable with the production of market goods and services. But competition and its corollary, choice, are increasingly seen as antidotes for the failings of public education systems in relation to learning standards and equity gaps.

(UNESCO, 2008, p. 159)

But as we saw in Chapter 1, there is no compelling evidence that parental choice and school competition in a marketised education system have 'delivered' in their own terms, and indeed may have exacerbated inequalities, middle-class parents being better equipped than others to play the markets and win their choices. We might add, too, that parental choice policies too often end up as school choice policies, in which schools choose pupils, so creating a vicious circle of a coterie of 'successful' schools picking the most academically able children from an ever-growing body of parent suitors so producing ever better examination results, ever greater demand

and growing dissatisfaction among the many parents whose children must go to other schools.

So, it seems to us, an education system centred around competition and individual choice is not free of its own thorny issues, struggling to deliver its own promises. We are not contesting a well-functioning system, but offering an alternative to a decidedly rickety system, which does not work very well in its own terms and has socially dysfunctional consequences. We would argue, instead, for putting this aspect of individual choice (parental selection of schools in a competitive market) in its place, as a lesser value, rather than treating it as a self-evidently central value.

One implication of the common school is a reining back on parental choice of school, and the importance attached to shopping around in an educational market. Instead, parents (and others) are encouraged to participate in the collective life of a democratic institution, building on but going far beyond the collective decision-making role of school governors. Can there be any significant scope left for parents to choose between schools in an education premised on the common school? Can shopping around co-exist with the idea of the common school? The only possibility we can see to explore is the possibility of choice where the common school is organised on a 'schools-within-school' basis, where different school units may develop distinct pedagogical approaches and parents and pupils may have some choice between them, either for their whole school career or for certain parts of it; the Morialta High School featured in Box 3.3 offers one example of how this might work.

Another implication of the common school is that it provides no public encouragement and little public support to so-called faith schools. The common school recognises and respects religious affiliation as one of many dimensions of diversity and identity, and treats religion, in its many forms, as a feature of the community and wider society in which it is situated. But it is not the task of the common school either to inculcate or uphold a particular set of beliefs and values for a particular group of children nor, by implication, to attach primacy to one aspect of identity over others. Indeed, following the argument of Unger (developed further in Chapter 4) that schools should give children 'powers of insight and action and the access to alien experience', we would argue that the essential tasks of the school in radical education are to expose children (and parents) to diversity and otherness, to enable them to think for themselves, and to equip them to live in a democracy of plural values, multiple identities and diverse ways of life. This is what John Gray terms a democracy of *modus vivendi*, in contrast to a democracy based on the ideal of rational consensus. Democracy based on the principle of *modus vivendi* starts from recognising, even welcoming, an irreducible plurality of values and perspectives. The aim:

> is to reconcile individuals and ways of life honouring conflicting values to a life in common. We do not need common values in order to live together in peace. We need common institutions in which many forms of life can coexist.
>
> (Gray, 2009, p. 25)

We might, therefore, consider the common school as one of these common institutions. Parents and confessional communities may strive, if they so choose, to reproduce their beliefs, practices and identities through their children – but it is not the job of the state nor the common school to involve themselves in furthering such sectional projects.

This does not mean, we repeat, a school that ignores the sensibilities of different faith groups, for example with respect to diet or dress. It does not mean a school that seeks to replace one set of parental beliefs, practices and identities with another 'authorised' set. Nor does it mean a school without values or ethics; we have emphasised the importance of a national framework of values and ethics in our concept of radical education. But these are democratically agreed values and ethics, collective choices, values that attach importance to justice, solidarity, experimentation and democracy; and ethics that are 'non-denominational' and relational, foregrounding care and respect for diversity, and developing the capacity for all members of the school community to make responsible, contextualised ethical judgements.

The common school and the school of diversity

Today in England, we have the worst kind of school system. On the one hand, it offers a dizzying array of different types of school and different providers, responding to the market imperative of consumer choice and competition, and expressing a political desperation that if only the right market mix can be found, everything else will fall into place. On the other hand, the system develops increasingly strong methods – technologies – for control and standardisation. The result is a mixture of social fragmentation and pedagogical normalisation; the diverse school system and the school of uniformity. Underpinning all is the 'silver bullet' mentality, a belief that the hard and sustained work of thought, deliberation and practice – the 'secrets' to the achievements of St George's and Reggio Emilia – can be avoided by buying-in to some wonder technology, some guaranteed panacea or some new form of management theory.

The common school, by contrast, offers a more uniform system, networks of smaller, age-integrated and self-governing schools serving local communities and in a close, mutual and democratic relationship with their local authorities. But it combines this with a strong commitment to diversity – or, we should say, diversities. This commitment is expressed through a recognition of singularity, a resistance to working with predefined categories and outcomes, support for the construction of identities and solidarities, and a desire to experiment in learning and other projects.

4 Transforming education

What is pragmatically possible is not fixed independently of our imaginations, but is itself shaped by our visions . . . What we need, then, is 'real utopias': utopian ideals that are grounded in the real potentials of humanity, utopian destinations that have accessible waystations, utopian designs of institutions that can inform our practical tasks of navigating a world of imperfect conditions for social change.

(Wright, 2009a, pp. 1, 4)

Every programmatic proposal worth thinking about marks out a path leading from where we are, in some desired direction, through a succession of steps. A deterministic social theory, and one embracing the idea of indivisible institutional systems succeeding one another according to a preestablished script, leaves no room for thinking about alternatives: necessity occupies the space of proposal.

(Unger, 2004, p. lxxvi)

'What is to be done?' The question can sound a cry of despair and hopelessness. Or, which is our choice for this chapter, it can be the starting point for a hopeful discussion of transformation. Here, we will open up a discussion about possible processes for transformation, how to move in the direction of radical education and the common school. That discussion will be modest, for we have no fully formulated and confident answer to the question, being only too well aware of the objections and obstacles in the way and the uncertainties and unintended consequences that are ever-present.

Our discussion will also be aware of the need for the process of transformation to be imbued with the values, relationships and ethics of our objectives. Even if feasible, we cannot seek radical democratic education by means of centralised diktat or techno-bureaucratic programming. So there will be no authorial and authoritative commandments, setting out what must be done to replace one system by another. We lack the confidence, but more important the inclination, to do this. Instead, we explore more modest possibilities for moving towards one of many alternatives: those possibilities include radical reform, democratic experimentalism and prefigurative practice, through which a willingness for transformation, where it exists, can be nurtured and put to work in stages to produce cumulative change. This is step-by-step as a deliberate strategy, in which each step brings new learning and worthwhile change.

We are guided in our thinking about transformation by the two social theorists introduced at the start of the book, Erik Olin Wright and Roberto Mangabeira Unger.

From their work, we take three main points. First, rejection both of necessity and determinism: the dictatorship of no alternative and the seductions of inevitable change and infallible planning. Second, the importance of ideas: we need imagination, vision and alternatives to throw off the dead hand of dictatorship. Third, transformation as a cumulative, piecemeal process: we move steadily but surely, we aim for accessible waystations or intermediate steps and stages, we adjust our direction in the light of experience and circumstances.

We end by arguing that the time is right for change since, returning to our theme in Chapter 1, we cannot continue as we are. Or put another way, there is no alternative to an alternative.

More poetry, less prose

In preceding chapters, we have set out a critique of what we term 'mainstream education' and of the school in which much formal education takes place. Our criticism is neither personal – aimed at individual educators and schools – nor blind to the many instances of innovative, caring and democratic practice and projects that have existed or currently exist, which show the great potential for transformation and give cause for hope. Our criticism is instead levelled at the prevailing discourse, both at its values, assumptions and images and at its stifling of alternatives under the weight of best practice, evidence-based policy and an array of human technologies intended to impose conformity to the norm. This gives us an education that is rooted in outmoded understandings, that has failed to engage with the rich complexity and diversity of our world, and that is ill-equipped to strengthen the ability of society – local, national and global – to address the profound discontent and species-threatening dangers facing us. When we need to nurture diversity, complexity and connectedness, it forces standardisation, reductionism and compartmentalisation; when we need to grow solidarity and democracy, it sows competition and individualism. The motto seems to be more of the same – but better.

The result has been that education, which should be such a source of excitement, enjoyment and emancipation, has been reduced too often to a dismal subject. It is a prime example of Edgar Morin's contention that today human life is unbalanced. Human life, he argues, is a mixture of prose and poetry, both necessary, both woven together, the prose side encompassing work, survival and aiming at targets, the practical, utilitarian and technical; while poetry is a way of life involving participation, love, eagerness and joy. But today the relationship between the two is out of kilter. Having separated prose and poetry, modern western civilisation has relegated poetry to private life. We need a powerful counteroffensive of poetry, at a time when human beings spend most of their lives surviving and where the future on offer seems to be ever more prose as we look forward to more years of paid work in an ever more competitive economy, where the constant cry of the manager is more productivity and the constant cry of government and business is to compete better and consume more.

Loris Malaguzzi also saw a world dominated by prose. He chose to write poetically about how the rich potential with which human beings are born is taken from us, with education complicit in this loss:

The child has a hundred languages
(and a hundred hundred hundred more)
but they steal ninety-nine
the school and the culture
separate the head from the body. . . .
They tell the child that
work and play
reality and fantasy
science and imagination
sky and earth
reason and dream
are things
that do not belong together.
And thus they tell the child
that the hundred is not there.
The child says:
No way. The hundred is there!

Our hopes could perhaps be summed up as for an education that values poetry as well as prose, conserves the hundred languages of childhood and enhances connections.

An exercise in utopian thinking

> Serious utopianism is a kind of speculative sociology, in that it is both systemic and institutionally specific. It embeds both a philosophical and anthropological quest for the substance of human flourishing, and a sociological quest for its conditions. It is a process of the imaginary reconstitution of society, which involves looking holistically at alternative modes of livelihood and social organisation, exposing them to public debate – as utopian proposals have always done – and considering means of transition.
>
> (Levitas, 2008, p. 90)

Drawing on and inspired by a variety of examples and mentors, we have attempted to create an alternative to education as a dismal subject: a *radical education* with democracy at its core, connected to a network of other values, understandings and sensibilities; and a *common school* for the whole community and person-centred learning in democratic fellowship. The two are viewed as complementary, the common school being best-suited to the practice of a radical education. We have touched, too, on some of the conditions that may foster this alternative, emphasising that the development of such education and schools cannot just be willed into being by laws and other central fiats:

- recognition that education is a deeply political and ethical matter so that politics and ethics precede policy-making and other technical practices, which proceed from political and ethical answers to critical questions – about purposes and about fundamental values, about the meaning of concepts such as education itself, learning, knowledge and care, and about understandings such as our image of the child, parents, and educators;

- developing strong and equal relationships between national government, local government and schools, based on a common national framework with local interpretation and experimentation, strong formal and everyday democracy, and a clear role for each in a decentralised system;
- a local project of education and a local infrastructure to enable schools to participate in the creation and implementation of that project in relationship with their local community, other schools and their local authority.

Two other conditions strike us as particularly important. First, re-balancing the role, type and uses of research to support radical education and the common school. This includes greater paradigmatic diversity, turning away from scientism and the repositivisation process that has occurred under neoliberalism, with greater attention being paid to paradigms that recognise the inevitability of complexity, context, uncertainty, perspective and interpretation; greater emphasis on the cultural role of research and less on the technical role;[7] more strategically chosen case studies and applied work with a critical edge (Lather, 2006); and the adoption of a 'phronetic model of social science' whose purpose:

> is not to develop epistemic theory, but to contribute to society's practical rationality by elucidating where we are, where we want to go, and what is desirable according to different sets of values and interests . . . [and] to society's capacity for value-rational deliberation and action . . . [through] a combination of concrete empirical analyses and practical philosophical-ethical considerations.
>
> (Flyvbjerg, 2006, p. 42)

A social science that, in short, contributes to – but does not seek to supplant – public and democratic deliberation.

A further condition, frustratingly vague but nonetheless vital, is faith in human potential and qualities, treating people as citizens to participate not as consumers to be served nor as human resources to be managed. John Dewey's thinking about democracy was shaped by such faith. As we have seen, he was clear that democracy was more than a form of government, but 'a way of life controlled by a working faith in the possibilities of human nature . . . [and] faith in the capacity of human beings for intelligent judgement and action if proper conditions are furnished' (Dewey, 1939). Roberto Unger, whose ideas we return to later, echoes this belief. For him, the essential doctrine of democracy is about 'faith in the constructive powers of ordinary men and women, and commitment to lift them up, to make them greater' (Unger, 2005a, p. 63). Of course, faith is a choice not a necessity, and many will not share ours; but many we think will do so, giving great hope for a better world.

In working up our alternative, and the conditions that might support it, we have engaged in unashamedly utopian thinking. Utopian thinking can, we acknowledge, be dangerous. This is especially true of 'classical "blueprint" utopianism [which] has been at best eliminative of difference and at worst authoritarian' (Anderson, 2006, p. 691), leading all too readily, as some have feared, to totalitarianism (Gray, 2007). This totalitarian idea of utopia is, Ruth Levitas observes, 'implicit in most lay usage of the term [and] is of a perfect society which is impossible and unattainable. It is either an idle dream or, if attempts are made to create that society, a dangerous illusion' (Levitas, 2003, p. 3). If not dangerous, such grand utopian plans can end up as no more than 'vague utopian fantasies [which] may lead us astray, encouraging us to embark on trips that have no real destinations at all, or worse still, which lead us toward some unforeseen abyss' (Wright, 2009b, p. 4).

But our approach to utopian thinking is, we hope, less grandiose, less totalising, less fundamentalist and, therefore, less dangerous; it is also, we think, a condition for truly democratic politics and policy-making, which acknowledges and values plurality and alternatives. For us, utopian thinking is an expression of desire and imagination, an exploration of possibilities and potentialities, an affirmation of alternatives, and an attempt to anticipate the 'not yet'. Levitas describes this approach to utopian thinking as 'an intrinsic part of what it means to be human' and that '[f]rom this a much wider view of utopia emerges, in which it becomes not a blueprint or prescription but the expression of desire for a better way of living' (Levitas, 2003, p. 4). Working with the ideas of Ernst Bloch, Tim Anderson develops this emancipatory and immanent concept of utopian thought:

> Utopic processes are immanent to a world that contains 'something that has not yet realised itself' (Bloch 1986: 193) . . . I define the utopic as a type of process in which plural 'goods' or 'betters' are 'not-yet' but immanent to life and therefore have disruptive, interrogative qualities. It is the intuition that utopic processes are connected to life through an intensification of its excessive possibilities and potentialities that gives the concept of the not-yet its importance and, subsequently, the reworked concept of utopia its value . . . utopia is always to-be rather than truly there.
>
> (Anderson, 2006, pp. 693, 697)

Viewed in this way, utopian thinking is not a road map to a certain and fixed destination. It is more, as we quoted from Erik Olin Wright in Chapter 1, a 'voyage of discovery' that sets off in a direction of travel, with limits on how far we can go, and the destination 'always to-be', either receding into the distance or taking new forms as the voyage gets underway. What such thinking offers is the opportunity to enter into a thought experiment, a valuable process in the struggle against 'the dictatorship of no alternative' and a cause for hope. Taking this approach, and contrary to classical 'blueprint' utopianism, our utopian thought has experimented with dynamic, open-ended conceptions of utopia, in line with Pinder's argument that utopianism should be valued as part of radical thought because it 'creates space for challenging what is, for disrupting dominant assumptions about social and spatial organisation, and for imagining other possibilities and desires' (Pinder, 2002, p. 238).

So we are not set in our ways, our utopian thinking being more of a sketch than blueprint, with further drafts quite conceivable. Our utopian project has been an exercise in subverting the dominant discourse by imagining and looking holistically at an alternative, just one of many possible, exploring the immanent potential of education and school, a potential which we see as full of possibilities. We do not put it forward as perfect or as the only utopia, but as one utopian alternative that expresses certain hopes and desires. And while we would like to carry some readers with us, we would also settle for stimulating utopian thinking in others that envisages other alternatives. For our main objective is twofold: to contribute to renewing a democratic politics of education, contested around different answers to critical questions; and to nurture hope that alternatives are possible, and that we therefore have choices to make, both individually and collectively.

How transformation might happen

> Transformative politics changes, part by part and step by step, the context of institutional arrangements and enacted belief that shapes the practical and discursive routines of social life . . . the central question is; where to?
>
> (Unger, 2004, pp. xxv, xxvi)

What sort of process?

Simply to promote utopian thinking is important but not enough. We need to pay attention to activation: how might transformation happen, what sort of process is envisaged? Not, we hasten to add, that we claim to have a complete theory of transformation, which would tell us what is to be done, by whom and when. If only!

All we are able to offer here are some fragmentary thoughts on what transformation might look like, drawing in particular on the work of Erik Olin Wright and Roberto Unger. Both Wright and Unger are concerned with exploring ways in which transformative social and political projects can not only provide alternative intellectual models to the global dominance of neoliberalism, but also offer practical stepping stones, alternative practices and ways of being within our current societies that might provide the vision and the means to bridge to a more just, more humanly enabling and ennobling future. What we see in the work of both is a concern with how utopian possibilities and substantive change might be realised in practice through processes that contain stages and steps, rather than relying on some unspecified and unlikely 'big bang'.

As we have already seen, Wright is dismissive of what he terms 'vague utopian fantasies'. His grounded approach is captured by the title of his Real Utopias Project which embraces 'the tension between dreams and practice'. It is, he observes, 'much easier to be a realist about what exists than about what could exist, and much easier to dream of a better world without worrying about the practical problems of unintended consequences and perverse dynamics'. So central to his approach are practical considerations: institutional design; identifying accessible waystations – 'intermediate institutional innovations that move us in the right direction but only partially embody those values' (Wright, 2007, p. 38); attention to navigating imperfect conditions; and criteria for elaborating and evaluating real utopias. As we also saw in Chapter 1, he has developed three such criteria – desirability, viability and achievability.

Desirability is about laying out values, ethics and goals:

> one asks the question: what are the moral principles that a given alternative is supposed to serve? This is the domain of pure utopian social theory and much normative political philosophy. Typically such discussions are institutionally very thin, the emphasis being on the enunciation of abstract principles rather than actual institutional designs.
>
> (Wright, 2007, p. 27)

Viability is about designing new policies and institutions based on desirable principles. It is:

> a response to the perpetual objection to radical egalitarian proposals 'it sounds good on paper, but it will never work' . . . [The exploration of viability focuses] on the likely dynamics and unintended consequences of the proposal if it were to be implemented. Two kinds of analysis are especially pertinent here: systematic theoretical models of how particular social structures and institutions would work, and empirical studies of cases, both historical and contemporary, where at least some aspects of the proposal have been tried.
>
> (Wright, 2007, p. 27)

Achievability is about the process of transformation and the practical political work of strategies for social change: 'It asks of proposals for social change that have passed the test of desirability and viability, what it would take to actually implement them' (Wright, 2007, p. 27).

Wright argues that these three criteria are 'nested in a kind of hierarchy: Not all desirable alternatives are viable, and not all viable alternatives are achievable' (Wright, 2006, p. 96). All three are crucial, but, in his view, the most important has to do with viability:

> Central to the problem of envisioning real utopias concerns the viability of institutional alternatives that embody emancipatory values, but the practical achievability of such institutional designs often depends upon the existence of smaller steps, intermediate institutional innovations that move us in the right direction but only partially embody those values.
>
> (Wright, 2007, p. 38)

In developing this notion of intermediate institutional innovation, he coins the term 'waystations'. Acknowledging difficult theoretical and practical problems, particularly to do with the fact that partial reforms often have different consequences than larger scale changes, he nonetheless argues for intermediate reforms that have two main characteristics:

> First, they concretely demonstrate the virtues of the fuller programme of transformation, so they contribute to the ideological battle of convincing people that the alternative is credible and desirable; and second, they enhance the

capacity of action for people, increasing their ability to push further in the future. Waystations that increase popular participation and bring people together in problem-solving deliberations are particularly salient in this regard. This is what in the 1970s was called 'non-reformist reforms': reforms that are possible within existing institutions and that pragmatically solve real problems while at the same time empowering people in ways which enlarge their scope for action.

(Wright, 2007, p. 38)

What makes viability so important is not only that it provides a bridge between desirability and achievability, showing the way from principle to actualisation, but also that it can restore hope among those who have lost belief in the possibility of alternatives and 'lost confidence in the workability of visions beyond the existing social order' (Wright, 2007, p. 28). From a Wrightian perspective, we have said from the start of Chapter 1 that this book is primarily focused on desirability and viability. Moreover, we think there is much productive work to be done here and now on this strand of utopian thinking, 'to develop in as systematic a way as possible a scientifically grounded conception of viable alternative institutions' (Wright, 2006, p. 99).

Roberto Unger shares Wright's concern for realism and pragmatism. He dismisses what he terms two styles of politics, the 'revolutionary' with its desire for sudden, violent and total change, typically the wholesale substitution of one institutional order for another in a national crisis; and the 'reformist', in which marginal and essentially trivial responses are offered to public anxieties, what he describes as a 'pessimistic reformism' in which 'we are left to humanise the inevitable' (Unger, 1998, p. 20). Instead, he argues for 'radical' or 'revolutionary reform', structural change taken step-by-step, bringing gradual but cumulative and substantive change: 'Reform is radical when it addresses and changes the basic arrangements of a society: its formative structure of institutions and enacted beliefs. It is reform because it deals with one discrete part of this structure at a time' (ibid., pp. 18–19). The emergent, restless dynamic of radical reform entails both a permanent provisionality and a cumulative accomplishment of significantly changed ways of being in the world that presage fundamentally different personal, social and political realities: 'It is the combination of parts and the succession of steps, reaching far beyond the starting point, and changing along the way our understanding of our interests, ideas and identities, that makes a reform project relatively more radical' (ibid., p. 19). Central to his ideal is the question 'where to?', foregrounding the need for a clear sense of direction: a 'programmatic argument', he proposes, 'is a vision of a direction and the next steps' (Unger, 2005a, p. 164).

Unger identifies several components in this process of revolutionary reform. In his book *False Necessity*, he insists on the importance of visionary language. In this context, language is 'a tool for persuasion and a device for discovery' (Unger, 2004, p. 430) that should, wherever possible, have a freshness and an intelligible immediacy that engages with the subtleties of personal experience. Thinking and doing differently needs to be matched with different forms of expression, both verbal and also (taking up Malaguzzi's hundred languages) in other forms. This resonates with the argument by the authorial duo of Gibson-Graham, that their project to reinvigorate our economic imaginations and to enact alternative economies requires:

producing a language of economic difference to enlarge the economic imaginary, rendering visible and intelligible the diverse and proliferating practices that the preoccupation with capitalism has obscured; we see this language as a necessary contribution to a politics of economic innovation.

(Gibson-Graham, 2006, p. x)

Substitute 'education' and 'educational' for 'economics' and 'economic', and the parallel becomes clear – a language of educational difference for a politics of educational innovation.

An insistence on the intellectual and practical reciprocity between matters of structural and strategic importance and what he sometimes calls a 'personalist vision' (strongly reminiscent of our discussion of a 'personalist' education in Chapter 2) is also central to Unger's work. This is elegantly exemplified in his advocacy of 'role defiance and role jumbling' that we have also referred to earlier. Roles too often imprison and diminish human capacities and capabilities in the interest of those in power. In developing radical reform, we thus need 'a cultural-revolutionary attack on rigid roles . . . a practice of role-defiance and role jumbling . . . a loosened sense of what it means to occupy a role . . . [that] helps to disrupt frozen connections among social stations, life experiences, and stereotyped forms of insight and sensibility' (Unger, 2004, pp. 563–64).

There is a profound and persistent emancipatory energy that drives through all of Unger's work and much of it has to do with that imprecise but crucial quality, the importance of which we highlighted earlier: faith. He is insistent on both the specialness and deep creativity of the ordinary man and woman, on their capacity to become so much more than systems and structures allow them to be. Many of his most eloquent, moving and insightful passages return to the specialness of ordinary men and women; to their betrayal and belittlement by so many regimes and ways of life; to the necessity and possibility of their fulfilment in arrangements and processes that release and enhance their creative powers. It is thus imperative that the cultural-revolutionary:

carries into the drama of everyday personal relations the effort to free sociability from its script and to make us available to one another more as the originals we all know ourselves to be and less as the placeholders in a system of group contrasts.

(Unger, 2004, p. 564)

An important role for democratic experimentalism

Another component in Unger's thinking about revolutionary or radical reform, which we think merits particular attention, is democratic experimentalism. In *False Necessity* (Unger, 2004), he suggests we need to establish 'small-scale, fragmentary versions of future society because without these kinds of experimental anticipations . . . there would be no way to pass from one set of assumptions about group interests, collective identities, and social responsibilities to another' (Unger, 2004, pp. 411–12). To be effective, these 'experimental anticipations' must satisfy two qualifying criteria. First, they must have what one might call transgressive significance, i.e. 'represent a step on a possible passage from the present formative order to the desired order' (Unger, 2004, p. 412). Second, they 'should contribute to the solution of the over-riding problem of means and ends by serving both as an anticipatory image of broader transformations and as a strategic tool' (Unger, 2004, p. 412).

Experimentation for Unger means vastly expanded opportunities to try out different ways of doing things, for example in particular parts of the country or in particular sectors. It involves making good use of imagination and creativity, thereby pushing incremental change beyond the boundaries of even the most innovative developments of the *status quo*. It expresses his faith in people's capacities, Unger's valorisation of democratic experimentalism resting in significant part on his insistence that we need to develop arrangements that do justice to each person's creative potential and the necessary connection to our capacity to lead good lives together. Hence his continuing attack on 'depersonalisation under the weight of frozen social roles' (Unger, 1998, p. 8) and his insistence that:

> [o]ur capacity for love and solidarity grows through the strengthening of our ability to recognise and to accept the otherness of other people . . . [to] radically accept one another as the original, context-transcending beings we really are, rather than as placeholders in a social scheme, acting out a script we never devised and barely understand.
>
> (Unger, 1998, p. 9)

Unger insists on the importance and synergy of both parts of his concept – democracy and experimentalism:

> The provision of public services must be an innovative collective practice, moving forward the qualitative provision of the services themselves. That can no longer happen in our current understanding of efficiency and production by the mechanical transmission of innovation from the top. It can only happen through the organisation of a collective experimental practice from below . . . Democracy is not just one more terrain for the institutional innovation that I advocate. It is the most important terrain.
>
> (Unger, 1995, pp. 179, 182)

He views democratic experimentalism as an essential element of what he terms 'high energy democracy', which is about releasing the creative powers of ordinary people by eradicating the distortions and subjugations of class, hierarchy and the myopic presumptions of prescribed role, or, as he so elegantly puts it, 'the abandonment of ordinary humanity to perpetual belittlement' (Unger, 1995, p. 46). For Unger, as we have already seen, the essential doctrine of democracy is 'faith in the constructive powers of ordinary men and women' (ibid., p. 63) and 'recognition of the genius of ordinary men and women' (Unger, 2004, p. lxxii). High energy democracy encourages a high level of organised civic engagement and 'seeks to strengthen our experimental capacities – our ability to try out alternative arrangements among ourselves'; and this assumes, finds and nourishes 'greatness in ordinary humanity' (ibid.).

Unger's writing here refers to democratic experimentalism as more than just *ad hoc* local projects that occasionally and by their own exertions break free from the constraints of orthodoxy, examples of which are always around us. He envisages the possibility of a state that actively encourages experimentation as part of a commitment to high energy democracy, in short an emancipatory state at ease with diversity. The state can act in various ways to achieve this end, including 'producing new social agents' that can create innovative services; monitoring and helping 'to propagate the most successful practices, accelerating the process of experimental winnowing out of what does not work'; and last, and perhaps most surprising in the current climate, by providing services directly but only 'those services which are too innovative, too difficult or too unrewarded by the market to be provided directly' (Unger, 2005b, p. 179) – government itself as a social agent of experimentation.

Another Brazilian social thinker, Boaventura de Sousa Santos, envisages something similar, the state assuming a new purpose and ethos:

> Rather than impose one form of sociability, the state must be made to create the conditions for social experimentation, that is, the conditions necessary so that alternative sociabilities may be credibly experimented with in each of the six structural spaces [household, work, market, community, citizenship, world]. This implies a profound transformation of the welfare state. In the paradigmatic transition, the welfare state is the state form that guarantees social experimentation.
>
> (Santos, 1995, p. 483)

We can see the early childhood education in the municipal schools of certain Italian towns and cities, such as Reggio Emilia, as an example of government-promoted experimentation, the local authority (municipality) in this case being the government source of support for experimentation in pedagogical work. A second example, this time at the level of national government, was the Centres of Innovation action research programme, launched in 2002 by the New Zealand government as part of the quality goal of the ten-year strategic plan for early childhood education, *Pathways to the Future: Ngā Huarahi Arataki*. Funded by the New Zealand Department of Education, the aim of the initiative was to challenge teachers' practice and foster teachers' research development by building innovative approaches, facilitating local action research and sharing the resulting knowledge, understanding and practice with others in the early childhood sector. There have been five rounds of this programme, each round focused on innovation in specified areas, for example, improved links between services developing as 'learning communities', infants' and toddlers' care and education, and inclusive early childhood education for diverse children and families. The successive rounds have involved practitioner teams in 20 early childhood services, each team working with a research associate to 'promote a deeper exploration of innovative teaching and learning processes' (for more information, see http://www.educate.ece. govt.nz/Programmes/CentresOfInnovation.aspx; and the series of publications on the Centres of Innovation programme available at http://www.nzcer.org.nz/default. php?products_id = 2445).[8]

The role of the school in democratic experimentalism

For Unger, 'the emancipatory school' has a key role in the process of deepening democracy through the kind of 'radicalised experimentalism' he advocates. Indeed, he insists that '[n]o organisation is more important to the progress of democratic experimentalism than the school' (Unger, 1998, p. 229). This has partly to do with his view that 'the democratic school as a maker of rebellious minds' (ibid., p. 220) should provide an education whose distinguishing traits are:

> to be analytical and problematic rather than informational; to prefer exemplary selective deepening to encyclopaedic coverage; to encourage cooperation, rather than isolation or authoritarianism, in learning and in teaching; and to proceed dialectically – that is to say, by the exploration of contrasting methods and views rather than by appeal to a closed canon of right doctrine.
>
> (Unger, 2005a, p. 61)

Interestingly, and immensely pertinent to the thorny issues of locality and parental choice with which we struggle in Chapter 3 of this book, Unger also includes a further key requirement of the emancipatory school:

> It is to give children the powers of insight and action and the access to alien experience enabling them to become little prophets. The remaking of our understanding of the actual by the imagination of the possible requires a large measure of detachment from the now dominant culture.
>
> (Unger, 1998, p. 231)

Indeed, his renewed insistence that '[t]he school must be the voice of the future' (Unger, 2005a, p. 71) returns to this third, distancing requirement of the radical imagination and is unswerving in its demand that the school 'must rescue the child from its family, its class, its culture, and its historical period. Consequently, it must not be the passive tool of either the local community or the government bureaucracy' (ibid.).

One should not be misled by the exuberance of Unger's advocacy here. Although, arguably, an overstatement it is important to remember the foundational values of his work, which prevent an atomistic or crude self-improvement reading of what is, in fact, a deeply relational account of 'high-energy democracy'. The imperative to transcend the inevitable constraints of location – in particular, the 'frozen roles' that define and confine who we are and who we might wish to become – is matched by a companion insistence that we are guided by the lodestar of ordinary humanity transformed not only by the work of the imagination but also by the new realities of felt encounter. The point is to deepen democracy in ways which transform not just the mechanics of joint action, 'the habits of human connection' (Unger, 1998,

p. 256), but also 'the quality of personal life and personal encounter [which] remains the ultimate prize of politics . . . The progress of democracy must bring about change in the character as well as the content of ways in which people deal with one another' (ibid., pp. 256, 257).

The need to detach oneself from dominant contemporary culture does not amount to a disavowal or a denial of one's roots. Nor does the need to resist the gravitational pull of the present deny the inevitable situatedness of human action: 'We are capable of finding genealogies rather than merely inheriting them' (Unger, 1998, p. 235). Rather, both recognise the extreme difficulty and absolute necessity of a practice that seeks to bridge the chasm between, on the one hand, the timorous betrayal of merely humanising the present and, on the other hand, the insistent subjugation of living humanity to the arrogance of millennial abstraction.

The point of democratic experimentalism, and its key part in transformatory processes, is that it attempts to break the stalemate of 'no alternatives' in ways which inspire and enact a utopian realism that is mindful of inevitable dangers and disappointments, but equally resolved to enact new 'narratives of human possibility' (Unger, 1998, p. 258) through the dynamics and aspirations of a radical incrementalism. At the heart of Unger's proposals lies a substantial faith in the power of emancipatory institutions, including but not only the democratic school. It is through our use of 'the tools of the institutional imagination' (ibid., p. 15), through our recognition that 'by enriching institutional possibilities, and pushing them in one direction rather than another, that we make them – and therefore ourselves – into one thing rather than another' (ibid., p. 17). His faith in radical, incremental institutional change is thus substantial.

However, as we would expect from someone for whom the point of politics requires external justification, that faith is not unqualified in either its structural or its cultural articulation. How we experience innovative structural change and the possibilities it opens up and closes down are important. Our individual stories are not minor organisational footnotes to a more substantial collective narrative: rather they carry with them the weight and texture of institutional legitimacy that weaves its way through the fabric of social and political change. Thus, the 'narratives of human possibility' enacted, for example, by the feminist movements illustrate why extra-institutional politics of personal relations must work together with the politics of institutions. Neither can achieve its objectives without help from the other. Each will find its work limited by the other's accomplishments and failures (Unger, 1998, p. 258). Emancipatory institutions are hugely, at times even overwhelmingly, important, but their legitimacy and their power to transform human lives remains derivative. For Unger, 'the most important fact about us [as human beings is] that we are greater than the institutions and cultures we build' (Unger, 1998, p. 260).

Prefigurative practice

Exploring the writings of Wright and Unger has rung bells for us about another concept highly relevant to the theme of transformation. When Wright writes of 'reforms that are possible within existing institutions and that pragmatically solve real problems while at the same time empowering people in ways which enlarge their scope for action' (Wright, 2007, p. 38); and when Unger writes of 'small-scale, fragmentary versions of future society . . . kinds of experimental anticipations', then we have been reminded of and drawn back to the concept of 'prefigurative practice'. It seems to us that they share some important ideas about the possible relationship between local projects or experiments and wider social goals, a relationship we consider central to transforming education and schooling, and between work in progress and a utopian destination. All value 'work in progress' and blur the distinction between process and outcome.

One of the key texts of the New Left that subsequently influenced writers such as Wini Breines (Breines, 1980) and, within the field of education, Roger Dale (Dale, 1988) was a paper on prefigurative practice by the Gramscian scholar, Carl Boggs. His account describes it as 'the embodiment within the ongoing political practice of a movement, of those forms of social relations, decision making, culture and human experience that are the ultimate goal' (Boggs, 1977/78, p. 100). Similar kinds of arguments were also being made and lived out in internal socialist struggles within the ascendant feminist movement. Pre-eminent amongst those advocating and practising prefigurative politics were feminists such as Sheila Rowbotham. Interestingly, her arguments acknowledge the importance of anarchist influences which stress 'the transformation of values and relationships in the process of making the new world' (Rowbotham, 1979, p. 121). She insists that the prefigurative practices of the women's movement recognised the importance of 'making something which might become the means to making something more . . . [S]ome changes have to start now else there is no beginning for us' (ibid., p. 140). In arguing that '[w]e need to make the creation of prefigurative forms an explicit part of our movement against capitalism' (ibid., p. 147), she was not insisting on a utopian project that would bring everyone to their knees. Rather, it was about consolidation and the need to 'release the imagination of what could be. The effort to go beyond what we know now has to be part of our experience of what we might know' (ibid.).

This insistence that we 'release the imagination of what could be'; and this anticipation of future modes of being through processes and relations, not just structures, that exemplify and embody the viability and desirability of radical alternatives – these are some of the most important past and continuing contributions of progressive traditions of public education to the furtherance of democracy in this country. Thus, Roger Dale, writing in 1988, argued that:

> The more radical, recent and professionally initiated concepts of comprehensive education . . . contain . . . a view of education's role in social change which sees it as prefigurative. That is to say, rather than waiting until all the necessary social engineering has been done, and the planned widespread social change brought about, this approach to social change suggests that education through its processes, the experiences it offers, and the expectations it makes, should prefigure, in microcosm, the more equal, just and fulfilling society that the originations of comprehensivism aimed to bring about. *Schools should not merely reflect the world of which they are a part, but be critical of it, and show in their own processes that its shortcomings*

are not inevitable, but can be changed. They aim to show that society can be character-ised by communal as well as individual values, that all people merit equal treat-ment and equal dignity, that academic ability is not the only measure of a person, that racism and sexism are neither inevitable nor acceptable.

(Dale, 1988, p. 17; emphasis added)

What prefigurative practice opens up is a further rationale for local educational (and other) projects and experimentation as part of a contribution to wider change, in edu-cation but also beyond. It affirms the wider and longer-term importance of the exam-ples discussed earlier, which have shown 'in their own processes that [the world's] shortcomings are not inevitable, but can be changed'. It confirms, too, the idea that transformation is not a matter of waiting for sudden revolutionary rupture, which many see as never likely to happen; nor is it a long trek with no benefits until a dis-tant goal is, perhaps and hopefully, reached. Rather transformation is a complex and gradual process of steps taken, with refreshing and rewarding staging points reached en route, with some tacking of direction resulting from learning on the journey, and a synergy between strategic and local action. Prefigurative practice brings the prospect of hope from what has been achieved to date, and the opportunity for new knowledge and understandings.

Because of the potential importance we attach to it, we look now in more detail at what prefigurative practice might mean as part of a process of achieving a real utopia of radical education and the common school.

What is prefigurative about prefigurative practice?

Perhaps, the most compelling attraction of prefigurative practice is its utopian realism: its rejection on the one hand of waiting for the call to the barricades and, on the other hand, of simply rearranging the deckchairs on the Titanic, while insisting on the necessity of a radical break with the present. Its appeal lies in its commitment to a transitional practice that enables significant aspects of future ways of being to happen now, or, in the syndicalist phrase, 'to build a new world in the shell of the old'. What makes the work of Erik Olin Wright and Roberto Unger particularly relevant to our current dilemmas is that they successfully address the twin challenges of prefigurative practice that Carl Boggs so incisively identified nearly four decades ago. These are that due attention is paid, first, to the task of organisation and, second, to the exploratory, libertarian dynamic that jointly inform a socialist theory of democratic transition. As Boggs himself puts it, '[w]hat is required, and what the entire prefigurative strategy lacks, is a merging of spontaneism and the external element, economics and politics, local democratic and state power struggles' (Boggs, 1977/78, pp. 120–21).

Building on the recent work of Unger and Wright and on the socialist, Marxist and anarchist traditions within which their work is most appropriately situated, we have developed an analytic account of prefigurative practice which we suggest is not specific to education and allied fields, but of more generic significance to all those who wish to work here-and-now towards profound social and political change. Certainly, our intention is to offer an intellectual and practical tool that articulates a defensible and energising way of refusing the Scylla of neoliberalism and the Charybdis of revolutionary rupture, whilst yet retaining a serious commitment to a tectonic shift in the basic assumptions and aspirations of dominant ways of life in most technologically-developed countries around the world.

What, then, might a prefigurative practice of radical school education consist of? What would mark practice out as prefigurative, in relation to the goal of radical education? We have set out 12 criteria in the following pages,[9] organised into three groups, against which to judge the presence of a genuinely prefigurative practice, defined in terms of its capacity to make a contribution to revolutionary or radical educational reform. But the list is not only evaluative, telling us where an institution may have got to on its transformatory journey, it is also developmental in the sense of indicating areas that may need more attention. All three groups – practice, strategy and motivation – need to be addressed.

We begin at the level of conceptualisation, and in this section – *What is prefigurative about prefigurative practice?* – set out our current view of what we take prefigurative practice to be arguing for. This includes eight core criteria against which to evaluate practice as prefigurative:

Box 4.1 What is prefigurative about prefigurative practice?

1 Profound change
2 Education and radical social change
3 Positional restlessness
4 Permanent provisionality

5 Transgressive holism
6 Transformed community
7 Celebrating and contesting history
8 The persistent pull of personalism

In *Strategy matters*, we then underscore the importance of how prefigurative practice addresses issues of social and political change at a strategic level.

Box 4.2 Strategy matters

9 Radical incrementalism   10 Strategic engagement

Lastly, in *Having the conviction to act*, we attend to matters of motivational engagement, which provide the necessary bridge from macro-ideals to the meso-realities of the daily contexts of enactment.

Box 4.3 Having the conviction to act

11 Institutional transformation   12 Narrative engagement

---

1 Profound change

At a time when there is much talk about innovation, step change, twenty-first century thinking and other exhortations of an ever-resourceful capitalism to transgress boundaries and create new opportunities for consumption, it is important to underscore the ideological and actual distance between prefigurative practice and what, for example, the Innovation Unit in England calls 'Next Practice' (Hannon, 2007). Next Practice often has much to recommend it; but what it currently does not do is seriously challenge the deep presumptions of its host society.

The radical traditions with which we identify are those which reject the presumptions and aspirations not just of neoliberal forms of capitalism, but much of what capitalism itself stands for. Thus, in following Unger's account of radical reform as that which 'addresses and changes the basic arrangements of a society: its formative structure of institutions and enacted beliefs' (Unger, 1998, pp. 18–19), we would wish to support radical approaches to practice that, like Alex Bloom's work at St George-in-the-East and those at Reggio Emilia, call into question the moral and existential basis of acquisitive consumerism and economism; that celebrate diverse identities rooted in public service and the possibilities of relational forms of human fulfilment; that see emulation as a more creative and joyful form of mutual engagement and motivation than the zero-sum predations of competitive individualism; and that reject traditional power structures and the dominant presumptions of authority.

Prefigurative practice is thus not about ameliorative processes or faddish palliatives for the running sores of social injustice and impoverished expectation. Whilst radical change can be cumulative and incremental, it has also to address and challenge 'the basic arrangements of a society', not just its surface features or relational conventions. We are mindful of Quintin Hoare's cautionary remarks in this regard:

> The idea that *Daily Express* – or for that matter *Times* – journalists, if they controlled the paper democratically, would produce a 'democratic' newspaper ignores the obvious fact that social institutions of this kind – schools or press – produce the men to fit them.
>
> (Hoare, 1965, p. 51)

If schools and other social institutions are to prefigure radically different futures, they will need to do more than embrace consultative or participatory processes. The current co-option of 'student voice' by the energetic activities of government and the ambitions of schools conscious of their league table positions should alert us to the dangers of hegemonic incorporation. It should also alert us to the challenge of devising an incrementalism that remains permanently restless with its achievements, permanently committed to a future based on values and aspirations that require fundamental change if they are to be centrally, rather than peripherally or analgesically, present in day-to-day encounters.

By way of illustrative resistance, the following box briefly encapsulates two paradigmatically different ways of both conceiving and 'doing' student voice. The neoliberal market perspective presumes a predominantly individualistic view of human beings and puts a lot of emphasis on individual choice. Individuals are encouraged to see themselves as consumers or customers who need to make informed choices about opportunities for learning within the school, often connected with their future life chances within the job market.

Box 4.4 Neo-liberal and person-centred student voice

Neo-liberal student voice		Person-centred student voice	
Instrumental (solitary)	*Instrumental* (plural)	*Communal* (individual)	*Communal* (mutual)
Individual perspective Personalised learning	*Collective perspective* High performance schooling	*Personal perspective* Person-centred education	*Communal perspective* Democratic fellowship
Voice Individual voice	*Voice* Representative voice	*Voice* Relational conversation	*Voice* Restless dialogue
Main concern Instrumental outcomes	*Main concern* Utilise all perspectives to improve results	*Main concern* Lead a good life	*Main concern* Co-create a good society/ better world
Driver Individual ambition	*Driver* Fully informed accountability	*Driver* Personal development	*Driver* Shared responsibility for a better future
Dominant model Consumer choice	*Dominant model* Learning organisation	*Dominant model* Family/ friendship	*Dominant model* Learning community
Key question What job do I wish to do/ course do I wish to take?	*Key question* How can we learn from everyone to achieve better outcomes?	*Key question* What kind of person do I wish to become?	*Key question* How do we develop an inclusive society together?

At the collective level, a school committed to this way of working sees its main task as one of maximising its position in competitive league tables by producing better outcomes for students. Student voice is important because in listening to students, the school becomes a more accountable and more effective learning organisation and thus, better at meeting its core responsibilities. At the individual level, the main concern underpinning this model is with certain kinds of instrumental outcome; at the collective level, the main concern is how best to utilise all perspectives in order to improve results.

The person-centred, democratic fellowship perspective also starts with individuals, but its understanding of what it means to be an individual is quite different. It sees individuals as persons, not as isolated, self-sufficient beings, but as essentially relational. As John Macmurray once said, 'We need one another to be ourselves' (Macmurray, 1961, p. 211). A person-centred perspective does include the responsibility to make choices, but they are choices taken within the context of deeper aspirations than those of the market. They concern fundamental questions to do with how we become good persons and the means of answering those questions are essentially through dialogue with others whom we care for and respect.

At the communal level, a school committed to this way of working sees its main task as one of developing an inclusive, creative society through a participatory democracy which benefits everyone. Student voice is important here, not so much through representative structures (though it will have these and operate them well), but rather through a whole range of daily opportunities in which young people can listen and be listened to, make decisions and take a shared responsibility for both the here-and-now of daily encounter and for the creation of a better future. At the individual level, the main concern underpinning this model is how one lives a good and fulfilling life; at the collective level, the main concern is how best to co-create a good society and a better world.

2 Education and radical social change

Earlier, we approvingly cited Brian Simon's view of radicalism that 'sees educational change as a key aspect (or component) of radical social change' (Simon, 1972, p. 9) and in our short exposition of aspects of Roberto Unger's work, we warmed to his insistence that '[n]o organisation is more important to the progress of democratic experimentalism than the school' (Unger, 1998, p. 229).

Our strong support both of the key role of education *in* prefigurative practice and of education and schooling as forms *of* prefigurative practice not only rests on a presumption of a radical form of schooling, it also rests on a long-standing, but nonetheless foundationally important, distinction between schooling and education and an insistence on the primary importance of the latter over the former. Currently, as we have already made clear, we do wish to press for a particular image and form of schooling as a key form of personal, social and political transformation in our individual and communal search for the good life. However, we also acknowledge the permanently recurring contingencies of circumstance that require deep attention and concede that they might, in some foreseeable circumstances, require the abandonment of schools as an agent of democracy. For the moment, despite a possible resurgence of support for deschooling/homeschooling (see, for example Harber, 2009) as an alternative to an, admittedly, parlous *status quo*, we see radical education through the common school as a possibility worthy of support and struggle.

One of the many reasons we find Alex Bloom's work so appealing is the tenacity with which he hangs on to a clear view of a particular approach to education-in-its-broadest sense, one which constantly challenges those in school to understand and retain that orientation, one which insists it is the school's responsibility to earn the educational allegiance of the child, not presume it or despoil it through the arrogance or casual indifference of what is customary and too often crushing in its prescription. It is no accident that Bloom's work was lauded by the anarchist press and by a range of anarchist writers such as Leila Berg, Tony Gibson, Colin Ward (who wrote a moving obituary in the anarchist weekly, *Freedom*) and Tony Weaver (who later became the editor of the New Education Fellowship's journal, *New Era*). Anarchism's unease with most forms of authority and its implacable opposition to the state often gives it a keen sense of the distinction between education and schooling: the widespread support within the movement for the work of Alex Bloom rests in large part on his capacity to understand and realise the priority of education over schooling and create a community of learners that transformed the dominant presumptions of the time into something energising and liberating for all.

3 Positional restlessness – egalitarian possibility

As with Unger, our commitment is not just to radical change but to 'high-energy' democracy which, whilst retaining elements of representational arrangements, none-theless sees democracy's aspirations as more fully understood and more effectively realised through the wide-ranging expansion of opportunities and expectations of participation by all in communal as well as individual pursuit of a permanently restless, insistently inclusive common good.

Central to the emphasis on democratic radicalism is, of course, a presumption of both egalitarian and libertarian possibilities. Thus, at the heart of Unger's insistence on 'role defiance and role jumbling' and the need to reject 'frozen roles' is not just a refusal to diminish the dignity and existential stature of ordinary men and women. There is also a companion belief in their Promethean power that stands as a permanent rebuttal of the interpersonal and political legitimacy of hierarchy and the arrogant presumptions of labelling. Prefigurative practice must embrace a disruptive insistence on what one might call 'positional restlessness', a radical mistrust of hierarchy and a commitment to an openness of possibility that honours difference and denies deference. What democratic experimentalism argues for, and what our understanding of prefigurative practice wishes to advocate, is a set of personal, social and political arrangements enacted through new organisational and cultural forms that do not merely allow but enhance and celebrate 'the constructive powers of ordinary men and women' and demonstrate 'a commitment to lift them up, to make them even greater' (Unger, 2005, p. 63).

Thus the more radical forms of student voice, which are beginning to challenge the manipulative mendacity of neoliberal incorporation, offer examples of prefigurative practice in the form of suggestive alternatives to voice as a disciplinary device operating simultaneously on adults and young people alike. In its place, we are beginning to see a return to more collaborative, exploratory pedagogy, a more emergent curriculum and the increasing resonance of inter-generational learning. Particularly impressive are values-led developments like Students-as-Learning Partners (see SSAT, 2009) within which staff invite young people not only to observe their practice, but, through that process and through the richness of the partnerships that invariable emerge, begin to blur role boundaries and become mutual advocates and supportive critics of each other's work.

Many of these desiderata have been illustrated by the work of Alex Bloom and his colleagues at St George-in-the-East with its twin emphasis on a negotiated, project-led curriculum in the mornings and a chosen series of electives in the afternoons; with its utilisation of London as a living resource; with its frequent use of residential camps on the coast of England; with its Weekly Reviews of teaching and learning; with its radical development of the whole School Meeting as the arbiter and enabler of the development of a democratic form of living and learning together. Similarly, the municipal schools of Reggio Emilia have adopted project work, which eschews predefined outcomes and welcomes the unexpected and the new; the atelier and atelieristas, which nurture the hundred languages and the emancipatory possibilities they open up for; and pedagogical documentation, which welcomes plurality of perspectives in a democratic process of interpretation, meaning-making and co-constructive learning, values dialogue, subjectivity and uncertainty, and makes space for amazement, surprise and wonder.

4 Permanent provisionality – the libertarian imperative

Central to the radical libertarian tradition is not only an understanding and enactment of freedom, which remains always apprehensive and often mistrustful of authority in all its forms and guises, there is also a particular insistence on opening up new spaces for exploration, new vistas of possibility. This restlessness, this 'permanent provisionality' (Fielding, 2006b) is central to the kinds of prefigurative practice we are advocating. It insists that democracy as a way of living in, apprehending and changing the world is never finished, but always open to the necessity of critique and transcendence in our quest for the good society.

The pedagogical practice of Reggio Emilia and St George's school, the two cases with which we began the book – with their openness to new thought and directions, their relish of experimentation and the unexpected, their adventurous roles and relationships, and their attention to a democratic framework of participation by children and adults alike – exemplify something of the permanent provisionality of radical democratic schooling. Here, the necessary and permanent provisionality of joint endeavour is subject to both the interrogation and the celebration of the values to which the school community aspires. Whilst the ethical and axiological bases of a school's work remains constant, their strength and suppleness are enhanced by the energy and imagination with which members of the school community explore new ways of coming to understand the world together.

5 Transgressive holism

Part of the power of prefigurative practice lies in the energising interconnectedness of its way of being, in the lived synergy of its holistic commitments. When Boggs's account of prefigurative practice talks of 'the embodiment . . . of those forms of social relations, decision making, culture and human experience that are the ultimate goal' (Boggs, 1977/78, p. 100), it is not just the range of practices he brings together but their relational interdependence. The holism we are arguing for brings together the structural and interpersonal elements of new ways of working and living. It is transgressive because, following the egalitarian and libertarian trajectories we have sketched in the preceding paragraphs, it requires a deep disruption of existing arrangements and dispositions.

Radical libertarians have always taken seriously the spirit and the substance of Gandhi's injunction that 'you must be the change you want to see in the world', and the need, therefore, to enact liberated forms of social and educational life in the here and now of a community explicitly set up to nurture such approaches. A similarly searching holism is characteristic of the socialist feminist movement exemplified by Sheila Rowbotham's reminder that '[i]t is important that we remember radical politics are also personal affairs' (Rowbotham, 1979, p. 142) and that we must 'find a way to meet person to person – an inward as well as an external equality' (Rowbotham, 1979, pp. 146–47). It is also something reflected in Unger's warning that:

> democratising reforms in government and the economy . . . will be frustrated or perverted if established within a society that continues, in the little, to operate on principles antagonistic to them . . . The progress of democracy must bring about a change in the character as well as the content of the ways people deal with one another.
>
> (Unger, 1998, pp. 256, 257)

One of the most impressive aspects of St George-in-the-East was the unity of its organisational structures and cultures. In this sense, it was both holistic and transgressive: holistic because the systems and organisational forms were expressive of a set of shared values that reinforced particular ways of working and certain kinds of interpersonal relations; transgressive because, as we have already seen, not only were traditional roles between pupils and staff blurred or transformed into more reciprocal ways of working, the entire educational undertaking of the school ruptured a wide range of conventional expectations and understandings of what a school was supposed to be doing and how it was expected to go about its work.

Holistic and transgressive, too, has been the educational project in Reggio Emilia. Practice is based on rich and interwoven theories about the child, knowledge, learning and relationships, and supported by structures and organisation that share the values and understandings that inscribe all aspects of this pedagogical work. A holistic approach to the child is expressed through the hundred languages of children and a recognition that 'the brains, hands, sensibilities, rationality, emotion and imagination all work together in close cooperation' (Vecchi, 2010, p. 2). While the transgressive element of the project is captured in the description of Loris Malaguzzi adopting 'a pedagogy of transgression', which:

> fights against routine and boredom, and pursues the transformation of the uto-pian into the possible, and the possible into the real . . . The important thing for him was to question the most rigid truths that curb the possibility of thinking differently. This represents his beloved concept of the new, of innovation, as strangeness and surprise.

> (Hoyuelos, 2004, p. 6)

6 Transformed conception of community

One of the dangers of holism is that it can often privilege wholeness over diversity. Likewise with community, although central to any convincing account of prefigurative practice or, indeed, any other account of human flourishing. Unger thus insists on a 'transformed conception of community' (Unger, 2004, p. 560) which is, in a sense, part of the same drive to destabilise and disrupt the accumulation of power and privilege within social and political processes. Unger's concern is to 'shift the gravitational centre of the communal ideal away from the sharing of values and opinions and the exclusion of conflict' in order to create a new form of community that 'although jeopardised by conflict, also thrives on it' (Unger, 2004, p. 560).

Whilst we would agree with his advocacy of an agonistic form of community and democracy, we feel less at ease with his summation of this approach as one that sees its central dynamic as 'the notion of a heightened vulnerability within which people get a chance to resolve more fully the conflict between the enabling conditions of self-assertion' (Unger, 2004, p. 560). Our preference is for an account of community such as that developed by John Macmurray (Macmurray, 1950), who takes what he considers to be the central principles of democracy – namely, equality and freedom – and places them at the heart of the developmental process. The foregrounding of a heightened vulnerability has too Hobbesian a feel to it and, in many respects, seems out of kilter with the spirit and direction of much of Unger's work – as, for example, his later insistence that '[o]ur capacity for love and solidarity grows through the strengthening of our ability to recognise and to accept the otherness of other people' (Unger, 1998, p. 9). Human aspiration deserves a more ennobling intellectual motif than the persistence of fear. Whilst the force of fear will always be present in the realities and narratives of human conduct, unless conditioned and controlled by the uniting force of love, it can never be an adequate dynamic, intellectual or experiential, for the creation of a just and joyful society (Macmurray, 1961).

One of the reasons the School Meetings at St George-in-the-East worked well was because all participants, students and staff, felt valued, felt significant and thus able and willing to make a personal contribution in the multiplicity of settings within which they did their daily work. This foundational basis of care and of what we have at different points in this book termed 'fellowship', or, more accurately, 'democratic fellowship' seems to us important. Commitment to a democratic fellowship is necessarily a commitment not only towards valuing difference, but to seeing difference as a necessary and residual requirement of a diverse, inclusive community. Such a community is both point and process, the end and the means of democratic living and learning together.

E. R. Braithwaite's description of a School Meeting at St George-in-the-East in his autobiographical *To Sir With Love* gives us a sense of how some of these matters worked themselves through in practice (see Fielding, 2009 for a fuller description and analysis). In the latter half of the Meeting, students move into a reciprocally demanding, sometimes critical, dialogue with three randomly chosen members of the staff who, with varying degrees of skill and conviction, seek to justify and, in some cases defend, the basis of the school curriculum on which the student body had earlier reflected in some detail. In this instance, one of the older boys challenged the nature of Physical Education or PE (at that time known as physical training or PT) that the school offered:

> He complained that the PT was ill-conceived and pointless, and the routine monotonous; he could see no advantage in doing it; a jolly good game was far better. Apparently, he was voicing the opinion of all the boys, for they cheered him loudly.
>
> (Braithwaite, 1969, p. 105)

There then follows a series of impassioned, thought-provoking exchanges between students and staff about the nature and possible justification of compulsion, the necessity of recognising differences in need and capacity, the importance of thinking about and helping others, and the relationship between school and wider society, particularly with regard to preparation for adult life. Whilst only a snapshot of one occasion at a particular point in its development, Braithwaite's account nonetheless helps us understand why the School Meeting had such felt significance for both students and staff and how the principles of freedom and equality which lie at the heart of democratic fellowship worked themselves through in the realities of time and circumstance. Purposes and aspirations, the touchstones of meaning-making, framed the opening and closing of the event; a framework of reflection, dialogue, disagreement and celebration enabled contributions from all ages and identities in ways which challenged traditional hierarchies within the context of an insistent, demanding mutuality. A range of voices were heard, not only through the narratives of learning, but also through the leveller of laughter and the eagerness of exploration. And all through this ran the excitement of the unpredictable and the reassurance of shared responsibility.

Reggio Emilia, too, is imbued with a concept of community at ease with diversity, *confronto* and sometimes, critical dialogue. Over the years, the project has developed a strong common vision, which includes ways of working, such as pedagogical documentation and a pedagogy of listening, that assume and respect multiple perspectives, diverse interpretations and the contestability of meanings – and refuse to privilege any one perspective, interpretation or meaning. Participation, as three *pedagogistas* write, is based:

> on the idea that reality is not objective, that culture is a constantly evolving product of society, that individual knowledge is only partial; and that in order to

construct a project, especially an educational project, everyone's point of view is relevant in dialogue with those of others, within a framework of shared values. The idea of participation [in Reggio Emilia] is founded on these concepts: and in our opinion, so, too, is democracy itself.

(Cagliari et al., 2004, p. 29)

7 Celebrating and contesting history

More often than not, radicalism is inseparable from history. As Tom Holland reminds us, '[w]hat has always been the key to understanding radicalism in [England] is that it looks for inspiration not in the future, but in the past' (Holland, 2008/09, p. 56). A pre-eminently important strand of our advocacy argues strongly for the necessity not just of history, but of history's pluralities, for a radical chosen genealogy. Unger's powerful insistence that the school helps young people to transcend the familial, class, cultural and historical contexts of their location is not a denial of their roots, but a plea for radical new identities fashioned by a transformational energy and understanding they are invariably denied. The point is not to deny location but to transcend it by creating new ones, by choosing or 'finding genealogies rather than merely inheriting them' (Unger, 1998, p. 235).

The ahistorical presumptions of neoliberalism are a consequence both of its arrogance and its fearful insistence on denying the possibility of alternative ways of being. By contrast, history matters for radical education, not history as the kings and queens of England, but history as a rich narrative of people and places, ideas and struggles, which can speak to us today, helping us to learn, building our confidence and giving us inspiration and hope. So the practices we prefigure will be rooted in a chosen past, whose radical continuities we wish to explore, celebrate and extend.

It is no accident that we chose to foreground the work of Loris Malaguzzi and Alex Bloom in Chapter 1. The traditions to which they belong stretch back through history and forward through the intervening years since their untimely deaths. They stretch across sectors and national boundaries and remind us not only that the world has been different, but that it could be so again. They remind us not only of the importance of retelling their stories and other stories that have also been shamefully forgotten; they also remind us of the need to tell each other our own stories and in so doing, weave our own narratives into the fabric of the future.

8 The persistent pull of personalism

One cannot read Unger's work without being drawn back again and again to the personalist anthropology that underpins his view of democracy. Many of his most eloquent, moving and insightful passages return to the specialness of ordinary men and women; to their betrayal and belittlement by so many regimes and ways of life; to the necessity and possibility of their fulfilment in arrangements and processes that release and enhance their creative powers.

The Promethean aspirations we have alluded to earlier cannot be realised through politics alone. Indeed, as, for example, the anarchist and feminist movements have long argued and as we suggested in our advocacy of transgressive holism, this is not something that politics can do on its own. It requires what Unger calls 'the extra-institutional politics of personal relations' working hand in hand with 'the politics of institutions' (Unger, 1998, p. 258). The justification of politics, its ultimate *raison d'être*, has to do with the nature and quality of the lives we are able to lead. Emancipatory politics is a necessary but not a sufficient condition of human flourishing. Whilst we are the creatures of a particular time and a particular place, we are also 'context-transcending beings' (ibid., p. 9):

> To challenge and to revise the context, even in little, piecemeal ways, is not only the condition for a fuller realisation of our ideals and interests; it is also an indispensable expression of our humanity as beings whose powers of experience and initiative are never exhausted by the social and cultural worlds into which we happen to have been born.
>
> (Unger, 2005a, pp. 70–71)

Democratic politics must, thus, always be a personalist politics. Following similar directions to those of John Macmurray in Chapter 2, Unger's argument and ours is that whilst the personal is through the political, fundamentally the political is for the sake of the personal. This is not a denial of civic virtues or a sentimental or parochial erosion of the public realm that has rightly worried many writers on the left. Rather, it is an insistence on the relational nature of a self that is communal rather than collective. It affirms both the ethical and inevitable nexus of politics and social justice. It also insists on their fulfilment in the felt realities of human encounter.

Within the context of a school, the pull of personalism draws us back, once again, to the centrality of educational purposes, a relational view of the self and the felt realities of human encounter that inform shared aspiration and daily reality. It insists on the constant demystification of organisational and policy discourse and its unremitting interrogation from the standpoint of an embodied, diverse humanity. It insists, as we have argued earlier in this book, that 'the functional is for the sake of the personal' and not, as neoliberalism would have us believe, the other way around. Indeed, at the heart of a personalist dynamic is a commitment, not just to the presence of the personal in educational arrangements but to its imminent insistence, to 'the functional as expressive of the personal'.

Thus, the underpinning educational beliefs of St George-in-the-East and the size of the school enabled a structural and cultural responsiveness to individuals as known and significant persons within a community that paid reciprocal and equal attention to their uniqueness and their relatedness to others. It encouraged, if not a transgression of roles and relations, then an account of both that enabled students and teachers to see each other as persons, to be surprised by each other's multi-sidedness. It developed a curricular approach that was not only values-driven and emergent rather than economically inscribed and efficiently 'delivered', but one within which the enthusiasms and curiosities of young people and adults formed the basis of shared enquiry. It modelled, in the wake of a terrible World War, in which the continued existence of democracy was under serious threat, an understanding of democracy, not primarily as a representative device, but rather as a participatory form of living and learning together that valued and nurtured the uniqueness of individual persons and the richness and diversity of their relatedness and interdependence in the quest for a good life in a just and creative society. In sum, it modelled and developed democratic fellowship.

Strategy matters

Having suggested eight defining characteristics that give a sense of what is prefigurative in prefigurative practice, we now turn to two essential companion arguments that insist on the need in prefigurative practice, not just for radicalism's internal synergy and integrity, but also for attentiveness to external contexts and conditions. These concern commitment to a radical incrementalism and to the importance of strategic alliances as key levers of sustainable change.

9 Radical incrementalism

What both Wright through 'waystations' and Unger through 'democratic experimentalism' are urging us to consider is a radical incrementalism in prefigurative practice, an incrementalism that, perhaps counter-intuitively and certainly contrary to much of the socialist and Marxist traditions, argues for the possibility of a deep break with the hegemonic dominance of capitalism through anticipatory enactments of fundamentally different ways of being in the world.

Incrementalism should not be seen, as it has been so often in the past, as synonymous with a compliant gradualism or a 'pessimistic reformism' that is left to 'humanise the inevitable' (Unger, 1998, p. 8). The claims not only of prefigurative practice but also of democratic experimentalism to radical credentials rest on their cumulative and transgressive persistence, on their achievement of changed understandings of 'interests, ideas and identities' (ibid., p. 19), and ultimately, on their contribution to the possibility of 'non-reformist reforms'.

In Chapter 3, we cited Boaventura de Sousa Santos's insistence that 'the state must be made to create the conditions for social experimentation'. We are aware of a plethora of difficulties here and are not in a position to suggest concrete ways forward with the same kind of conviction as we have with regard to our other propositions; this is exactly the kind of area that requires more work under Wright's heading of 'viability', including 'systematic theoretical models of how particular social structures and institutions would work, and empirical studies of cases, both historical and contemporary'. We are, however, strongly persuaded by the merits of the kind of case that Boaventura de Sousa Santos, Roberto Unger and Erik Olin Wright are urging us to consider and would argue, at the very least, for serious attention to be paid to the notion of democratic experimentalism as a companion to current market-driven or philanthropic approaches. We are further persuaded, from the many local examples, both past and present, of educational experimentation that the state which assumes a role of actively supporting social experimentation would find no shortage of takers for developing radical democratic education and the democratic common school.

10 Strategic engagement

It is important to recognise that the cumulative ambitions of radical incrementalism operate as much at a horizontal as a vertical level. The hope is not just to intensify the commitment and resilience of those who are involved, but also to reach out to those who are not, to connect to others in an ongoing, cumulative way, 'to increase popular participation and bring people together in problem-solving deliberations' (Wright, 2007, p. 38). This catalytic power goes beyond the generation of transgressional energy and its cumulative incorporation in radical incremental change. It underscores the importance of strategic circumspection.

For Wright, waystations must 'demonstrate the virtues of the fuller programme' (Wright, 2007) and for Unger, the small-scale fragmentary versions of the future must 'represent a step on a possible passage from the present formative order to a desired order' (Unger, 2004, p. 412). In doing so they not only provide 'an anticipatory image of broader transformations', they also act as a 'strategic tool' (ibid.). Without wider strategic engagement, whether through social movements, political alliances or local, regional, national and international networks, prefigurative practice is unlikely either to be successful in keeping the formal and informal intrusions of the *status quo* at bay or in learning from solidary organisations and movements and thus sustain the necessary processes of learning how to live and work differently, how to enable the future to grow in the present.

At the end of Chapter 2, we gave a number of examples, both from St George-in-the-East and from Reggio Emilia, of the essential role that regional, national and global solidarities played in their development and, in the case of Reggio, in its remarkable, still-evolving continuity. Contemporary developments in communication and the rise of networks and transnational movements insist on and enhance the strategic imperatives which radical democratic education needs to embrace if it is to achieve its promise and its larger aspirations.

Having the conviction to act

If the substance and direction of our arguments for prefigurative practice are largely right there still remains the challenge of how to connect macro-level aspiration to meso-level participation, how to encourage action and engagement at the level of daily practice. It seems likely that there are two complementary ways of doing this. One has to do with the transparent articulation of core institutional characteristics with the grounded nature of prefigurative practice. The other has to do with a more overtly motivational strategy and the nature of the language used to describe it.

11 Institutional transformation

In order to fulfil its emancipatory potential, prefigurative practice – in our case, the radical democratic school – must, in Sheila Rowbotham's phrase, 'release the imagination of what could be' (Rowbotham, 1979, p. 147) or, as Unger has it, provide 'an anticipatory image of broader transformations' (Unger, 2004, p. 412). Creating 'an anticipatory image of broader transformations' is not just an aesthetic matter: it is in large part a psychological matter – it must, in Wright's terms, be viable and, above all, achievable. If people are to act, if they are to risk the rupture of new ways of working and relating on a day-to-day basis, they need practical instantiations of lived alternatives. Transformative alternatives must thus illustrate, albeit in small, ongoing ways, the grounded possibility of doing things significantly differently: in Sarah Benton's words,

> [i]t's not enough for the individual woman to 'know' she is possessed or dominated; in order not to be possessed or dominated, indeed in order not to want to be there, there must be an alternative culture in which such values are seen to be dominant and to be practised (in however erratic a way) in relations to which she can define herself.
>
> (cited in Rowbotham, 1979, p. 129)

For Roberto Unger, one of the most important defining levers of democratic experimentalism has to do with the power of organisations, with 'the tools of institutional imagination' (Unger, 1998, p. 15), to shape not just the way we work, but also who we are and who we might wish to become. However, institutional transformation is always more than that: it is an enactment of a different reality that has the power to suggest wider possibilities, interconnections and ways of being. Counter-hegemonic institutional practices and aspirations – prefigurative practices – are likely to have pride of place in any radical strategy because they have the power of presence, the irrefutability of contemporary reality, that gives the lie to the familiar fabrications of 'there is no alternative'.

If Stuart Hall is right in suggesting that 'subordination is constantly and effectively *realised* in the real structures and relationships in which they [the subordinate classes] are obliged to live out their relations to the requirement of the whole system' (Hall, 1977, p. 55), then we have to create and live by new ones as part of our challenge. When we actually encounter these radical alternatives it is in large part their brute reality, their enacted denial of injustice and inhumanity and their capacity to live out a more fulfilling, more generous view of human flourishing that in turn moves us to think and act differently. This is the emotional and political power of places like Reggio Emilia and St George's, vivid examples of prefigurative practice and sources of inspiration to others to think and act differently in their own prefigurative practice.

Thus, the educational project of Reggio Emilia, whilst drawing on many important historical traditions, has created a distinct identity that shows the possibility of both thinking and acting significantly differently to the prevailing educational discourse inscribed as it is with managerialism, neoliberalism and positivism. That this has happened can be explained, in part at least, by the democratic commitment and practice present from the start of the project and the nurturing of deeply collegial relationships involving children, parents, educators, politicians and other citizens. The scale of this divergence from the educational mainstream, which we repeat combines thought with action, has been summed up by Dahlberg and her colleagues:

> Choosing to adopt a social constructionist approach; challenging and deconstructing dominant discourses; realising the power of these discourses

in shaping and governing our thoughts and actions, including the field of early childhood pedagogy; rejecting the prescription of rules, goals, methods and standards, and in so doing risking uncertainty and complexity; having the courage to think for themselves in constructing new discourses, and, in so doing daring to make the choice of understanding the child as a rich child, a child of infinite capabilities, a child born with a hundred languages; building a new pedagogical project, foregrounding relationships and encounters, dialogue and negotiation, reflection and critical thinking; border crossing disciplines and perspectives, replacing either/or positions with an and/also openness; and understanding the contextualised and dynamic nature of pedagogical practice, which problematises the idea of a transferable 'programme'.

(Dahlberg *et al.*, 2007, p. 122)

St George-in-the-East similarly prefigured a profound change in relationships, values and practices, exemplified by the decision to eradicate competition, an ethical and political decision that not only ruled out certain kinds of relationships and practices, but ruled in others. In going against the grain of dominant, taken-for-granted ways of living and learning, it also developed counter-practices that exemplified and enacted the validity and desirability of creative alternatives. Thus, on one famous occasion A. S. Neill visited the school for the annual 'prize-giving'. Given Bloom's aversion to competition, the 'prize' – some tablecloths for the school's lunchtime arrangements – was agreed by the School Council and presented to the whole school by the head teacher of one of the most famous radical private schools in the western world.

The point here is not only that the prize was a communally agreed gift that contradicted the dominant paradigms of the day. It is also that a range of other practices made such an event a natural enactment of an alternative set of values and practices. These included playing of competitive games with local schools whilst insisting the results be treated as a friendly (i.e. no winners and losers), absence of ability grouping, the celebration of an individual achievement as a matter of communal joy and personal recognition, and so on in a myriad of ways, all woven together and made universally visible in the tapestry of the school's values. In the words of the radical reformer, Marjorie Franklin, who knew the school well, Bloom's work at St George-in-the East was 'a balanced unity and not just a collection of unrelated good ideas' (Consultant Psychiatrist [Marjorie Franklin] 1962, p. 41).

12 Narrative engagement

Despite its pre-eminent power, the concrete fact of profoundly different ways of working and of creating alternative realities cannot bear all the weight of radical emancipatory ambition. The alternative realities they present and presage must also be morally and politically desirable in a range of ways, including their potential to excite our narrative sensibilities. Here language has a key role to play, language as 'a tool for persuasion and a device for discovery' (Unger, 2004, p. 430). In order to fulfil this role, Unger insists the articulation of institutional proposals must not only connect to the here-and-now of current debates and pre-occupations, it must also suggest a strong sense of future possibility and thereby exercise a visionary pull. Key in all this is his insistence that it is the personal, the felt reality of human encounter, that provides the gravitational dynamic of the discourse:

> the emphasis of language must always fall on the subtleties of personal experience rather than on the more impersonal aspects of dogma and practice. For one thing, only the reference to detailed, person-to-person relations can give the discourse of the movement an intelligible and persuasive immediacy. For another thing, only the test of personal experience . . . can ultimately validate our ideas about possibility and empowerment.
>
> (Unger, 2004, p. 431)

Our examples, particularly those from Reggio Emilia, amply testify to the importance of Unger's case. Not only do the concrete instances of lived inspirational practice shine through the prose of its proponents, the prose itself often verges on the poetic, with a vocabulary and style of writing that combines clarity with an emotional and aesthetic sensibility that makes reading the prose a joyful and life-enhancing experience. And this writing, it bears reiterating, is just one of many languages that they work with to communicate experience and emotion, ideas and relationships. Their narrative engagement is truly multi-lingual, as the only way to express fully the complexity, joy and constant amazement of their educational project.

Whilst Alex Bloom's prose is less adventurous than the range and flair of the Reggio literature, it nonetheless carries conviction. Its practical exemplification of ways of working quite different from the norms of the time have enough grounded credibility to resonate with those whose school experience was dominated by quite other realities. Equally important, it also articulated a moral conviction and imaginative richness that carried its own powers of persuasion.

Why transformation might happen: an age of multiple crises

> Many of us are consuming well beyond our economic means and well beyond the limits of the natural environment, yet in ways that fail to improve our well being – and meanwhile many others suffer poverty and hunger. Continuing economic growth in high-income countries will make it impossible to achieve urgent carbon reduction targets. Widening inequalities, a failing global economy, critically depleted natural resources and accelerating climate change pose grave threats to the future of human civilisation.
>
> (New Economics Foundation, 2010b, p. 2)

Throughout this book, we have begun to sketch out some parts of a process of transformation towards a utopian destination, paying particular attention to an incremental and cumulative process, the key roles in this process of waystations, democratic experimentalism and prefigurative practice, and the potential positive contribution of an enabling state – both national and local government – as an agent of innovation and a sustainer of experimentation. Transformation cannot be imposed uniformly from above, though it may be articulated and supported by democratic deliberation and governance at the national level, just as the national level provides that framework of entitlements, understandings, values and goals that gives shared meaning to citizenship in a particular society. Rather, transformation is a process of recognising and backing social agents capable of taking forward change in particular places or sectors, be they local authorities (like Reggio Emilia), local community organisations or cooperatives (like the Sheffield Children's Centre) or local schools (like St George-in-the-East or the many examples of 'schools-within-schools').

Despite these beginnings of a plausible narrative of transformation, drawing from a widening body of work on utopian thinking and transformations, there are also strong reasons for saying that transformation of education and the school will not happen, and therefore for 'radical pessimism'. Current education and schooling are not accidental. They are socially reproduced by powerful discourses and institutions, which education and schooling in turn help to reproduce. Education cannot be seen in isolation from wider social and economic forces, and the former cannot change substantially without change in the latter. The Thatcherite assertion that 'there is no alternative' is still capable of casting its malign spell, reducing us to immobility and despair.

But as Wright reminds us, processes of social reproduction are never omnipotent and irresistible. They are beset by tensions and weaknesses, and so there are always possibilities for transformation:

> There are reasons to be sceptical of this radical pessimism. One of the central tasks of emancipatory social science is to try to understand the contradictions, limits and gaps in systems of reproduction which open up spaces for transformative strategies . . . even when the spaces are limited, they can allow for transformations that matter.
>
> (Wright, 2009c, p. 203)

In fact, as we argued in Chapter 1, there is good reason to think that these 'spaces for transformative strategies' are today not as limited as they have been, indeed that such spaces are opening up and widening all the time. Since the 1980s, state socialism has failed and collapsed, whilst its triumphant successor, neoliberal capitalism, has once again (as it did in the nineteenth century) disqualified itself by revealing its destructive nature and its irrelevance to both human survival and flourishing. Conditions continue to change and with them the equation of viability and achievability for radical social alternatives also reconfigures.

Confronted by the personal, social, cultural and environmental costs of the *status quo*, one message emerges more clearly and more insistently by the day: we cannot carry on as we are! A way of life premised on constant growth, relentless consumerism, hypermarket capitalism, high inequality, competitive individualism and weakening public responsibility is not only inimical to individual and collective flourishing, it is also environmentally unsustainable. If humankind is to have a future worth living, indeed any future at all, we need not only to rethink but transform the economy, to change our relationship to the environment in a fundamental way, to reduce inequalities that are unjust and damaging, and to renew and deepen democracy as the means to address these challenges collaboratively.

We may appear to belabour this point. We think not. Indeed if anything, we under-play the seriousness of the situation confronting us individually and as a species. We are in the midst of multiple and growing crises, that put not only our well-being but very survival at risk. As Morin reminds us, our 'number one vital problem' is the sheer multiplicity and inexorable growth in the crises that confront us. We need collabora-tive, systemic and long-term responses and education must be part of that. Yet while part of our collective brain acknowledges something unprecedented and alarming is taking place, the other part seeks the solace of normal service, including an education devoted to producing a capitalist workforce whose main qualities are unquestion-ing flexibility and an unresisting responsiveness to whatever conditions capitalism ordains as necessary for competitive success and continuing growth.

As well as painfully coming to terms with the seriousness of the state we are in, we need also to hold on to a sense of historical perspective and what that tells us about past transformations and future possibilities: times do change, transformations do occur, the unpredicted comes to pass, and nothing is forever. Today's rampant neo-liberalism, as Susan George reminded us earlier, would have seemed crazed during the early post-war years. Indeed, in an excellent example of Wrightian and Ungerian thinking about the process of transformation, the neoliberal world that today we too often take for granted began its modern renaissance among a scattering of radical thinkers and organisations, such as thinktanks, in the late 1960s and 1970s, who began to answer the questions of desirability and viability – 'where to?' and 'how?' – before governments incrementally implemented measures to bring about sweeping radical reform in practice. Mrs Thatcher may have had an idea of the direction she and her circle favoured; but she had no grand road map for getting to the market nirvana, her policies being introduced piecemeal and, often, opportunistically and accumulating until they had begun to change the political, economic and social landscape in fun-damental ways. In this context, we can in fact read the school reforms of the 1980s and 1990s as an instance of Unger's 'radical reform', and examples of prefigurative practice for a full-blown neoliberal society.

The upsurge of neoliberalism in the 1970s was triggered by large crises, not least in the prevailing form of Fordist capitalism (Harvey, 1989), and today we face again a transformatory crisis, or rather that multiplicity of crises, more complex and threaten-ing than any before. So if governments were able to spend several decades promoting transformation, through competitive individualism and market solutions for every problem, it is neither unrealistic nor unreasonable to argue, as the New Economics Foundation does, that governments and societies should 'spend the next few decades promoting the benefits of cooperation and interdependence' (New Economics Foundation, 2009, p. 53). The transformation of education and schooling can and must be seen as part of a larger process of transformation that is increasingly apparent, increasingly possible and increasingly urgent. Education and schooling are part of the current problem, but must also be part of the future solution.

So, rather than expecting education to fix society, we should see it as an active part of the wider and very urgent transformation of society and an active partner in that societal transformation alongside other social actors. Its contribution is, in Dale's words, 'to prefigure, in microcosm, the more equal, just and fulfilling society'. But also to create and sustain an institution – the common democratic school – essential to the practice of democracy and democratic experimentalism that is needed to bring about a more sustainable, more just and more solidaristic society.

That role in transformation may be limited initially to individual projects and schools, with the courage to think and do differently, those democratic experimenters who are always to be found, no matter how harsh the environment, like Loris Malaguzzi and his colleagues in Reggio Emilia or Alex Bloom and St George's school or the Schools-within-Schools pioneers. But such projects can proliferate, develop and survive where local government takes up its responsibilities, for education and for transformation to a better life for its citizens, as Reggio Emilia has demonstrated so superbly. Lastly, democratic experimentalism as part of a transformatory process would thrive further if it was recognised, welcomed and supported by the nation state, through a welfare state that sought a politics, provision and practice of education that would contribute to a sustainable, flourishing, democratic – and yes, poetic – society.

We began with a quotation from Edgar Morin and end with one, or rather one taken from a preface to his essay for UNESCO, *Seven complex lessons in education for the future*. It captures our own beliefs and hopes about the future of the world and about the place of a radical education in creating the transformation needed to secure that future:

> When we look to the future we confront many uncertainties about the world our children, grandchildren and great grandchildren, will live in. But we can be certain of at least one thing: if we want this earth to provide for the needs of its inhabitants, human society must undergo a transformation. The world of tomorrow must be fundamentally different from the world we know . . . We must strive to build a 'sustainable future'. Democracy, equity, social justice, peace and harmony with our natural environment should be the watchwords of this world to come . . . Education, in the broadest sense, plays a preponderant role in this development aimed at fundamental changes in our ways of living and behaving . . . One of the greatest challenges we face is how to adjust our way of thinking to meet the challenge of an increasingly complex, rapidly changing, unpredictable world. . . . This means breaking down traditional barriers between disciplines and conceiving new ways to reconnect that which has been torn apart . . . [W]e have to keep our sights on the long term and honour our tremendous responsibility for future generations.
>
> (Morin, 2001, pp. 5–6)

A post-electoral post-script

We have written this book for an international readership and have tried to adopt a broad historical and territorial perspective. So we hope readers outside England will bear with this short and insular reflection on recent events – perhaps if for no other reason than that developments in England seem on occasion to have a disproportionate influence on policy and practice elsewhere.

The sophistry of independence

We finished our manuscript before the latest (May 2010) election in the United Kingdom. This ended 13 years of Labour government, replacing it by a coalition Conservative and Liberal Democrat government, which has been conspicuously active on the education front in England. It has pushed through at great speed, with no public consultation and little Parliamentary scrutiny, new legislation primarily intended to establish more 'independent', publicly-funded schools: more 'academy' schools and the introduction of a new kind of school, the so-called 'free' school, which (to quote the government website) 'will be set up by a wide range of proposers, including charities, universities, businesses, educational groups, teachers and groups of parents'.

'Independent' though is a misnomer. Proliferating academies and 'free' schools may be unfettered by democratic obligations to elected local authorities. But they will, instead, be wholly dependent on central government, giving 'any future education secretary, in England, unprecedented powers, exercisable without reference to any elected body' (letter by Peter Newsam, *The Guardian*, 28 July).

Despite the Labour party's opposition to aspects of the legislation, what is striking is the continuity of policy. This latest round of educational legislation tightens the grip of a regime that first began to seize power in the 1980s, a regime based on an ideological belief in markets, competition and consumer choice – a neoliberal utopian dream gradually made reality.

For 'big society' read ubiquitous market

Just as the duplicitous discourse of 'independence' masks the deeper realities of neoliberal imperatives, so the new government's unctuous advocacy of the 'big society' ushers in the increasingly visible hand of market fundamentalism. As Peter Wilby has so insightfully observed, the Coalition Prime Minister, David Cameron, may be keen that

> we 'don't always turn to officials, local authorities or central government'. [But h]e doesn't want to stop us turning to business. On the contrary, Cameron wants to connect 'private capital to investment in social projects'. That, I suspect, is what the 'big society' is really all about. Parents may decide to start a school, but they will soon find it's best to bring in private money and hire private management if it is to get off the ground and survive as a going concern . . . For 'big society' read big bonanza for big business.
>
> (Wilby, 2010a)

Spawning more independent schools develops the market. Weakening still more the educational role of democratic local authorities removes a potential obstacle to marketisation. Education is further privatised, not just by opening up new opportunities for businesses, but more insidiously by privatising perception. For as an active role for local authorities in education withers and the role given to interest groups – parents, private providers and other 'proposers' – flourishes, the idea that education is a common responsibility and community project, a public matter conducted in public spaces, becomes more and more alien. Society and government are increasingly separated and placed in opposition to each other, the public sphere rendered suspect.

The English education system has always been a vehicle for the pursuit of private interest and the hindrance of social justice. Consider the newly elected UK Parliament and government: thirty-five per cent of MPs are privately educated, compared to seven per cent of all children, with the figure rising to fifty per cent for MPs from the two governing coalition parties and an astonishing sixty per cent of all ministers (Sutton Trust, 2010). But rather than tackle the central role that education plays in reproducing hierarchy and inequality, successive governments vie to sustain and enhance that role. The new schools pushed through by the new government 'like most school types recently invented, will tend to favour the middle classes, who have the time and know-how to take advantage of "diversity"' (Wilby, 2010b).

Emaciated politics, healthy dictatorship

The indecent haste of new government legislation and the absence of substantive political opposition reveal the emaciated state of the politics of education in England and the rude good health of the dictatorship of no alternatives. The signs are everywhere. The unchallenged triumphalism of the dominant market discourse; the silence over private schooling and the growing privatisation of the former public system; and the absence of any serious debate about critical educational questions such as those proposed in this book. Taking up two key themes of our book, there is not even a passing recognition that democracy might be an important issue in education nor that type of school should go well beyond questions of governance and finance.

The emaciated state of the politics of education shows too in continuing indifference to the serious state we are in – environmentally, democratically, socially and economically – and what this state might mean for education. As a society, we seem unable to face up to the serious questions confronting us and start the process of thinking how education might contribute to answering these questions: questions about survival, questions about an economy not premised on growth or endless consumption, questions about solidarity and justice, care and responsibility, questions about democracy and diversity. Just as we seem unable to envisage a just, equitable, sustainable, democratic society, so too we seem unable to open up debate about what sort of education and what sort of school this might mean.

Reclaiming education as a democratic project and a community responsibility

Our intention in writing this book was never to influence the details of particular policies in particular countries; there are plenty of others better equipped and better placed than us to do so. Our intent, as we make clear from the start, is to develop *an* alternative that seeks to reclaim education as a democratic project and a community responsibility and the school as a public space of encounter for all citizens.

By so doing we have sought to diversify utopian thinking and prefigurative practice, away from the current monopoly held by markets. By arguing for a return to fundamental questions of human purpose and to envisioning social, political and educational spaces where these matters can once again be discussed, understood and acted on in the search for an inclusive, elusive common good we have sought to contest the dispiriting and destructive obsession with an overly-instrumental, reductionist form of schooling that distorts the present and betrays the future. We have sought to contest the dictatorship of no alternatives by feeding the emaciated politics of education and in doing so rekindle hope in the possibilities of education in its broadest and fullest sense. The recent election in England only confirms for us the urgency of this task.

Notes

1 Nikolas Rose describes 'human technologies' as a technical means for acting on human capacities, including

> forms of practical knowledge, with modes of perception, practices of calculation, vocabularies, types of authority, forms of judgement, architectural forms, human capacities, non-human objects and devices, inscription techniques and so forth, traversed and transacted by aspirations to achieve certain outcomes in terms of the conduct of the governed.
>
> (Rose, 1999, p. 52)

2 The same is true of the English government's 2007 statement of aims for secondary education. Three broad aims, with statutory force, are stated – successful learners, confident individuals and responsible citizens – followed by a series of brief criteria defining each aim. Once again, this is a management rather than a political exercise, neither encouraging nor allowing any reflection or deliberation about meanings or alternatives (for further information, see http://curriculum.qcda.gov.uk/key-stages-3-and-4/aims-values-and-purposes/aims/index.aspx).

3 The Czech philosopher and educator, John Amos Comenius (1592–1670) observed that

> The proper education of the young does not consist in stuffing their heads with a mass of words, sentences, and ideas dragged together out of various authors, but in opening up their understanding to the outer world, so that a living stream may flow from their own minds, just as leaves, flowers, and fruit spring from the bud on a tree.
>
> (http://en.wikiquote.org/wiki/John_Amos_Comenius)

4 Ransom (2003) argues that there are various forms of accountability, including 'professional', 'neoliberal' and 'democratic', and argues for 'democratic accountability', which he argues is constituted by a number of principles and practices. Apple adds that 'the issue is not whether or not we need accountability, but what the logics of the accountability should be' (2005, p. 23).

5 By contrast, independent state-funded schools, which have attracted a lot of political attention in England, account for less than ten per cent of Swedish school children. English politicians have shown no awareness of or interest in the far more innovative developments underway in Sweden's local authority-run schools, which we discuss in this chapter.

6 The Italian concept of confrontation – *confronto* – is very different in meaning to the English 'confrontational', with its connotation of hostility, even aggression. It is seeking people out because we want their point of view or to look at something we are or do in the light of another way of being or doing. It is an important word in Reggio Emilia.

7 In the *technical role*, research is a producer of means, strategies and techniques to achieve given ends. De Vries argues, however, that this is only one of the ways in which research can be

practically relevant, and there is at least one other way in which research can inform practice. This is by providing a different way of understanding and imagining social reality. He refers to the latter as the *cultural role* of research (Biesta, 2007, pp. 18–19).

8 However, in May 2009, the newly-elected right wing New Zealand government announced the termination of the programme as a cost-cutting measure, with the two current rounds of research on innovative pedagogy having to end within five weeks.

9 For a good recent contribution to the educational literature on prefigurative practice, see McCowan (2010).

Bibliography

Åberg, A. (2005) 'A knowledge building project about birds', *Children in Europe*, 9, 20–21.

Ackerman, B., Alstott, A. and van Parijs, P. (2005) *Redesigning Distribution: Basic Income and Stakeholder Grants as Cornerstones of a More Egalitarian Capitalism*. London: Verso.

Aldrich, R. (2010) 'Education for survival: an historical perspective', *History of Education*, 39 (1), 1–14.

Allen, R. and Vignoles, A. (2009) *Can School Competition Improve Standards? The Case of Faith Schools in England*. (DoQSS Working Paper No. 0904.) London: Institute of Education, University of London (http://repec.ioe.ac.uk/REPEc/pdf/qsswp0904.pdf, accessed 27 July 2010).

Anderson, B. (2006) '"Transcending without transcendence": Utopianism and an ethos of hope', *Antipode*, 38 (4), 691–710.

Apple, M. (2004a) *Ideology and Curriculum*. 3rd Edn, London: RoutledgeFalmer.

—— (2004b) 'Creating differences: neo-liberalism, neo-conservativism and the politics of educational reform', *Educational Policy*, 18 (1), 12–44.

—— (2005) 'Education, markets and an audit culture', *Critical Quarterly*, 47 (1–2), 11–29.

Apple, M. and Beane, J. (Eds) (2007) *Democratic Schools: Lessons in Powerful Education*. 2nd Edn, Portsmouth, NH: Heinemann.

Arendt, H. (1954) *Between Past and Future: Eight Exercises in Political Thought*. Harmondsworth: Penguin Books.

Armstrong, M. (1973) 'The role of the teacher', in P. Buckmann (Ed.) *Education Without Schools*. London: Souvenir Press.

Armstrong, M. and King, L. (1977) 'Schools within schools: the Countesthorpe "team" system', in J. Watts (Ed.) *The Countesthorpe Experience*. London: Allen & Unwin, 53–62.

Associació de Mestres Rosa Sensat (2005; English translation) *For a New Public Education System*. Barcelona: Associació de Mestres Rosa Sensat (http://www.rosasensat.org/documents/2/?tmplng = ca, accessed 27 July 2010).

Ball, S. (2003) *Class Strategies and the Education Market*. London: Routledge.

—— (2007) *Education plc: Understanding Private Sector Participation in Public Sector Education*. London: Routledge.

Ball, S., Bowe, R. and Gewirtz, S. (1994) 'Market forces and parental choice', in S. Tomlinson (Ed.) *Educational Reform and Its Consequences*. London: Institute for Public Policy Research.

Barrow, R. (1978) *Radical Education: A Critique of Freeschooling and Deschooling*. London: Martin Robertson.

Bentley, T. (2005) *Everyday Democracy: Why We Get the Politicians We Deserve*. London: Demos.

Berg, L. (1968) *Risinghill: Death of a Comprehensive School*. Harmondsworth: Penguin.

—— (1971) 'Moving towards self-government', in P. Adams, L. Berg, N. Berger, M. Duane, A. S. Neill and R. Ollendorff (Eds) *Children's Rights*. London: Elek.

Biesta, G. (2007) 'Why "what works" won't work: evidence-based practice and the democratic deficit in educational research', *Educational Theory*, 57 (1), 1–22.

Biesta, G. and Lawy, R. (2006) 'From teaching citizenship to learning democracy: overcoming individualism in research, policy and practice', *Cambridge Journal of Education*, 36 (1), 63–79.

Biesta, G. and Osberg, D. (2007) 'Beyond re/presentation: a case for updating the epistemology of schooling', *Interchange*, 38 (1), 15–29.

Bloch, E. (1986; English translation by N. Plaice, S. Plaice and P. Knight) *The Principle of Hope*. Oxford: Basil Blackwell.

—— (2006) 'Educational theories and pedagogies as technologies of power/knowledge: educating the young child as a citizen of an imagined nation and world', in M. Bloch, D. Kennedy, T. Lightfoot and D. Weyenberg (Eds) *The Child in the World/The World in the Child: Education and the Configuration of a Universal, Modern, and Globalized Childhood*. Basingstoke: Palgrave Macmillan.

Bloom, A. A. (n.d.) 'Our pattern', unpublished.

—— (1948) 'Notes on a school community', *New Era*, 29 (6), 120–21.

—— (1949) 'Compete or co-operate?', *New Era*, 30 (8), 170–72.

—— (1952) 'Learning through living', in M. Alderton Pink (Ed.) *Moral Foundations of Citizenship*. London: London University Press.

—— (1953) 'Self-government, study and choice at a secondary modern school', *New Era*, 34 (9), 174–77.

Boaler (2005) 'The "Psychological Prisons" from which they never escaped: the role of ability grouping in reproducing social class inequalities', *Forum*, 47, (2–3), 135–44.

—— (2008) 'Promoting "relational equity" and high mathematics achievement through an innovative mixed ability approach', *British Educational Research Journal*, 34 (2), 167–94.

Boddy, J., Cameron, C., Mooney, A., Moss, P., Petrie, P. and Statham, P. (2005) *Introducing Pedagogy into the Children's Workforce: Children's Workforce Strategy, Response to the Consultation Paper*. London: Thomas Coram Research Unit.

Boggs, C. (1977/78) 'Marxism, prefigurative communism, and the problem of workers' control', *Radical America*, 11.6–12.1, 99–122.

Bowles, S. and Gintis, H. (1999) *Recasting Egalitarianism: New Rules for Equity and Accountability in Markets, Communities and States*. London: Verso.

Braithwaite, E. R. (1969) *To Sir With Love*. London: New English Library.

Breines, W. (1980) 'Community and organization: the New Left and Michels' "Iron Law"', *Social Problems*, 27 (4) April, 419–29.

British Broadcasting Corporation (2008) Interview with Alan Bennett, Radio 4 'Today Programme', Thursday 24 January.

Broadhead, P., Meleady, C. and Delgado, M. A. (2008) *Children, Families and Communities: Creating and Sustaining Integrated Services*. Maidenhead: Open University Press.

Bruner, J. (2004) 'Reggio: a city of courtesy, curiosity and imagination', *Children in Europe*, 6, 27.

Burke, C. (2005) '"The school without tears": E. F. O'Neill of Prestolee', *History of Education*, 34 (3) May, 263–75.

Butt, R. (1981) 'Economics are the method: the object is to change the soul', *The Sunday Times*, 3 May 1981 (http://www.margaretthatcher.org/speeches/displaydocument.asp?docid = 104475, accessed 27 July 2010).

Cable, V. (2009) *A Perfect Storm: The World Economic Crisis and What it Means*. London: Atlantic Books.

Cagliari, P., Barozzi, A. and Giudici, C. (2004) 'Thoughts, theories and experiences: for an educational project with participation', *Children in Europe*, 6, 28–30.

Cambridge Primary Review (2009) *Introducing the Cambridge Primary Review*. Cambridge:

University of Cambridge Faculty of Education (http://www.primaryreview.org.uk/Downloads/Finalreport/CPR-booklet_low-res.pdf, accessed 27 July 2010).

Carr, W. and Hartnett, A. (1996) *Education and the Struggle for Democracy: The Politics of Educational Ideas*. Buckingham: Open University Press.

Case, H. (1966) 'A therapeutic discipline for living', *New Era*, 47 (7), 131–36.

Castells, M. (1997) *The Power of Identity, The Information Age: Economy, Society and Culture, Vol. II*. Oxford: Blackwell.

Catarsi, E. (2004) 'Loris Malaguzzi and the Municipal School Revolution', *Children in Europe*, 6, 22–23.

Central Advisory Council for Education (1967) *Children and their Primary Schools*. Plowden Report, London: Her Majesty's Stationary Office.

Chakrabortty, A. (2009) 'This unexpected radical shows up an abject failure to tame the banks', *The Guardian*, 28 August 2009.

Children in Europe (2008) *Young Children and their Services: Developing a European Approach. A Children in Europe Policy Paper* (http://www.childrenineurope.org/docs/PolicyDocument_000.pdf, accessed 27 July 2010).

Clark, A. (2010) *Transforming Children's Spaces*. London: Routledge.

Cohen, J. and Rogers, J. (1995) *Associations and Democracy*. London: Verso.

Cole, G. D. H. (1950) *Essays in Social Theory*. London: Macmillan.

Consultant Psychiatrist [Marjorie Franklin] (1962) 'Clinical aspects of the work of David Wills', *Anarchy*, 15 (5), 139–46.

Croall, J. (1983*) Neill of Summerhill: The Permanent Rebel*. London: Routledge and Kegan Paul.

Dahlberg, G. (2000) 'Everything is a beginning and everything is dangerous: some reflections on the Reggio Emilia experience', in H. Penn (Ed.) *Early Childhood Services: Theory, Policy and Practice*. Buckingham: Open University Press.

—— (2003) 'Pedagogy as a loci of an ethics of an encounter', in M. Bloch, K. Holmlund, I. Moqvist and T. Popkewitz (Eds) *Governing Children, Families and Education: Restructuring the Welfare State*. New York, NY: Palgrave.

—— (2004) 'Making connections', *Children in Europe*, 6, 22–23.

—— (2005) *Ethics and Politics in Early Childhood Education*. London: Routledge.

Dahlberg, G. and Bloch, M. (2006) 'Is the power to see and visualize always the power to control?', in T. Popkewitz, K. Pettersson, U. Olsson and J. Kowalczyk (Eds) *The Future Is Not What It Appears To Be: Pedagogy, Genealogy and Political Epistemology. In Honour and in Memory of Kenneth Hultqvist*. Stockholm: HLS Förlag.

Dahlberg, G. and Lenz Taguchi, H. (1994) *Förskola och skola – om två skilda traditioner och om visionen om en mötesplats (Pre-school and school – two different traditions and the vision of a meeting place)*. Stockholm: HLS Förlag.

Dahlberg, G., Moss, P. and Pence, A. (2007) *Beyond Quality in Early Childhood Education and Care: Languages of Evaluation*. 2nd Edn, London: Routledge.

Dale, R. (1977) *Liberal and Radical Alternatives: A Critique* (Course E202 Schooling and Society, Block VI Alternatives?) Milton Keynes: Open University Press.

—— (1979) 'From endorsement to disintegration: progressive education from the Golden Age to the Green Paper', *British Journal of Educational Studies*, 26 (3), 191–209.

—— (1988) 'Comprehensive Education', Talk given to Madrid Conference, April, unpublished.

Darling, J. and Norbenbo, S. E. (2003) 'Progressivism', in N. Blake, P. Smeyers, R. Smith and P. Standish (Eds) *The Blackwell Guide to Philosophy of Education*. Oxford: Blackwell.

Davies, M. (2005) 'Less is more: the move to person-centred, human scale education', *Forum*, 47 (2–3), 97–218.

—— (2009) *Human Scale by Design (Occasional Papers No. 2)*. London: Human Scale Education.

Deleuze, G. (1992) 'Postscript on the societies of control', *October*, 59, 3–7.

Deleuze, G. and Guattari, F. (1994; English translation by H. Tomlinson and G. Burchill) *What Is Philosophy?*, London: Verso.

Delgado, M. A. (2009) *Community Involvement in Services for Children, Families and Communities: Acceptance, Resistance and Alternatives to Mainstream Views in Education, Health and Childcare.* Saarbrücken: VDM Verlag Dr. Müller.

Department for Children, Schools and Families (2008) *Extended Schools: Building on Experience.* London: DCSF (http://www.teachernet.gov.uk/_doc/13061/esp2008.pdf, accessed 26 July 2010).

Dewey, J. (1939) 'Creative democracy – the task before us', address given at a dinner in honour of John Dewey, New York, 20 October 1939 (http://chipbruce.files.wordpress. com/2008/11/dewey_creative_dem.pdf, accessed 27 July 2010).

Dudley, P. (2007) *Lessons for Learning: Using Lesson Study to Innovate, Develop and Transfer Pedagogic Approaches and Metapedagogy.* London: TLRP (http://www.bera.ac.uk/lesson-study/, accessed 27 July 2010).

Dyson, A., Goldrick, S., Jones, L. and Kerr, K. (2010) *Equity in Education: Creating a Fairer Education System.* Manchester: Centre for Equity in Education, the University of Manchester (http://www.education.manchester.ac.uk/research/centres/cee/publications/, accessed 27 July 2010).

Edmiston, B. (2008) *Forming Ethical Identities in Early Childhood Play.* London: Routledge.

Eichsteller, G. and Holthoff, A. (forthcoming) 'Conceptual foundations of social pedagogy', in C. Cameron and P. Moss (Eds) *Social Pedagogy and Working with Children.* London: Jessica Kingsley Publishing.

English Department for Education and Skills (2005) *Extended Schools: Access to Opportunities and Services for All: A Prospectus.* London: DfES (http://www.teachernet.gov.uk/_doc/8509/ Extended-schools%20prospectus.pdf, accessed 27 July 2010).

Evans, R. (1983) Countesthorpe College, Leicester. The Countesthorpe team system: towards the 'mini school', in B. Moon (Ed.) *Comprehensive Schools: Challenge and Change*, Windsor: NFER-Nelson.

Facer, K. and Sandford, R. (2010) 'The next 25 years? Future scenarios and future directions for education and technology', *Journal of Computer Assisted Learning*, 26 (1), 74–93.

Fendler, L. (2001) 'Educating flexible souls: the construction of subjectivity through developmentality and interaction', in K. Hultqvist and G. Dahlberg (Eds) *Governing the Child in the New Millennium.* London: RoutledgeFalmer.

Fielding, M. (1976a) 'Against competition: in praise of a malleable analysis and the subversiveness of philosophy', *Proceedings of the Philosophy of Education Society of Great Britain*, X (July), 124–46.

—— (1976b) 'Competition and ideology', *Cambridge Journal of Education*, 6 (3), 135–38.

—— (1999) 'Radical collegiality: affirming teaching as an inclusive professional practice', *Australian Educational Researcher*, 26 (2), 1–34.

—— (2000) 'Community, philosophy and education policy: against effectiveness ideology and the immiseration of contemporary schooling', *Journal of Education Policy*, 15 (4), 397–415.

—— (Ed.) (2001a) *Taking Education Really Seriously: Four Years Hard Labour.* London: Routledge Falmer.

—— (2001b) 'OFSTED, inspection and the betrayal of democracy', *Journal of Philosophy of Education*, 35 (4), 695–709.

—— (2004a) '"New Wave" student voice and the renewal of civic society', *London Review of Education*, 2 (3), 197–217.

—— (2004b) 'Transformative approaches to student voice: theoretical underpinnings, recalcitrant realities', *British Educational Research Journal*, 30 (2), 295–312.

—— (2006a) 'Leadership, personalisation and high performance schooling: naming the new totalitarianism', *School Leadership and Management*, 26 (4), 347–69.

—— (2006b) 'Leadership, radical student engagement and the necessity of person-centred education', *International Journal of Leadership in Education*, 9 (4), 299–313.

—— (2007a) 'On the necessity for radical state education: democracy and the common school', *Journal of Philosophy of Education*, 41 (4), 539–57.

—— (2007b) 'Collaboration, collegiality, community', paper presented to Philosophy Section Seminar, Institute of Education, University of London, 23 May.

—— (2008a) 'Personalisation, education and the market', *Soundings*, 38 (Spring): 56–69.

—— (2008b) 'Radical student engagement: the pioneering work of Alex Bloom', paper presented at the *European Conference on Educational Research*, University of Gothenburg, Sweden.

—— (2009) 'Public space and educational leadership: reclaiming and renewing our radical traditions', *Educational Management, Administration and Leadership*, 37 (4), 497–521.

—— (2011 forthcoming) 'Whole school meetings and the development of radical democratic community', *Studies in Philosophy and Education*.

Fielding, M. and Cunningham, I. (2009) 'Educational leadership as if people matter: supporting person-centred approaches to innovative school leadership, unpublished report on Innovative Headteachers' support programme funded by the Esmée Fairbairn Foundation.

Fielding, M., Bragg, S., Craig, J., Cunningham, C., Eraut, M., Gillinson, S., Horne, M., Robinson, C. and Thorp, J. (2005) *Factors Influencing the Transfer of Good Practice*. London: Department for Education and Skills.

Fielding, M., Elliott, J., Burton, C., Robinson, C. and Samuels J. (2006) *Less is More? The Development of a Schools-within-Schools Approach to Education on a Human Scale at Bishops Park College, Clacton, Essex*. Brighton: University of Sussex.

Fisher, B. and Tronto, J. (1990) 'Toward a feminist theory of caring', in E. Abel and M. Nelson (Eds) *Circles of Care, Work and Identity in Women's Lives*. New York: State University of New York Press.

Flyvbjerg, B. (2006) 'Social science that matters', *Foresight Europe* (October 2005–March 2006), 38–42.

Fortunati, A. (2006) *The Education of Young Children as a Community Project: The Experience of San Miniato*. Azzano San Paolo, Brazil: Edizioni Junior.

Foucault, M. (1988) in L. Kritzman (Ed.) *Politics, philosophy, culture: Interviews and other writings 1977–1984*. New York: Routledge.

Freire, P. (1996 Edn) *Pedagogy of the Oppressed*. London: Penguin Books.

—— (2004 Edn) *Pedagogy of Hope*. London: Continuum.

Fung, A. and Wright, E.O. (2003) *Deepening Democracy: Innovations in Empowered Participatory Governance*. London: Verso.

Galardini, A. (2008) 'Pedagogistas in Italy', *Children in Europe*, 15, 19.

Gardner, H. (2004) 'The hundred languages of successful educational reform', *Children in Europe*, 6, 16–17.

Gaudin, T. (2008) *The World in 2025: A Challenge to Reason*. Brussels: European Commission DG Research (http://2100.org/World2025.pdf, accessed 27 July 2010).

George, S. (1999) 'A short history of neoliberalism: twenty years of elite economics and emerging opportunities for change', paper presented at conference *Economic Sovereignty in a Globalising World*, Bangkok, Thailand, 24–26 March 1999 (www.globalexchange.org/campaigns/econ101/neoliberalism.html, accessed 27 July 2010).

—— (2009) *Too Young for Respect? Realising Respect for Young Children in Their Everyday Environ- ments*. Den Haag: Bernard van Leer Foundation.

Gibson-Graham, J.-K. (2006, 2nd edn.) *The End of Capitalism (As We Knew It): A Feminist Critique of Political Economy*. Minneapolis, MN: University of Minnesota Press.

Gibson-Graham, J. K. (1996) *The End of Capitalism (As We Knew It): A Feminist Critique of Political Economy*. Oxford: Blackwell.

Giroux, H. (2008) 'Rethinking the promise of critical education under an Obama regime', interview with Henri Giroux, 2 December 2008 (http://www.truthout.org/article/henry- giroux-rethinking-promise-critical-education, accessed 27 July 2010).

Glatter, R. (2010) *Towards a Fair and Coherent School System* (Much improved: should do even bet- ter, e-paper 8). London: New Visions for Education Group (http://www.newvisionsfore- ducation.org.uk/content/08%20-%20School%20System.pdf, accessed 27 July 2010).

Gornick, J. and Meyers, M. (2009) *Gender Equality: Transforming Family Divisions of Labor*. London: Verso.

Gray, J. (2007) *Black Mass: Apocalyptic Religion and the Death of Utopia*. London: Allen Lane.

—— (2009) *Gray's Anatomy: John Gray's Selected Writings*. London: Allen Lane.

Gribble, D. (1998) *Real Education: Varieties of Freedom*. Bristol: Libertarian Education.

Hall, S. (1977) *Review of the Course*. Milton Keynes: Open University Press.

Halpin, D. (2003) *Hope and Education*. London: Routledge.

Hannon, V. (2007) *'Next Practice' in Education: A Disciplined Approach to Innovation*. London: Innovation Unit.

Harber, C. (2009) *Toxic Schooling: How Schools Became Worse*. Nottingham: Educational Heretics Press.

Hardt, M. (2008) 'For the love of the multitude: a conversation with Michael Hardt', *the t- machine*, 9 August 2008 (http://the-t-machine.blogspot.com/2008/08/for-love-of-multi- tude-discussion-with.html, 27 July 2010).

Hardt, M. and Negri, A. (2005) *Multitude: War and Democracy in the Age of Empire*. London: Penguin Books.

Hargreaves, A. (1999) 'Fielding errors? Deepening the debate about teacher collaboration and collegiality: response to Fielding', *Australian Educational Researcher*, 26 (2), 45–54.

Hart, S., Dixon, A., Drummond, M. J. and McIntyre, D. (2004) *Learning without Limits*. Buckingham: Open University Press.

Hartley, D. (2007) 'Personalisation: the emerging "revised" code of education?', *Oxford Review of Education*, 33 (5), 629–42.

Harvey, D. (1989) *The Condition of Postmodernity*. Oxford: Blackwell.

—— (2005) *A Brief History of Neoliberalism*. Oxford: Oxford University Press.

Hatcher, R. (2007) '"Yes, but how do we get there?" Alternative visions and the problem of strat- egy', *Journal of Critical Education Studies*, 5 (4) (www.jceps.com/?pageID=article&articleID=98, accessed 27 July 2010).

Hoare, Q. (1965) 'Education: programmes and men', *New Left Review*, 1/32 July–August, 40–52.

Holland, T. (2008/09) 'Golden thread, national myth', *New Statesman*, 22 December–9 January, 53–56.

Hoyuelos, A. (2004) 'A pedagogy of transgression', *Children in Europe*, 6, 6–7.

Hutton, W. and Schneider, P. (2008) *The Failure of Market Failure: Towards a 21st Keynesianism*. London: NESTA.

Innovation Unit (2006) *All Age Schooling: A Resource*. London: DfES Innovation Unit (http:// www.innovation-unit.co.uk/images/stories/files/pdf/allage_booklet2.pdf, accessed 27 July 2010).

Jackson, T. (2009) *Prosperity without Growth? The Transition to a Sustainable Economy*. London:

Sustainable Development Commission (http://www.sd-commission.org.uk/publications/downloads/prosperity_without_growth_report.pdf, accessed 27 July 2010).

Jacoby, R. (1977) *Social Amnesia: A Critique of Conformist Psychology from Adler to Laing*. Hassocks: Harvester Press.

—— (1997) 'Revisiting "Social Amnesia"', *Society*, 35 (1), 58–60.

Jenkins, S. (2009) 'Holy texts and lineage are no way to assemble state schools', *The Guardian*, 30 October.

Johansson, I. and Moss, P. (forthcoming) 'Reforming the school: taking Swedish lessons', *Children & Society*.

Judt, T. (2009) 'What is living and what is dead in social democracy?', *New York Review of Books*, 56 (20), 86–97.

Langsted, O. (1994) 'Looking at quality from the child's perspective', in P. Moss and A. Pence (Eds) *Valuing Quality in Early Childhood Services: New Approaches to Defining Quality*. London: Paul Chapman Publishing.

Lather, P. (2006) 'Foucauldian scientificity: rethinking the nexus of qualitative research and education policy analysis', *International Journal of Qualitative Studies in Education*, 19 (6), 782–91.

Lauder, H. and Hughes, D. (1999) *Trading in Futures: Why Markets in Education Don't Work*. Buckingham: Open University Press.

Leadbeater, C. (2008) *What's Next? 21 Ideas for 21st Century Learning*. London: The Innovations Unit (www.innovation-unit.co.uk/images/stories/whats_next – 21_ideas_final.pdf, accessed 27 July 2010).

Lenz Taguchi, H. (2009) *Going Beyond the Theory/Practice Divide in Early Childhood Education*. London: Routledge.

Levitas, R. (2003) 'Introduction: the elusive idea of utopia', *History of the Human Sciences*, 16 (1), 1–10.

—— (2008) 'Be realistic: demand the impossible', *New Formations*, 65, Autumn, 78–93.

Little, J. W. (1999) 'Colleagues of choice, colleagues of circumstance: response to M. Fielding', *Australian Educational Researcher*, 26 (2) August, 35–44.

Lubienski, C. (2008) 'School choice research in the United States and why it doesn't matter: the evolving economy of knowledge production in a contested policy domain', in M. Forsey, S. Davies and G. Walford (Eds) *The Globalisation of School Choice*. Oxford: Symposium Books.

McCowan, T. (2010) 'School democratization in prefigurative form: two Brazilian experiences', *Education, Citizenship and Social Justice*, 5 (1), 21–41.

Macmurray, J. (1938) *The Clue to History*. London: Student Christian Movement Press.

—— (1943) *Constructive Democracy*. London: Faber & Faber.

—— (1945) 'A philosopher looks at human relations', conference address, Sunday 26 August, unpublished.

—— (1950) *Conditions of Freedom*. London: Faber & Faber.

—— (1961) *Persons in Relations*. London: Faber & Faber.

Mac Naughton, G. (2005) *Doing Foucault in Early Childhood Studies: Applying Post-structural Ideas*. London: Routledge.

Malaguzzi, L. (1993) 'For an education based on relationships', *Young Children*, 11/93, 9–13.

Martin, R. and Smith, J. (1979) 'A case for conversation: teams at Countesthorpe', in G. Haigh (Ed.) *On Our Side: Order, Authority and Interaction in School*. London: Maurice Temple Smith.

Meade, A. and Podmore, V. (2010) *Caring and Learning Together: A Case Study of New Zealand*. Paris: UNESCO (http://unesdoc.unesco.org/images/0018/001872/187234e.pdf, accessed 27 July 2010).

Ministry of Education (1948) *Report by H.M. Inspectors on St. George-in-the East County Secondary School, Stepney, London*; Inspected 25–27 February, 1948.

Morin, E. (1999) *Homeland Earth: A Manifesto for the New Millennium.* Cresskill, NJ: Hampton Press.

—— (2001) *Seven Complex Lessons in Education for the Future.* Paris: UNESCO.

Mosher, R. (Ed.) (1980) *Moral Education: A First Generation of Research and Development.* New York: Praeger.

Moss, P. (Ed.) (2009) *International Review of Leave Policies and Related Research 2009 (Employment Relations Research Series No. 102).* London: Department for Business, Innovations & Skills (http://www.berr.gov.uk/files/file52778.pdf, accessed 27 July 2010).

Moss, P. and Haydon, G. (Eds) (2008) *Every Child Matters and the Concept of Education.* London: Institute of Education, University of London.

Moss, P. and Petrie, P. (2002) *From Children's Services to Children's Spaces: Public Policy, Children and Childhood.* London: RoutledgeFalmer.

Mouffe, C. (2000) *The Democratic Paradox.* London: Verso.

Mundy, H. (1991) *No Heroes, No Cowards.* Milton Keynes: Living Archive Project.

Mursell, J. (1955) *Principles of Democratic Education.* New York: Norton.

NCSL (2005) *Getting Started with Networked Learning Walks.* Nottingham: National College for School Leadership.

Neill, A. S. (1968) *Summerhill.* Harmondsworth: Penguin.

New Economics Foundation (2009) *The Great Transition: A Tale of How It Turned Out Right.* London: New Economics Foundation.

—— (2010a) *Growth Isn't Possible: Why We Need a New Economic Direction.* London: New Economics Foundation.

—— (2010b) *21 Hours: Why a Shorter Working Week Can Help Us All to Flourish in the 21st Century.* London: New Economics Foundation.

New Zealand Ministry of Education (1996) *Te Whāriki: He Whāriki Matauranga mo nga Mokopuna o Aotearoa.* Wellington: Learning Media (http://www.educate.ece.govt.nz/learning/curriculumAndLearning/TeWhariki.aspx, accessed 27 July 2010).

Noddings, N. (2005) *The Challenge to Care in Schools.* 2nd Edn. New York: Teachers College Press.

Nuffield Review (2009) *Education for All: The Future of Education and Training for 14–19 Year Olds.* London: Routledge.

Oberhuemer, P. (2005) 'Conceptualising the early childhood professional', paper presented at *15th Annual EECERA Conference*, Malta, 3 September 2005.

OECD (2001) *Starting Strong I.* Paris: Organisation for Economic Cooperation and Development.

—— (2003) *The OECD Schooling Scenarios in Brief.* Paris: OECD/CERI (http://www.oecd.org/document/10/0,3343,en_2649_39263231_2078922_1_1_1_37455,00.html).

—— (2006) *Starting Strong II.* Paris: OECD.

—— (2007) *PISA 2006: Science Competencies in Tomorrow's World. Volume 1-Analysis.* Paris: OECD.

Olsson, L. M. (2009) *Movement and Experimentation in Young Children's Learning: Deleuze and Guattari in Early Childhood Education.* London: Routledge.

Osberg, D. and Biesta, G. (2007) 'Beyond presence: epistemological and pedagogical implications of "strong" emergence', *Interchange*, 38 (1), 31–51.

Pascal, C. (2009) *With our Best Future in Mind: Implementing Early Learning in Ontario.* Toronto: Queen's Printer for Ontario (http://www.ontario.ca/ontprodconsume/groups/content/@onca/@initiatives/documents/document/ont06_018899.pdf, accessed 27 July 2010).

Peacock, A. (2005) 'Raising standards: what do we really want?' *Forum*, 47 (2–3), 91–96.

—— (2006) 'Escaping from the bottom set: finding a voice for school improvement', *Improving Schools*, 9 (3), 251–59.

Penn, H., Burton, V., Lloyd, E., Potter, S., Sayeed, Z. and Mugford, M. (2006) *Systematic Review of the Economic Impact of Long-Term Centre Based Early Childhood Interventions*. London: Social Science Research Unit, Institute of Education (http://eppi.ioe.ac.uk/cms/LinkClick. aspx?fileticket = rWneSIRuVac%3d&tabid = 676&mid = 1572&language = en-US).

Petrie, P. (forthcoming) 'Children's associative spaces and social pedagogy', in C. Cameron and P. Moss (Eds) *Social Pedagogy and Working with Children*. London: Jessica Kingsley Publishing.

Pinder, D. (2002) 'In defence of utopian urbanism: imagining cities after "the end of utopia"', *Geografisker Annaler, Series B 84*, B: 3–4, 229–41.

Power Inquiry (2006) *The Report of Power: An Independent Inquiry into Britain's Democracy*. London: The Power Inquiry.

Prieto, H. P., Sahlström, F., Calander, F., Karlsson, M. and Heikkilä, M. (2002)'Together? On childcare as a meeting place in a Swedish city', *Scandinavian Journal of Educational Research*, 47 (1), 43–62.

Pring, R. (2007) *John Dewey*. London: Continuum.

Ransom, S. (2003) 'Public accountability in the age of neoliberal governance', *Journal of Educational Policy*, 18 (5), 459–80.

Readings, B. (1996) *The University in Ruins*. Cambridge, MA: Harvard University Press.

Reed, D. C. (1997) *Following Kohlberg: Liberalism and the Practice of Democratic Community*. Notre Dame, IN: University of Notre Dame Press.

Rinaldi, C. (1993) 'The emergent curriculum and social constructivism', in C. Edwards, L. Gandini and G. Forman (Eds) *The Hundred Languages of Children*. Norwood, NJ: Ablex.

—— (2005) 'Is a curriculum necessary?' *Children in Europe*, 9, 15.

—— (2006) *In Dialogue with Reggio Emilia: Listening, Researching and Learning*. London: Routledge.

Roemer, J. E. (1996) *Equal Shares: Making Market Socialism Work*. London: Verso.

Rose, N. (1999) *Powers of Freedom: Reframing Political Thought*. Cambridge: Cambridge University Press.

Rowbotham, S. (1979) 'The women's movement and organizing for socialism', in S. Rowbotham, L. Segal and H. Wainwright (Eds) *Beyond the Fragments: Feminism and the Making of Socialism*. London: Merlin Press.

Roy, K. (2004) 'Overcoming nihilism: from communication to Deleuzian expression', *Educational Philosophy and Theory*, 36 (3), 297–312.

St. Pierre, E. A. and Pillow, W. S. (2000) 'Inquiry among the ruins', in E. A. St. Pierre and W. S. Pillow (Eds) *Working the Ruins: Feminist Post/Structural Theory and Methods in Education*. New York: Routledge.

Sample, I. (2009) 'World faces "perfect storm" of problems by 2030, chief scientist to warn', *The Guardian*, 18 March 2009 (http://www.guardian.co.uk/science/2009/mar/18/perfect-storm-john-beddington-energy-food-climate, accessed 27 July 2010).

Sandel, M. (2009a) 'Markets and morals', Lecture 1, BBC Reith Lectures, 9 June 2009.

—— (2009b) 'A new politics of the common good', Lecture 4, BBC Reith Lectures, 30 June 2009.

Santos, B. de S. (1995) *Towards a New Common Sense: Law, Science and Politics in the Paradigmatic Transition*. London: Routledge.

Shah, H. and Goss, S. (Eds) (2007) *Democracy and the Public Realm*. London: Compass and Lawrence & Wishart.

Simon, B. (1972) *The Radical Tradition in Education in Britain*. London: Lawrence & Wishart.

—— (1977) 'Countesthorpe in the context of Comprehensive development', in J. Watts (Ed.) *The Countesthorpe Experience*. London: George Allen & Unwin.

—— (2009) 'The school and the architecture of time: beyond pedagogic baptism', paper presented at Philosophy of Education Society of Great Britain Conference, Gregynog, 26–28 June 2009.

Sizer, T. R. (1984) *Horace's Compromise*. Boston: Houghton Mifflin.

Skidmore, P. and Bound, K. (2008) *The Everyday Democracy Index*. London: Demos.

Skolverket (2006) *School Choice and its Effect in Sweden; Summary in English of Report 230*. Stockholm: Skolverket (http://www.skolverket.se/sb/d/355, accessed 27 July 2010).

—— (2009) *Descriptive Data on Pre-school Activities, School-Age Childcare, Schools and Adult Education in Sweden, 2008*. Stockholm: Skolverket.

Spring, J. (1975) *A Primer of Libertarian Education*. Montreal: Black Rose Books.

SSAT (2009) *Students as Learning Partners*. London: Specialist Schools & Academies Trust.

Stephens, P. (2009) 'The nature of social pedagogy: an excursion in Norwegian territory', *Child and Family Social Work*, 14 (3), 343–51.

Sutton Trust (2010) *Education Background of Government Ministers in 2010*. http://www.suttontrust.com/reports/MPs_educational_backgrounds_2010.pdf (accessed 1 August 2010).

Swedish Ministry of Education (1998; English translation) *Curriculum for Pre-school*. Stockholm: Ministry of Education and Science.

Tasker, M. (2008) *History, Values and Practice (Occasional Papers No. 1)*. London: Human Scale Education.

Taylor, W. (1994) 'Prospects for progressive pedagogy in England's schools in the late 20th century', *New Era in Education*, 75 (1), 7–11.

Thomson, P. and Gunter, H. (2007) 'The methodology of students-as-researchers: valuing and using experience and expertise to develop methods', *Discourse*, 28 (3) September, 327–42.

Tobin, J. (2007) 'Rôle de la théorie dans le movement RECE', in G. Brougère and M. Vandenbroeck (Eds) *Repenser l'éducation des jeunes enfants*. Brussels: P. I. E. Peter Lang.

Turner, T. and Wilson, D. G. (2010) 'Reflections on documentation: a discussion with thought leaders from Reggio Emilia', *Theory Into Practice*, 49 (1), 5–13.

UNESCO (2008) *Overcoming Inequality: Why Governance Matters*. (Education for All global monitoring report 2009). United Nations Educational, Scientific and Cultural Organization (UNESCO). Oxford: Oxford University Press.

Ulmer, G. L. (1985) *Applied Grammatology: Post(e)-pedagogy from Jacques Derrida to Joseph Beuys*. Baltimore, MD: John Hopkins University Press.

Unger, R. M. (1998) *Democracy Realized*. London, Verso.

—— (2004) *False Necessity: Anti-necessitarian Social Theory in the Service of Radical Democracy*. 2nd Edn, London: Verso.

—— (2005a) *What Should the Left Propose?*, London: Verso.

—— (2005b) 'The future of the Left: James Crabtree interviews Roberto Unger', *Renewal*, 13 (2/3), 173–84.

UNICEF (2007) *An Overview of Child Well-Being in Rich Countries: Innocenti Report Card 7*. Florence: UNICEF Innocenti Research Centre.

Vecchi, V. (Ed.) (2002) *Theatre Curtain: The Ring of Transformations*. Reggio Emilia: Reggio Children.

—— (2004) 'The multiple fonts of knowledge', *Children in Europe*, 6, 18–21.

—— (2010) *Art and Creativity in Reggio Emilia: Exploring the Role and Potential of Ateliers in Early Childhood Education*. London: Routledge.

Vidal, J. (2009) 'Asia facing unprecedented food shortage, UN report says', *The Guardian*, 17 August 2009.

Wagner, J. T. (2006) 'An outsider's perspective: childhoods and early education in the Nordic countries', in J. Einarsdottir and J. T. Wagner (Eds) *Nordic Childhoods and Early Education:*

Philosophy, Research, Policy and Practice in Denmark, Finland, Iceland, Norway, and Sweden. Greenwich, CT: Information Age Publishing.

Walkerdine, V. (1992) 'Progressive pedagogy and political struggle', in C. Luke and J. Gore (Eds) *Feminisms and Critical Pedagogy.* London: Routledge.

Wallis, S. (2010) 'Radical road to a greener economy', in M. Bunting, A. Lent and M. Vernon (Eds) *Citizen Ethics in a Time of Crisis.* London: Citizens Ethics Network (http://mcdonald-centre.files.wordpress.com/2010/02/citizen-ethics.pdf, accessed 27 July 2010).

Wasserman, E. (1980) 'An alternative high school based on Kohlberg's Just Community approach to education', in R. Mosher (Ed.) *Moral Education: A First Generation of Research and Development.* New York: Praeger.

Watts, J. (1977) (Ed.) *The Countesthorpe Experience.* London: Allen & Unwin.

—— (1980a) *Towards an Open School.* London: Longman.

—— (1980b) 'A further consideration of Sub Schools', *PRISE News*, Winter, 15–23.

White, J. (2005) *The Curriculum and the Child: The Selected Writings of John White.* London: RoutledgeFalmer.

—— (2007) *What Schools Are For and Why? (IMPACT Paper No. 14).* London: Philosophy of Education Society of Great Britain.

Whitty, G. (1974) 'Sociology and the problem of radical educational change', in M. Flude and J. Ahier (Eds) *Educability, Schools and Ideology.* London: Croom Helm.

Whitty, G., Power, S. and Halpin, D. (1998) *Devolution and Choice in Schools.* Buckingham: Open University Press.

Wilby, P. (2009) 'Parents' admissions trauma is down to gross inequality outside the school gates', *The Guardian*, 5 March.

—— (2010) 'New schools, same results', *The Guardian*, 26 July, p. 27 (http://www.guardian.co.uk/commentisfree/2010/jul/26/schools-new-names-same-results, accessed 1 August 2010).

—— (2010a) 'The big society and the media 100', *The New Statesman*, 26 July, p. 8 (http://www.newstatesman.com/society/2010/07/society-private-government, accessed 1 August 2010).

Wilkinson, R. and Pickett, K. (2009) *The Spirit Level: Why More Equal Societies Almost Always Do Better.* London: Allen Lane.

Williams, H. (2000) 'Schools that teach children to lie', *New Statesman*, 9 October.

World Health Organisation (2008) *Closing the Gap in a Generation: Health Equity Through Action on the Social Determinants of Health.* Geneva: World Health Organisation.

Wright, E. O. (2006) 'Compass points: towards a Socialist alternative', *New Left Review*, 41 (September–October), 93–124.

—— (2007) 'Guidelines for envisioning real utopias', *Soundings*, 36 (Summer), 26–39.

—— (2009a) 'Introduction: Why real utopias?', Chapter One of final pre-publication draft of *Envisioning Real Utopias* (http://www.ssc.wisc.edu/~wright/ERU_files/ERU-CHAPTER-1-final.pdf, accessed 27 July 2010).

—— (2009b) 'The tasks of emancipatory social science', Chapter Two of final pre-publication draft of *Envisioning Real Utopias* (http://www.ssc.wisc.edu/~wright/ERU_files/ERU-CHAPTER-2-final.pdf, accessed 27 July 2010).

—— (2009c) 'Elements of a theory of transformation', Chapter Eight of final pre-publication draft of *Envisioning Real Utopias* (http://www.ssc.wisc.edu/~wright/ERU_files/ERU-CHAPTER-8-final.pdf, accessed 27 July 2010).

Wright, N. (1989) *Assessing Radical Education: A Critical Review of the Radical Movement in English Schooling 1960–1980*. Milton Keynes: Open University Press.

Wrigley, T. (2007) 'Another school is possible', the *Caroline Benn Memorial Lecture* for the Socialist Educational Association, 2007 (http://www.socialisteducation.org.uk/CB7.htm, accessed 27 July 2010).

Yeatman, A. (1994) *Postmodern Revisionings of the Political*. London: Routledge.

Zigler, E. (2003) 'Forty years of believing in magic is enough', *Social Policy Report*, 17 (1), 10.

Additional web resources

All web addresses correct at time of print.

Brookline High School, http://bhs.brookline.k12.ma.us/Programs/SWS/

Bulletin of the Atomic Scientists, http://www.thebulletin.org/content/doomsday-clock/overview

Calouste Gulbenkian Foundation, http://www.gulbenkian.org.uk/publications/education/urban-village-schools

ECE Educate, http://www.educate.ece.govt.nz/Programmes/CentresOfInnovation.aspx

Every Child Matters, http://www.dcsf.gov.uk/everychildmatters/http://publications.every-childmatters.gov.uk/eOrderingDownload/DCSF-00331-2008.pdf

Living Archive, www.livingarchive.org.uk

National Curriculum, http://curriculum.qcda.gov.uk/key-stages-3-and-4/aims-values-and-purposes/aims/index.aspx

New Zealand Council for Educational Research, http://www.nzcer.org.nz/default.php?products_id = 2445

Wikiquote, http://en.wikiquote.org/wiki/John_Amos_Comenius

Index